Conceptualizing Cultural and Social Dialogue in the Euro-Mediterranean Area

This collection critically analyzes the dynamics and complexities of the wider Euro-Mediterranean area on the basis of individual theory-informed designs and conceptual frameworks.

Since the predominant focus has been on the first (political and security partnership) and the second baskets (economic and financial partnership) of the Barcelona Process, our contributors analyze social and cultural issues (the third basket of the Euro-Mediterranean Partnership), drawing upon linkages between concepts, structures and policy outcomes.

Some articles focus on the impact of the EU's actor capability in the area of EU policies towards the South in enhancing interregional dialogue, understanding and cultural cooperation. Others focus on a critical discourse analysis of dialogue, identity, power, human rights and civil society (including Western and non-Western conceptions). Finally, it culminates with discussions at roundtables organized by the EuroMedCultur network (in the making) on culture and community in the Euro-Mediterranean area. This network brings together civil society activists, policy makers and academics working on social and cultural issues in the area.

This book was previously published as a special issue of *Mediterranean Politics*.

Michelle Pace is Research Fellow in the Department of Political Science and International Studies, European Research Institute, University of Birmingham, Birmingham, UK

Tobias Schumacher is Research Fellow and Coordinator in the European University Institute, Florence, Italy

Conceptualizing Cultural and Social Dialogue in the Euro-Mediterranean Area

A European Perspective

Edited by Michelle Pace and Tobias Schumacher

LONDON AND NEW YORK

First published 2007 by Routledge
2 Park Square, Milton Park, Abingdon, Oxfordshire OX14 4RN

Simultaneously published in the USA and Canada
by Routledge
711 Third Avenue, New York, NY 10017, USA

First issued in paperback 2016

Routledge is an imprint of the Taylor & Francis Group, an informa business

© 2007 Taylor & Francis Ltd

Typeset in Times 10/12pt by the Alden Group, Oxfordshire

All rights reserved. No part of this book may be reprinted or reproduced or utilised in any form or by any electronic, mechanical, or other means, now known or hereafter invented, including photocopying and recording, or in any information storage or retrieval system, without permission in writing from the publishers.

British Library Cataloguing in Publication Data
A catalogue record for this book is available from the British Library

Library of Congress Cataloging in Publication Data
A catalog record for this book has been requested

ISBN 13: 978-1-138-97141-7 (pbk)
ISBN 13: 978-0-415-37129-2 (hbk)

CONTENTS

1 Preface: The Importance of Conceptualizing Cultural and Social Co-operation in the Euro-Mediterranean Area
GLENDA G. ROSENTHAL   1

2 Introduction: The Study of Euro-Mediterranean Cultural and Social Co-operation in Perspective
TOBIAS SCHUMACHER   3

3 Imagining Co-presence in Euro-Mediterranean Relations: The Role of 'Dialogue'
MICHELLE PACE   13

4 Setting the (Cultural) Agenda: Concepts, Communities and Representation in Euro-Mediterranean Relations
RAFFAELLA A. DEL SARTO   35

5 The Politics of De-Paradoxification in Euro-Mediterranean Relations: Semantics and Structures of 'Cultural Dialogue'
STEPHAN STETTER   53

6 Security through Intercultural Dialogue? Implications of the Securitization of Euro-Mediterranean Dialogue between Cultures
HELLE MALMVIG   71

7 Global Civil Society Across the Mediterranean: The Case of Human Rights
LAURA FELIU   87

8 EU Relations with Islam in the Context of the EMP's Cultural Dialogue
SARA SILVESTRI   106

9 Wounded by a Divide Syndrome. The Impact of Education and Employment on Euro-Med Cohesion
JOACHIM JAMES CALLEJA   127

10 Conclusion: Cultural Democracy in Euro-Mediterranean Relations?
MICHELLE PACE   147

Index   159

Preface: The Importance of Conceptualizing Cultural and Social Co-operation in the Euro-Mediterranean Area

Since its inception in November 1995, the Euro-Mediterranean Partnership has created various links between the now-35 member states of the European Union and the countries of the southern littoral of the Mediterranean. Little concern about the existence or the fostering of such links was shown by policymakers until then, although the occasional scholar tried to develop the notion that the countries bordering the Mediterranean constituted, particularly in historical times, an important strategic, political, economic and even a cultural entity. Fernand Braudel's seminal 1966 study of the Mediterranean and the Mediterranean World at the time of Philip II of Spain is the chief modern example of this. In classical times, Greek and Roman authors were also greatly interested in what brought the peoples of the Mediterranean littoral together – rather than what set them apart.

Today, in a post-9/11 context, a Madrid and London bombings era, we do not hear much about links and commonalities in this area. The tone of the discourse centres on 'clash of civilizations', threats, terrorism and irreconcilable political, economic and cultural differences. In the space of ten years since the start of the so-called Barcelona Process, an optimistic and far-reaching initiative undertaken by the European Union and its Mediterranean neighbours, efforts to create a 'common' area, a zone of 'shared' prosperity and a social, cultural and human 'partnership' have come to seem quixotic, even pointless, in the current international climate.

The third 'basket' of the Social, Cultural and Human Chapter of the Barcelona Agreement, whose achievements and failures these studies explore, represents a radical change in European thinking. It represents the ambitious idea promoted by European Union policy-makers that encouraging understanding between cultures and exchanges between civil societies is a necessary component of any political, strategic or economic programme aimed at promoting democracy in neighbouring Mediterranean countries. Testimony to the ongoing conviction in the crucial importance of all these components may be found in their incorporation in the more recent 2003 European Neighbourhood Policy.

Since the European Union has repeatedly declared that full membership in its institutions and full participation in its policies is restricted to 'European' countries only, any special relationship or privileged partnership has to be based on much more than mere trade preferences or opening of borders to immigrant workers. The key question is whether the EU can really cast off old, sometimes neo-colonial, attitudes and present-day fears and work toward the stated objective set forth by the European Commission in 2002 of bringing 'people on both sides of the Mediterranean closer together, to promote their mutual knowledge and understanding and to improve their perception of each other'. This collection presents a thorough analysis of how this objective can be implemented in practice and is a recommendable read for academics, civil society representatives, EU policy makers and students of Euro-Mediterranean studies who are keen to explore new theoretical and empirical grounds in this field.

Glenda G. Rosenthal
Institute for the Study of Europe,
Columbia University

Introduction: The Study of Euro-Mediterranean Cultural and Social Co-operation in Perspective

TOBIAS SCHUMACHER
European University Institute Florence, San Domenico di Fiesole, Italy

When the Foreign Ministers of the European Union (EU) and the then 12 Mediterranean Non-Member countries (MNC) in November 1995 met in Barcelona and solemnly inaugurated the Euro-Mediterranean Partnership (EMP), this event marked a turning-point in the history of Euro-Mediterranean relations.[1] For almost 40 years, Europe's policies towards its southern periphery were based on financial assistance and economic co-operation and thus characterized by most observers as a pure aid-and-trade approach (Gillespie, ed., 1997; Schumacher, 1998). With the entering-into-force of the Barcelona Process, however, Euro-Mediterranean relations were given a new framework which abolished the decade-old (European) pre-occupation with economic matters. In addition to a revised chapter on economic and financial co-operation, both the Barcelona Declaration and the new Euro-Mediterranean association agreements (EMAA), superseding the co-operation agreements concluded in the mid-1970s, provide for a political and security co-operation and, most of all, establish the so-called third basket which, in turn, allows for social and cultural co-operation and herewith a social and cultural dialogue. Given the popularity of frightening and actually unjustified assumptions that the two main religions along the northern and southern Mediterranean shores, i.e. Christianity and Islam, were in a continuing and deeply conflictual relation (Huntington, 1996) which supposedly precludes Western and Islamic societies from peaceful and collaborative co-existence, Euro-Mediterranean social and cultural co-operation was also conceived with the aim to dispel any putative clash of civilizations. Like the first basket, the creation of the third *volet* has been recognized right from the outset as a major component of the EMP, not least due to the fact that it is nowadays commonly acknowledged that political, economic, social and cultural behaviours are interlinked with each other (Martín and Byrne, eds., 2004). With its objective 'to bring people on both sides of the Mediterranean closer together, to promote their mutual knowledge and understanding and to improve their perception of each other' (European Commission, 2002: 5), as well as with its focus on the development of human resources, co-operation between municipalities and regions, a dialogue on cultures and civilizations, the media and youth, an exchange between civil societies, social development, health and migration, the scope of Euro-Mediterranean social and cultural co-operation is undoubtedly very ambitious.

Yet, ten years into 'Barcelona', not much is left of the original enthusiasm that encompassed the creation of the third basket. Instead, most critical observers agree that its pitfalls prevail (Panebianco, ed., 2003; Pace and Schumacher, 2004: 122–7). Certainly, the establishment and recent inauguration of the Anna Lindh Euro-Mediterranean Foundation for the Dialogue between Cultures in Alexandria put the EMP and herewith the third basket temporarily back into the international spotlight. Yet, although the Foundation must be considered as a long overdue measure to remedy the absence of a 'catalyst for all initiatives aimed at increasing dialogue and common understanding',[2] it cannot compensate for the fact that social and cultural co-operation in the framework of the EMP for most of the period since 1995 has been a sleeping beauty. The reasons for this failure are numerous and, most of all, due to structural deficiencies of both the Barcelona Declaration and the EMAA. Like the provisions on the political and security chapter, the relevant stipulations of the Declaration and its follow-up work programme, as well as of title VI of the EMAA, are vague and rather inexplicit. In a way, they can be characterized as a loose shopping list of principles and declarations of (good) intent, and lack any mention of concrete or at least potential implementation mechanisms.

Moreover, none of the objectives is linked to either the first basket or to the second basket, in spite of the alleged holistic character of the EMP (Barbé, 1996). As was already noted by one observer, the third basket can hardly be called coherent as it is guided by two structurally very different themes (Jünemann, 1997). On one hand, it reflects some laudable awareness on the part of the then 27, and nowadays 35, partners with regard to the socio-economic situation in the southern Mediterranean and the cultural differences between the societies of the two shores, and envisages progressive measures for closer co-operation. On the other hand, however, it has a rather harsh undertone as it relates to a-cultural issues such as the fight against illegal immigration, terrorism and international crime, drug trafficking and the fight against corruption. This division is highly problematic and has to be questioned. Of course, its proponents may argue that the Barcelona Declaration as well as the EMAA follow and, thus, subscribe to the enlarged understanding of security, which was introduced by Barry Buzan two decades ago (Buzan, 1983). Yet, this contrasts with the view that these issue-areas in the context of 'social' and 'cultural' co-operation appear as misplaced and somewhat alien. As the political elites in both the EU and the southern Mediterranean deal with them in the context of the chapter on political and security co-operation, it remains an open question why they had to be incorporated into the third basket. In addition, comparing the Barcelona Declaration with title VI of the EMAA reveals that the two provisions are not truly coherent with each other. Whilst title VI stipulates that all issues related to the fight against illegal immigration shall be incorporated into the social dialogue, all of the remaining topics, as outlined above, are not subsumed under this section. The fight against terrorism, for instance, was included under title V of the EMAA, which implies that it is part of economic co-operation and, hence, falls under the jurisdiction and scope of the second basket.

It is this ambiguity, i.e. the inclusion of issue-areas that neither are directly associated *with* nor necessarily pertain *to* social and cultural co-operation, that has impeded real progress in the third chapter and contributes to the low degree of awareness of its strategic importance on the part of policy practitioners, academics and civil society actors on both sides of the Mediterranean. As the first study by Michelle Pace reminds us, language matters with regards to meaning formation and the conceptualization of politics, and pre-determines the path that is eventually taken to implement the stipulations the parties in question agree upon. In this vein, both the Barcelona Declaration and the EMAA, however, encompass a multiplicity of languages and run short of clear-cut definitions and operational criteria. In the case of the third basket, this has not only provided many of the (nowadays) 35 partners with exit-options and a legitimate excuse to display a non-engagement policy, which, in turn, is simply due to a lack of knowledge and/or sufficient interest. Even worse, as the whole Barcelona Declaration represents the lowest common denominator of 27, rather diverging than overlapping, governmental positions, the implementation path taken since 1995 to develop, launch and sustain the third basket is not a straight and coherent one.

Hitherto, of the ten areas that are stressed in the follow-up work programme of the Barcelona Declaration as priority areas for action, only four have attracted attention in the capitals of the EU member states and the MNC, though with mixed results as they are based on highly questionable foundations and assumptions. These four areas are media, youth and herewith exchanges between civil societies, and the dialogue between cultures (and civilizations); in addition, emphasis has been laid on cultural heritage. With regard to the latter and media co-operation, it took the parties more than three and five years respectively, to launch two initiatives, namely the Euro-Med Heritage Programme (EMHP) and the Euro-Med-Audiovisual Programme (EMAP). Notwithstanding the praise these two programmes regularly receive by the European Commission for their impact on the preservation of the cultural heritage and their focus on the preservation, production and distribution of documentaries that supposedly capture the essence of people's lives and cultures, respectively (European Commission, 2002: 11–14), they hardly contribute to one of the third basket's major goals of bringing the 'peoples [of both shores of the Mediterranean] closer, promoting understanding between them and improving their perception of each other' (Barcelona Declaration, 1995). This can be explained by the fact that both initiatives are highly specific and a domain of a tiny circle of experts. In particular, the potential impact of the EMAP was overrated by many in Brussels, as it faces severe constraints which are due to the tight control and pressure the state bureaucracies in the MNC exert on their individual media systems.

Unsurprisingly, projects which aim to address topics such as democratization or human rights, both of which are key concerns of the EMP, in an artistic-cinematistic or simply properly journalistic way, have not yet had any chance of realization in the framework of the Barcelona Process. In contrast, the Euro-Med Youth Action Programme (EMYAP) with its focus on youth exchanges, volunteer work and support measures, has produced positive results in terms of confidence-building, empowerment of young people and the acquisition of inter-cultural competence. Yet, like the EMAP and the EMHP, the EMYAP, which entered into force only in 1999 and was suspended by the European Commission in early 2005 on the grounds of a putative need for restructuring, too often turned out to be a *domaine reservé* of co-opted, privileged and non-religious actors in the southern Mediterranean. This, in turn, is closely inter-linked to the problem of multiplicity of languages in the Barcelona Declaration, as mentioned above, and the different connotations and notions revolving around the meaning, actors and functions of key concepts such as culture, dialogue and civil society that, in fact, underpin the entirety of the third basket and the EU-sponsored so-called dialogue between cultures.

With regards to dialogue and civil society, no clear-cut and universally acceptable definition exists, as both concepts are highly value-laden and subject to different normative interpretations. Whereas, on one hand, this lack of consensus has obstructed Euro-Mediterranean cultural and social co-operation, it has not, on the other hand, provoked senior officials, which in a way do acknowledge the spoiler function of this deficiency,[3] to examine and map the different notions with a view to reaching a common vocabulary that could eventually guide all activities related to the third basket. Also the scientific community dealing with the EMP has shown only a rudimentary interest for the EMP's third basket and thus its underlying concepts. This can be explained by the fact that the vast majority of studies which are of an empirical and, too often, purely essayistic nature, have been pre-occupied with the political and security chapter and the economic and financial dimension, respectively. Although there is a growing interest among scholars to analyse cultural and social co-operation from a more general perspective (Colas, 1997; Jünemann, 1998; Peresso, 1998; Panebianco, ed., 2003), very few studies, mostly with a focus on civil society (Jünemann, 2003; Mouawad, 2003), have been published focusing on a more theory-informed, or at least analytical, examination of some of the shortcomings of the third basket. In a way, this assessment is rather surprising in the light of the current 'moment of robust intellectual openness' (Latham, 1994: 8) and herewith the undisputable fact that culture, identity and dialogue are staging an exciting and powerful comeback in both post-Cold War and post-9/11 International Relations (IR) theorizing and research. Even though, as Alexander and Smith remind us (Alexander and Smith, 1993: 151), some of these issues were already subject to intellectual scrutiny during the first 20–25 years following the Second World War, it is undoubtedly the epochal turbulences in the early 1990s and, even more so, the tragic events of 11 September 2001 that have promoted the scholarly re-orientation toward culture and the acknowledgment of its significance enormously. This applies particularly to the critical camp of the IR discipline as it has hitherto proven to be the circle that is most interested *in* and open *towards* a critical examination of culture as an important and influential factor of world politics.

It is in this light that this collection of studies has to be seen. While it certainly aims at shedding empirical light on the neglected and intellectually rather dark spot, called Euro-Mediterranean cultural and social co-operation, it sets out to provide for a more theory-informed and conceptual platform on which the latter, that is the study of the third basket, can be challenged, and, hence, inspired by, insights of critical thinking. Given the undisputable academic parochialism with regards to a theoretical and conceptual examination of the underlying building blocks of the third basket, the collection concentrates particularly on a critical analysis of the concept of Euro-Mediterranean (inter-)cultural and social dialogue. With this in view, and by considering the vivacious diversity of perspectives generally revolving around these issues, it follows the assumption that there is no one theory or methodology for the analysis of these concepts. Hence, it refrains from adhering to one particular notion of critical thinking and takes somewhat of a broader perspective, essentially allowing and thus 'leaving the door open' for a serious consideration of what could be labelled as mainstream positions. In order to minimize the problems of selection and coherence that almost every compilation inevitably faces, all contributions in this collection address the issue of dialogue, albeit from different angles and with different research agendas, and link their critical studies either implicitly or explicitly to the report of the high-level advisory group which was established at the initiative of the President of the European Commission (High-Level Advisory Group, 2003). Moreover, although it is undoubtedly tempting to anchor one's analysis to a certain concept of culture such as, for instance, Hall's and Hall's model of behavioural components of culture (Hall and Hall, 1990) or Hofstede's five-dimensional concept of cultural difference (Hofstede, 1991), each contribution is based on the awareness that any definition of culture is inevitably biased by the person doing the defining (Demorgon and Molz, 1996).

With the objective of bringing young, critical European Political Scientists together, the compilation opens with a contribution by Michelle Pace, Research Fellow at the European Research Institute at the University of Birmingham, that uncovers the multi-faceted challenges facing the 35 partners in developing mutual and sustainable relations through dialogue. Starting from the assumption that a systematic analysis of what Euro-Mediterranean dialogue actually implies and how it shapes Euro-Mediterranean relations as well as national agendas is lacking, she presents a theoretical discussion of the meaning of dialogue by drawing upon the work of Mikhail Bakhtin and the four-dimensional group development model of Bruce Tuckman. The application of this thinking enables her to divide Euro-Mediterranean relations into four analytical phases, namely a forming, a storming, a norming and, finally, a performing phase, which offer an empirical overview of the diversity of voices, that, in turn, have been constraining the imagined co-presence in the framework of the EMP. Moreover, it is advanced that, despite ten years of what is considered by the 35 partners as dialogue, ample space for critical self-reflection and an overlap of the Self and the Other is not discernable. Neither have the EU nor the MNC adapted to the language of the Other. Notwithstanding this shortcoming, it is concluded that the EMP, and herewith its institutional structures providing for dialogic encounters, is a process which has the potential to develop into an inter-subjective, meaning formation and perpetual cognition mechanism for all parties involved.

In the thrust to address the issue of (inter-)cultural dialogue from different perspectives, the following three contributions at first glance seem to be very similar as they all question and challenge the conceptual underpinnings, as well as the apparently accepted Euro-Mediterranean world view of dialogue. Yet, they differ largely as they approach the matter from different strands of critical thinking, thus travelling, to paraphrase the late Susan Strange, 'from different starting points and ending at different destinations' (Strange, 1994: 16), thereby occasionally crossing each other's path at highly illuminating intellectual junctures. In her essay, Raffaella Del Sarto, Marie Curie Research Fellow at the Mediterranean Programme at the Robert Schuman Centre for Advanced Studies at the European University Institute in Florence, concentrates her analysis on three intertwined issues, that is culture, community and representation in Euro-Mediterranean relations. To this end, her approach is three-fold: In a first step, she revisits Huntington's 'clash of civilizations paradigm' and its set of ontological foundations and implications for today's international relations because, as the author shows, it has increasingly taken hold of many public discourses in the 'West' and beyond. Revealing a growing tendency of depicting cultures and civilizations as autonomous agents engaging in dialogue with each other, Del Sarto shows that the process of defining communities in world politics is an arbitrary one that includes some actors while necessarily excluding others. Hence, 'the nation-state logic of community stands in contrast to the idea of global society and the universality of the rights of human beings'. This insight serves as the starting-point for the second step of her analysis whereby she discusses very important questions such as 'how are cultures and culture defined, how are meanings imposed, who represents the alleged cultures within the inter-cultural dialogue, and how do these patterns of representation affect both world politics and the EMP?' Based on these rather problematic and thought-provoking findings, she finally turns toward the Anna Lindh Foundation as a case study and concludes with a plea for a redrawing of the boundaries of difference and similarity in the EMP through the creation of a trans-cultural dialogue along clear-cut thematic lines.

Following it, Stephan Stetter, Research Associate at the Institute for World Society Studies at the University of Bielefeld, in his contribution on semantics and structures of cultural dialogue, adopts a systems theoretical perspective and looks into the construction of identity discourses in Euro-Mediterranean relations and explains how and to what extent these 'semantics of identity' relate to and impact upon cultural dialogue taking place in the framework of the Barcelona Process. By identifying the Self/Other distinctions that underpin the entire Process, he highlights the powerful role they play and argues that they cultivate and promote a semantic and, most importantly, hegemonic, construction of culture which eventually acts as a prime differential category between Europe and the southern Mediterranean. In more concrete terms, Stetter points out that the institutionalization of the Euro-

Mediterranean cultural dialogue is an example of the politics of de-paradoxification since its political significance rests on the 'conflictive fundaments inherent in this concept'. As alternative forms with which collective identity patterns in the Euro-Mediterranean area could be processed, his contribution offers three possible points of departure: First, integration could be achieved through less emphasis on value-laden and normative concepts, such as cultural dialogue. Second, picking up on one of the arguments of the first contributions of this volume, both the EU and the MNC are, in the view of the author, well advised to concentrate on the shared world societal reference point of their relations, rather than observing and instrumentalizing cultural differences. Third, more attention on the part of all parties involved is needed with regard to the divergent and cross-cutting debordering processes in Euro-Mediterranean relations.

In contrast, the next contribution authored by Helle Malmvig, Research Fellow at the Department of Conflict and Security Studies at the Danish Institute for International Affairs in Copenhagen, analyses the consequences of framing the Euro-Mediterranean inter-cultural dialogue within a context of security. Inspired by the Copenhagen School's conceptualization of security and by applying Habermas' theory of communicative action, she shows how inter-cultural dialogue is represented as a means to achieve security in the Euro-Mediterranean area and points to the implications of this representation. The application of Habermas' line of thinking, as well as the utilization of Critical Theory enable her to put forward the argument that a securitization of the dialogue takes place and that this phenomenon has provided Euro-Mediterranean cultural dialogue with 'extraordinary legitimacy and urgency, while at the same time compromising the very conditions of possibility for a dialogue along Habermasian lines.' Hence, it is contended that the dialogue has become extremely politicized and an object of tight control of governmental actors north and south of the Mediterranean sea. This, in turn, constrains the effective implementation of the dialogue to the extent that, according to Malmvig, only certain themes and some carefully selected civil society groups are considered. Given these rather sobering findings, it is not surprising that the current dialogue, in the words of the author, 'risks to be confined to intellectual exchanges and conferences rallying cosmopolitan elites, who are reinforcing their (similar) worldviews and values, leaving little impact on the general population.'

In a way, this contribution prepares the ground for the next article, entitled 'Global Civil Society across the Mediterranean: The Case of Human Rights', written by Laura Feliu, Lecturer on International Relations at the Universitat Autònoma de Barcelona (UAB). Against the backdrop of research on democratization and political transition, Feliu adopts a more actor-oriented approach and examines the scope and role of global civil society, with a special emphasis on human rights, in the context of the Euro-Mediterranean (inter-)cultural dialogue, both from a conceptual and empirical point of view. As the Anna Lindh Foundation, as well as the Barcelona Declaration and the EMAA, consider civil society groups as the most important agents of any dialogic encounter, Feliu's insights are extremely noteworthy and of particular importance for any political decision to be taken with respect to the third basket: Although the establishment of the EMP has significantly boosted the reinforcement and creation of new trans-national human rights networks in the Euro-Mediterranean area, trans-national links created by human rights civil society associations on the southern shore of the Mediterranean area are still weak and underdeveloped. Consequently, as is pointed out, southern Mediterranean NGOs are under-represented within international fora and, thus, limited in their scope of influence and agenda-setting. The most active southern civil society associations can be, according to Feliu, found in those MNC that she considers as liberalized autocracies. Yet, even within the context of a more open and less repressive environment, the members of these networks show signs of significant heterogeneity. Furthermore, trans-national civil society dialogue is additionally hampered by the fact that the direction of trans-national ties is vertical, that is between associations from the south and the north of the Mediterranean, but hardly horizontal across MNC borders.

Sara Silvestri, PhD researcher at the Centre of International Studies at the University of Cambridge, was invited to add a more empirical dimension to this volume and to shed some light on the recent EU attitudes and initiatives towards Islam, most of all in the context of the EMP, but also in policy areas, such as Justice and Home Affairs and Social Affairs, which both impact on the Barcelona Process and herewith its dialogic dimension. It becomes obvious from this contribution that any initiatives intended to promote civilizational, inter-cultural or inter-faith dialogue have neither produced any concrete results, nor led to a clear vision on how to improve relations with, as well as within, religious and ethnic communities in Europe and the Mediterranean. With this in view, Silvestri certainly joins the previous authors in their general critique of the Euro-Mediterranean dialogue's un-successful and exclusive world view and structure, but strikes a more optimistic chord to the extent that she regards more positively the symbolic meaning of the EU's efforts of disseminating a new attitude toward the use of dialogue as a tool of cultural rapprochement, and, most importantly, of democratic development and social justice.

Finally, the volume ends with a contribution by Joachim James Calleja, lecturer in the Department of International Relations at the University of Malta and acting Chief Executive Officer of the Malta Qualifications Council, who addresses the impact of education and employment on Euro-Mediterranean cohesion and identity. He convincingly argues that the Euro-Mediterranean space is exposed *to* and suffering *from* a divide syndrome which manifests itself through conflicts, prejudices, intolerance, neo-colonial patterns of behaviour, segregation and the lack of an endogenous approach to regional policies. This syndrome, the author argues, has been seen by many in the South 'as a means to protect conceptual, moral and behavioural patterns of the nation-state which either incarnated the principles of religion and made them its own or coexisted with such principles in order to secure its own existence.' As it is rightfully claimed that the EMP lacks a balanced and symmetrical ownership, Calleja borrows from Abel's Kantian-inspired concept of unlimited communities of communication and presents a framework, based on employment and education, which may have the potential to overcome this gap. Yet, as is contended, this may be the case only as long as the educational challenge starts as part of a community of communication of the Euro-Mediterranean area that, in turn, regards human beings as equals irrespective of ethnicity or creed.

This volume is the outcome of a series of workshops related to the dynamics of Euro-Mediterranean relations in general (ECPR, Bologna, June 2004) and to culture and community in the framework of the EMP in particular (Swedish Institute, Alexandria, October 2003 and Friedrich Ebert Foundation, Rabat, December 2004), co-organized by the two editors. Our thanks go to the Swedish Institute and the Friedrich Ebert Foundation, respectively, whose financial support was key to the workshops in Alexandria and Rabat. We would like to extend our gratitude to the participants of the meetings for their active participation and contributions, and, last but not least, to Richard Gillespie for his unconditional and invaluable support throughout the process of compiling and publishing this volume. As we are convinced that cultural co-operation must not and cannot be neither conducted in a voluntaristic fashion nor be achieved through central political decisions, we sincerely hope that this volume, with its inclination towards theory, comparative analysis and the evaluation of past practice, can shed some light on how best to achieve a true dialogue in an area of marked complexity and conflict such as the Mediterranean.

Notes

[1] The 12 MNC were Algeria, Morocco, Tunisia, Egypt, Israel, Palestine, Jordan, Lebanon, Syria, Turkey, Malta and Cyprus. Since May 2004, Malta and Cyprus became members of the EU and, thus, are not considered as MNC.

[2] Presidency Conclusions of the Euro-Mediterranean Conference of Minister of Foreign Affairs in Naples, 2–3 December 2003.

[3] See the Foreword, written by the former Italian Ambassador in charge of the Barcelona Process, Antonio Badini (in Panebianco, 2003: ix).

References

Alexander, J. C. & Smith, P. (1993) The discourse of American civil society: a new proposal for cultural studies, *Theory and Society*, 22(1), pp. 151–207.

Barbé, E. (1996) The Barcelona Conference: launching pad of a process, *Mediterranean Politics*, 1(1), pp. 25–42.

Buzan, B. (1983) *People, States and Fear* (Boulder: Westview).

Colas, A. (1997) The limits of Mediterranean partnership: civil society and the Barcelona Conference of 1995, *Mediterranean Quarterly*, 6(4), pp. 63–80.

Demorgon, J. & Molz, M. (1996) Bedingungen und Auswirkungen der Analyse von Kultur(en) und interkulturellen Interaktionen, in: A. Thomas (Ed.) *Psychologie interkulturellen Handelns* (Göttingen: Verlag für Psychologie).

European Commission (2002) *Dialogue between Cultures and Civilisations in the Barcelona Process* (Luxembourg: Office for Official Publications of the European Communities).

Gillespie, R. (Ed.) (1997) *The Euro-Mediterranean Partnership. Political and Economic Perspectives* (London: Frank Cass).

Hall, E. & Hall, M. (1990) *Understanding Cultural Differences: Keys to Success in West Germany, France and the United States* (Yarmouth: Intercultural Press).

High-Level Advisory Group (2003) Dialogue between peoples and cultures in the Euro-Mediterranean area, *Euromed Report*, 68 (Brussels: EuropeAid Cooperation Office DG).

Hofstede, G. (1991) *Cultures and Organisations: Software of the Mind* (London: McGraw-Hill).

Jünemann, A. (1997) Die Mittelmeerpolitik der Europäischen Union: Demokratisierungs programme zwischen normativer Zielsetzung und realpolitischem Pragmatismus, in: Deutsch-Französisches Institut (Eds) *Frankreich Jahrbuch 1997* (Opladen: Leske & Budrich).

Jünemann, A. (1998) Cultural aspects of Euro-Mediterranean cooperation and the German point of view, in: S. Hegazy (Ed.) *Egyptian and German Perspectives on Security in the Mediterranean* (Kairo: FES).

Jünemann, A. (2003) The forum civil Euromed: critical watchdog and intercultural mediator, in: S. Panebianco (Ed.) *A New Euro-Mediterranean Cultural Identity* (London: Frank Cass).

Latham, R. (1994) Moments of transformation, *Items*, 47, pp. 1–8.

Linklater, A. (1994) Dialogue, dialectic and emancipation in international relations at the end of the post-war age, *Millenium*, 22, pp. 119–131.

Martin, I. & Byrne (Eds), I. (2004) Economic and social rights in the Euro-Mediterranean Partnership, special issue, *Mediterranean Politics*, 9(3).

Mouawad, Youssef (2003) Civil society, God and cousins: the case of the Middle East, in: S. Panebianco (Ed.) *A New Euro-Mediterranean Cultural Identity* (London: Frank Cass).

Pace, M. & Schumacher, T. (2004) Culture and community in the Euro-Mediterranean Partnership: a roundtable on the third basket, Alexandria 5–7 October 2003, *Mediterranean Politics*, 9(1), pp. 122–127.

Panebianco, S. (Ed.) (2003) *A New Euro-Mediterranean Cultural Identity* (London: Frank Cass).

Peresso, E.-M. (1998) Euro-Mediterranean cultural cooperation, *European Foreign Affairs Review*, 3(3), pp. 135–156.

Schumacher, T. (1998) *Die Maghreb-Politik der Europäischen Union. Gemeinschaftliche Assoziierungspraxis gegenüber Algerien, Marokko und Tunesien* (Wiesbaden: Deutscher Universitäts-Verlag).

Schumacher, T. (2005) *Die Europäische Union als internationaler Akteur im südlichen Mittelmeerraum. 'Actor Capability' und EU-Mittelmeerpolitik* (Baden-Baden: Nomos).

Strange, S. (1994) Prologue: some desert island tales, in: S. Strange (Ed.) *States ands Markets* (London: Pinter Press).

Imagining Co-presence in Euro-Mediterranean Relations: The Role of 'Dialogue'

MICHELLE PACE
European Research Institute, University of Birmingham, UK

Introduction

A key external relations priority for the European Union (EU) is the creation of an area of dialogue, co-operation and exchange in the South and East Mediterranean and the Middle East – an area of vital strategic importance for the EU. With the Euro-Mediterranean Partnership (EMP), the EU created an innovative policy basket, in that, through the Barcelona declaration, the 27 signatories recognized that for the Euro-Mediterranean relationship to work, dialogue between people (not just the elite) was essential. Activities under the third (social, cultural and human affairs) basket of the EMP have since flourished (MEDA-Democracy, Euro-Mediterranean Heritage, Euro-Mediterranean Audiovisual, Euro-Mediterranean Youth Action Programme, etc). These have been complemented (since 1995) by the Forum Civil Euro-Mediterranean (FCE) through civil society conferences that run alongside all Euro-Mediterranean Ministerial Conferences. One of the main functions of the FCE is to encourage and enhance intercultural dialogue between the Mediterranean partners and the EU member states. Other turning-points in Euro-Mediterranean relations were the launching of the Euro-Mediterranean Parliamentary Assembly, the Euro-Mediterranean Non-Governmental Platform and the setting up of the

'Anna Lindh Euro-Mediterranean Foundation for the Dialogue between Cultures'. Despite these various activities, there has been no systematic analysis of what the Euro-Mediterranean dialogue actually implies and how it increasingly shapes EU-Mediterranean agendas. At a time when the perception of the irreconcilable nature of cultures is growing it is important to take seriously the concept of dialogue between European and Mediterranean cultures. This essay aims to fill this gap in the literature by critically examining the role of dialogue in Euro-Mediterranean relations. It first establishes the nature of dialogue and its significance for Euro-Mediterranean relations. For this purpose, it draws upon the work of a key thinker on dialogue, Mikhail Bakhtin. The theoretical section also draws upon the work of Bruce Tuckman's 1965 forming, storming, norming and performing group development model and adapts these theoretical frameworks to the EMP. The empirical section, which follows, sketches out what Euro-Mediterranean dialogue actually entails, analyses what dialogue seeks to attain, and finally concludes with some implications for the future of Euro-Mediterranean dialogic relations.

Nature of Dialogue and Significance for Euro-Mediterranean Relations

The nature and utility of dialogue in international politics and in the Euro-Mediterranean process in particular cannot be underestimated. Indeed, nowhere is the need for, and the difficulty of, achieving dialogue more evident than in the Euro-Mediterranean space. Emanating from the cleavages in this area – the cultural confrontations and the economic gap between the North and the South (to mention just a few) – are the central securitization discourses of our time: radical fundamentalism, proliferation of weapons of mass destruction, international terrorism, migration, the drug trade, and interstate conflicts. The task of bridging the cleavages that give rise to these securitized practices is both urgent and long overdue. The EMP represents a radical departure from past EU efforts to achieve security through alliances, economic interdependence and other conventional practices. The thrust of the Barcelona Declaration is one of community and region-building and the creation of a security partnership, eventually leading to a security community through, among other instruments, a dialogue in the sense of the progressive development of shared understandings (Habermas, 1984 and Malmvig in this volume). Certainly, the Euro-Mediterranean process has the potential to develop into a 'dialogue of partners' that could replace or at least weaken discourses on the 'clash of civilizations' in this challenging area (Huntington, 1993). But, in practice, could dialogue instead lead to a 'convergence of differences' between the factions participating in the dialogue? Do participants really engage in processes that allow them to put themselves in the shoes of the 'other'? How can the participants create the needed sense of equality so necessary for dialogue when the economic gap between the Mediterranean and European partners is so glaring? Some of the participants in the Barcelona process are states that are weak. Can their representatives be partners in the dialogue? These are just a few of the questions which shed light on the importance of a better understanding of the nature of successful dialogue which, in turn, is crucial to our understanding of the success or failure of the EMP itself. In fact, the Barcelona process is a laboratory where one of the most ambitious experiments in international relations may have started to take place.

The need for increased dialogue arose following the end of the Cold War, the EU's shift Eastward and the new post-Cold War securitization discourses of the region that motivated the EU to look to enter into dialogue with the Mediterranean in the early 1990s. During 1992 and 1993 the Commission proposed that future relations with Mediterranean Non-Member Countries (MNCs) should go beyond the financial sector and economic sphere to include a dialogue between the parties, the creation of a Euro-Mediterranean free-trade area and social, economic and cultural cooperation. These recommendations, initially looking just to a Euro-Maghrebi partnership, were approved at the Lisbon summit in June 1992 and confirmed at the Corfu summit in June 1994 (these summits are in fact European Council meetings). In the meantime, negotiations got underway with Tunisia, Morocco and Israel on the basis of mandates specifying these four basic elements. With the launching of the EMP in November 1995 and the European Neighbourhood Policy (ENP) in 2003, it has become commonly accepted that the EU's 'dialogue' with Mediterranean partners is one of the main instruments as well as achievements in EU-Mediterranean cooperation. However, although the term appears in virtually all EMP/ENP documentation, there seems to be no coherent understanding of what dialogue actually means. Its meaning is therefore in need of clarification (Monar, 1997).

Understanding 'Dialogue'

In our day-to-day interpretation of the term 'dialogue', we usually refer to dialogue as communication or discussion between people or groups of people such as governments or political parties (Collins, 1987). By means of the EMP, the EU aims to promote dialogue across the Euro-Mediterranean area on political, economic and social themes. The EMP marked a move from Euro-Mediterranean contacts, of an ad hoc and formal nature, to somewhat regular and institutionalized contacts. According to one author, three conditions have to be met for the effective use of the term dialogue:

- A formal decision of the (Euro-Mediterranean) Committee and/or the ministers to engage in a 'dialogue';
- A formal agreement with the (Mediterranean) partners concerned;
- In addition to normal diplomatic relations, regular political contacts have to be provided for at one or various levels.[1]

In Euro-Mediterranean affairs, relations are governed broadly by the EMP, of which the Euro-Mediterranean Association Agreements (EMAA) are a vital feature. The Partnership provides for a comprehensive framework for Euro-Mediterranean relations structured along three pillars: a political and security partnership, an economic and financial partnership and a partnership in social, cultural and human affairs. The three pillars or baskets offer different forms of dialogue: political/security, economic and social.

In its most recent initiative, the Neighbourhood Policy, the EU aims to deepen its relations with Mediterranean partners through 'a more intensive political dialogue' (Council of the European Union, 2002; European Commission, 2003 and 2004). The main instruments for the deepening of this dialogue are Action Plans which aim at enhancing the Barcelona Process.

Theorizing Euro-Mediterranean Dialogic Relations

Euro-Mediterranean politics have few resources to assess the quality of Euro-Mediterranean cultural interactions that shape and are shaped by the changing structures and processes of the EU system, as well as the wider international system. One way of arriving at a potential framework for critically thinking about Euro-Mediterranean dialogic relations is to draw upon the work of the critical thinker, Mikhail Bakhtin.

Despite Bakhtin's acknowledged relevance to the social sciences, Euro-Mediterranean politics have been relatively unreceptive towards his thinking. Drawing upon literary theory, Bakhtin's theories focus primarily on the concept of dialogue, and on the notion that language (that is, any form of speech or writing) is always a dialogue. Acknowledged as the philosopher of dialogue, he evolved a view of dialogue (from his earliest writings in pre-revolutionary Russia through his last unfinished manuscript in the mid-1970s), as a human condition, as an ethical imperative, and even as a prerequisite for thinking.[2] Thus, his notion of dialogue focuses on the idea of the social nature of dialogue, and the idea of struggle inherent in it. For Bakhtin, dialogue consists of three elements:

- a speaker,
- a listener/respondent, and
- a relation between the two.

Language and the outcome of language (or what language says; ideas, characters, forms of truth) are always thus the product of the interactions between (at least) two people or two groups.

Bakhtin contrasts the notion of dialogue with what it is not, that is, the idea of monologue, or what he terms as the *monologic*, which refers to utterances by a single person or entity. For Bakhtin, ideas about language have always postulated a unitary speaker, a speaker who has an unmediated relation to 'his unitary and singular "own" language.' Like Derrida's 'engineer', this speaker claims to 'produce unique meaning in [my] own speech; [my] speech comes from [me] alone.' Hence, according to Bakhtin, this way of thinking about language focuses on two pillars: language as a system, and the individual who speaks it. For Bakhtin, both pillars, however, produce monologic language: a language that seems to come from a single, unified source (Bakhtin, 1981: 666).

Bakhtin develops his work on dialogue further by arguing that there are two principal forces in operation whenever language is used: a centripetal force and a centrifugal force (ibid.: 667–8). Drawing upon physics, Bakhtin argues that, on the one hand, a centripetal force tends to push things toward a central point; on the other

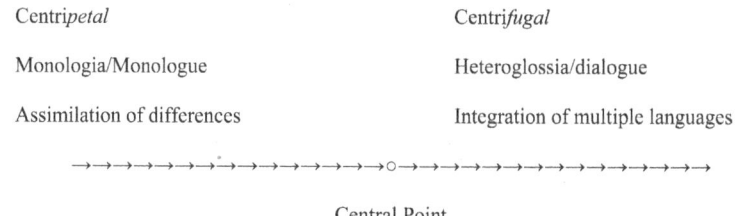

Figure 1. Bakhtin's chosen site for intercultural dialogue.

hand, a centrifugal force tends to push things away from a central point and out in all directions (see Figure 1).

According to Bakhtin, monologic language (monologia) operates according to centripetal forces: the speaker of monologic language attempts to push all the elements of language and all its various rhetorical modes (the journalistic, the religious, the political, the economic, the academic, the personal) into one single form or utterance, converging into one central point. The centripetal force of monologia tries to get rid of differences between languages (or rhetorical modes) in order to present one unified language. Monologia is a system of norms, of one standard language, or an 'official' language, a standard language that everyone would have to speak (and which would then be enforced by various mechanisms).

An alternative form of dialogue is *heteroglossia,* which attempts to encompass a multiplicity of languages, that is by including a wide variety of different ways of speaking, different rhetorical strategies and vocabularies. In Bakhtinian terms, dialogue is therefore not understood in terms of multiple meanings for individual words or phrases, by disconnecting the signifier and the signified. Thus, instead of racing towards consensus, we may pause for reflection on the meanings conveyed by the Other.

Bakhtin argues that in any utterance, both monologia and heteroglossia, both the centripetal and the centrifugal forces of language are at work. 'Every concrete utterance of a speaking subject serves as a point where centrifugal as well as centripetal forces are brought to bear' (ibid.: 668). Language, in this sense, is always both anonymous and social, something formed beyond any individual, but also concrete, filled with specific content which is shaped by the speaking subject. Thus, for Bakhtin,

> the idea *lives* not in one person's *isolated* individual consciousness; if it remains there only, it degenerates and dies. The idea begins to live, that is, to take shape, to develop, to find and renew its verbal expression, to give birth to new ideas, only when it enters into genuine dialogic relationships with other ideas, with the ideas of *others*. Human thought becomes genuine thought, that is, an idea, only under conditions of living contact with another and alien thought, a thought embodied in someone else's voice, that is, in someone else's consciousness expressed in discourse (Todorov, 1984: 87–8).[3]

A heteroglossic view of dialogue points to a conceptualization of politics and the social focusing on the crucial importance of language for politics. Language is a creative force rather than an empty vehicle for consensus-building. Moreover, such a conception of dialogue emphasizes the inter-subjective and perpetual cognition and meaning formation inherent in this process. It also stresses that *everybody*, every member of the polity, has a voice, not only the decision makers and those who have their ear (Neumann, 2003).

This brings us to the discussion of the Self and the Other through the dialogic interaction of the two. In this context, dialogue plays itself out at various degrees. The first degree of dialogue requires the unity of the Self (Hanafi, cited in Pace and Schumacher, 2004). The dialogic process thus requires reconciliation with the Self before interaction with an Other. At the second level of dialogue, an acceptance of the Other in dialogue has to be in place. To come back to Bakhtin's work, critics interested in seeing the heteroglossia in Euro-Mediterranean relations would seek to encourage a dialogic relation embedded in social relations, which can be described as a relation with a distinct social purpose. As Neumann argues, it is precisely because dialogue plays itself out at different levels that social practices become crucial. Dialogue places subjects along a process of inter-action with others that constitute the Self (Neumann, cited in Pace and Schumacher, 2004). As the colonizer defined the colonized, so too, the colonized defined the colonizer. This mirror-image of the Self through the Other, à la Lacan, sheds light on societal codes and the way in which these are shaped, reshaped and lived out. Dialogue therefore involves a dynamic interplay of cultures between discourse (being) and practice (becoming) (ibid.: 123). Cultures are distinctive in the sense that there cannot be a one-to-one relationship between the respective phenomena that comprise them, but if a person is grounded in one culture, they can begin to grasp another by melding its phenomena into their own cultural horizon. Communication then becomes a possibility (ibid.: 123) and postulates a 'fusion of horizons' which signifies the growing 'convergence of our *and* their perspectives through a process of reciprocal learning' (Dallmayr, 2001: 341).

In aiming to understand the mythical aspect of the Other's (social) personality, a dialogical dialogue thus seeks a *common* horizon. Hence, dialogue, of necessity, must be never ending (Neumann, cited in Pace and Schumacher, 2004: 123). The process of a dialogical dialogue itself aims to bring about *a* horizon, defined as a new, emerging understanding through the exploration by imagination of new modes of human possibilities. Bakhtin argues that all utterances are directed toward an answer, a response. (In everyday speech, words are understood by being taken into the listener's own conceptual system, filled with specific objects and emotional expressions, and being related to these); the understanding of an utterance is thus inseparable from the listener's response to it. All speech is thus oriented toward what Bakhtin calls the 'conceptual horizon' of the listener; this horizon is comprised of the various social languages the listener inhabits/uses. This is why Bakhtin argues that 'discourse lives on the boundary between its own context and another, alien, context' (Bakhtin, 1981: 672–3).

A good model for what a heteroglossic Euro-Mediterranean dialogue could look like is the language of democracy. As argued by one author:

We also need to be modest about our ability to find the answers for other societies. Liberal democracy is the best form of government yet discovered. But if you rush to a multi-party election without first developing the underpinnings of liberal democracy – the rule of law, civil society, private property, independent media – you can end up with what Fareed Zakaria has called 'illiberal democracy'. We can, and should, offer a toolbox of experiences in all aspects of transition, from how to write a constitution to how to deal with a difficult past. But then it's up to them (Garton Ash, 2004a and 2004b).

Thus, there is no single, unified language of democracy but many languages of democracy. In using all these languages, the aim is to increase the potential options for Mediterranean partners, as the democratic norm probably contains some kind of language which every Mediterranean partner has as part of their existing vocabulary or 'horizon'. In recognizing its post-colonial role, Europe has to bring together the best of Europe as well as the best of the Mediterranean. It is therefore helpful for analytical, as well as practical purposes, to interpret dialogue not just as conversation but also as process (Guillaume, 2002; Inayatullah and Blaney, 2004). To avoid criticisms of Eurocentrism or elitism, inter-cultural dialogue must therefore, of necessity, be the product of an *inter-action* between the parties concerned: a process of self-criticism and self-reflection through imagining the Other. A dialogic dialogue opens up the possibility for learning, so that different languages may be reconfigured through the process and may be modified (no one language emerges as triumphant). The logic of a dialogic encounter is, then, an integrationist logic. Rather than claiming to have a dialogue on Mediterranean issues, Euro-Mediterranean relations should aim for that to which the dialogue converges.

As noted earlier, another way of arriving at this conclusion is to look at 'dialogue' in a Habermasian way. A main theme running through Habermas' critical theoretical works is that valid knowledge can only emerge from a situation of open, free and uninterrupted dialogue. His chosen site for intercultural imagination is the public sphere. He argues that the idea of a neutral apolitical science, based on a rigid separation of facts and values, is untenable since questions of truth are inextricably bound up with the political problems of freedom to communicate and to exchange ideas (Habermas, 1971 and 1974). Thus, 'dialogue' is not a neutral concept; many preconditions have to be met in order to have a conversation appropriately called a dialogue. One of these is the equality of the participants. Habermas is also critical of Western social theory for its failure to avoid reductionism and to develop a valid theory of communication and rationality (Habermas, 1984 and 1987). Thus, the nature of social science, being inherently a 'Western' *praxis*, is a means to the end of an intercultural dialogue. With such frameworks for thinking about dialogue it is difficult to find the terms through which one seeks to explore Others through inter-actions, without falling in the trap of ethnocentrism. In order to ensure an equitable climate for dialogue, there need to be some ground 'rules for practical discourse' that demand objectification, justification and non-contradiction in order to structure dialogue as debate. If dialogue with Mediterranean partners is to inform the EU's democratic decision-making, EU-Mediterranean actors themselves have to contribute to establishing the conditions for dialogue, particularly in those cases where such conditions are not already present. A prerequisite for dialogue is that a lot of common ground already exists. Dialogue should aim at freedom, that is, to 'call something into being which did not exist before, which was not given, not even as an object of cognition or imagination' (Arendt, 1961: 151). Theorizing Euro-Mediterranean politics is not only about ordering a set of already existing signs but also about creating new ones. A dialogic dialogue requires enlightenment beyond preconceived ideas of the Other. Different and mutually exclusive universalisms have to be reconciled in order to enter into a dialogue. Every worldview, whether European or Mediterranean, can construct its own reasons to enter into dialogue, with its own historically defined meanings attached to it. Thus we will be rid of the paradoxical task of being 'objective' in defining the terms of the dialogue (Griffioen, 2002).

As Bakhtin argues, the alternative to dialogue is monologue. In this context, the appeal of dialogue as a mode for being-in-the-world is particularly strong. In the complex reality of Euro-Mediterranean relations, however, the question remains: to what degree does this choice really exist? The conceptualization of dialogue, as developed by Bakhtin, is an ethically stimulating one but tells us little by way of the role of power in politics. Likewise, Habermas's ideal speech situation falls short of the reality of such a situation. This is particularly pertinent in Euro-Mediterranean relations where the EU's hegemony adds challenges to the development of real dialogue between the partners.

In theorizing Euro-Mediterranean politics, particularly the role of dialogue in Euro-Mediterranean relations, it is the task of social scientists to embrace the role of empirical studies on how dialogue actually ensues. We need to observe how Euro-Mediterranean dialogic practices interact with other practices and how power relations (specifically the EU's hegemony) are immersed within these practices. If we are to celebrate differences and to offer a space for alternative voices to be heard, dialogue has a crucial role to play both in our intellectual conceptualizations and even more so in policy-making circles which impact on people's social lives. Keeping in mind Bakhtin's conception of dialogue as a description of the human condition, we recognize that meaning formation is an intersubjective phenomenon and therefore does not exclude the possibility of monologue. For this reason, it is even more pertinent to engage in dialogue and open up to alternative 'languages'. Rather than losing ourselves in translation, let us lose ourselves in a truly dialogic relationship with others.

Bruce Tuckman's 1965 Forming Storming Norming Performing Development Model

Before moving on to analyse aspects of existing dialogic efforts in Euro-Mediterranean relations and examining whether dialogue is really taking place in the Barcelona process, a synthesis of the theoretical arguments, developed above, into a workable model is called for. The key to ongoing dialogue processes is equal access to participation under conditions of mutual recognition and the possibility for contestation, allowing possibilities to agree to disagree (Tully, 1995 and 2004). Bruce Tuckman developed a stage-model for group development through his Forming, Storming, Norming and Performing model (Tuckman, 1965). Most analysts assume that groups go through a number of phases or stages if they exist for an extended period. Tuckman's influential model exposes four stages going from (1) orientation/testing/dependence (forming) to (2) conflict (storming) to (3) group cohesion (norming) and to (4) functional role-relatedness (performing). We can apply this model to European-Mediterranean group development but before that the next section will briefly expand Tuckman's model.

In the forming phase, groups orient themselves through testing to identify the boundaries of their behaviour. Through this process, one group establishes a dependency relationship with other group members. This phase can be linked to Bakhtin's inter-action stage in which language and the outcome of language is understood as the product of these inter-actions. The second phase is characterized by polarization and conflict around issues with behaviours serving as resistance to group influence and task requirements. If we link this to the dialogic process, it includes contestation which, as Antje Wiener argues, involves the possibility of (1) dialogue and deliberation and subsequent agreement (logic of arguing); (2) dialogue and disagreement; (3) disagreement and conflict among negotiating elites, and (4) contentious action in the respective elite negotiators' root cultural spheres (Tarrow, 1998: 12–13 in Wiener, 2005). In Bakhtinian terms this phase would include centripetal as well as centrifugal forces. The third phase is one where resistance is overcome and in which in-group feeling and cohesiveness develops, new standards evolve, and new roles are adopted. Groups are now better able to express opinions. Thus, in dialogic terms:

> genuine dialogue or consensus requires a reciprocity of understanding, in the sense that it is not up to others ('them') to understand 'our' perspective, but it is equally up to 'us' to grasp things from 'their' perspective' (Dallmayr, 2001: 341). This phase would eventually lead to Bakhtin's heteroglossia in which diversity of voices becomes the fundamental characteristic of group dynamics.

In the final phase, the groups work towards achieving task activities. Functional and flexible roles are in place, and group energies are channelled towards targeted objectives. The resolution of structural issues is in place and the structures become supportive of group performance. In Bakhtin's terminology, this would be the phase where groups seek a 'common' horizon and group inter-actions reach a level of maturity.

Having examined the various stages that group development experiences à la Tuckman and how these phases are linked to Bakhtin's work on dialogue, it is important to highlight that occasionally groups may revert to an earlier phase, particularly if the context is unfavourable to dialogic relations. With this dual conceptual framework in mind, we now turn to the empirical sites of dialogue in Euro-Mediterranean relations.

Theory and Practice: A Review of Ten Years of Euro-Mediterranean Dialogue

This section attempts an examination of how the partners in the Barcelona process feel about dialogue and an exploration of what kind of relationship both parties want and how the dialogue that exists reflects these objectives. It brings to the fore views of existing governments and organizations involved in the process of Euro-Mediterranean dialogue. Through an application of the conceptual frameworks on dialogue presented above, this section seeks to uncover the real meaning of dialogue in Euro-Mediterranean relations and the ensuing experience of the participants involved in this process.

The Forming Phase/Bakhtin's Inter-action Stage of Euro-Mediterranean Relations

Euro-Mediterranean affairs stretch back to the Treaty of Rome in 1957 when a series of policy initiatives were designed to regulate relations between Europe and its southern periphery (Joffé, 2005). When applying the stages of dialogue to Euro-Mediterranean relations, a pertinent question to ask is how far is the dialogue, in this context, shaped by Europe's colonial past in the Mediterranean area, and how extensive is the legacy of this historical period on the struggles Mediterranean partners have had to undergo through decolonization? In conventional theoretical frameworks, Euro-Mediterranean politics seem to miss the legacy of colonial rule which formed competitive cultures and which sanctified inequality and subjugated those outside the European centre. If Euro-Mediterranean relations are to engage in a truly dialogic dialogue, our theoretical frameworks must seriously and critically confront the role of colonialism, various responses to colonialism, neocolonialism and its legacies (Inayatullah and Blaney, 2004). As Joffé claims:

> In some respects, these (EU) initiatives represented a continuation of the experiences of the colonial era, especially the French relationship with its former colonies in North Africa. In reality, however, they reflected the inevitable and vital need for collaboration in view of European dependence on migrant labour from the Southern Mediterranean region, European dominance in the economic relationship across the Mediterranean and European involvement in regional security (Joffé, 2005).

The EU (previously EC) has thus held a hegemonic position in the Mediterranean area for a long time, and EU-superiority and Mediterranean-inferiority and dependency has been the order of their relations (Pace, 2005a). Moreover, although the EU member states and the Mediterranean partners share to some extent a common or at least a closely interrelated history – a shared language à la Bakhtin – as far as economic and social development is concerned, the Mediterranean countries, particularly the Arab partners, do not constitute a homogenous group (ibid.). One of the reasons for the hegemony of the European Union, vis-à-vis the Mediterranean area, is related to the levels of economic development between

North and South. With Europe being so well integrated and the South so divided, the gap in degrees of regional integration between the two areas is evident (Moré, 2004). The EU is the largest provider of financial aid to some Mediterranean partners including Jordan and the Palestinian Territories (West Bank and Gaza Strip), while the other Mediterranean partners are also beneficiaries of financial aid from the EU. Morocco has been the leading recipient among the Mediterranean partners in terms of total funds received from the MEDA programme.

Moreover, while EU member states have a high Gross Domestic Product (GDP) per capita, attaining a maximum of $53,780 in the case of Luxembourg, this is not the case for Arab countries; for example, Morocco's GDP per capita is approximately 1/15th of Luxembourg's and 1/9th of Ireland's (Pace, 2005a). This disparity is also reflected in the Human Development Index (HDI) established by the United Nations Development Programme (UNDP, 2003).

To sum up, the forming phase of EU-Mediterranean dialogic relations is very much characterized by the EU taking the lead, while Mediterranean partners have been attempting to adapt to this new context in their relations with the EU. The gaps and discrepancies in the two groups' relations often lead to the next stage of group development (see below). The forming stage is also a process through which Euro-Mediterranean partners test the grounds and boundaries of their behaviour. In Bakhtinian terms, this is a stage at which European and Mediterranean partners formulate ideas about the other group, through inter-action.

The Storming Phase: Bakhtin's Stage of Centripetal Forces in Euro-Mediterranean Relations

The declared objectives of the third basket of the EMP raised high expectations with regards to the creation of closer links between peoples in the region through a social, cultural and human partnership designed to encourage mutual understanding and cooperation between civil societies in the Euro-Mediterranean space.

It is still, however, often argued that civil society is underdeveloped in the Mediterranean partner countries (see Feliu in this volume). Arab voices acknowledge, for example, that Arab civil societies have so far played a weak role during the course of the EMP's third basket implementation process (Ammor and Shalaby, cited in Pace and Schumacher, 2004). Although several programmes have been launched under the third basket umbrella, the mobility of human beings from the South to the North remains a major obstacle and bone of contention. To make human exchange opportunities viable, certain constraints have to be addressed. To take one example, the key to lively and significant international cultural (culture defined in a narrow sense) and educational exchanges and cross-fertilization is mobility. The current visa regulations to enter the Schengen zone provide huge bureaucratic hurdles to the free flow of ideas and intellectual and artistic stimulation. The actual process of acquiring a visa is not just cumbersome and time-demanding but also very discouraging not just for an artist but also for an inviting institution. The latter is faced with some considerable challenges: an invitation letter to an artist from a neighbouring Mediterranean country has to include a written guarantee of being solely responsible for the invitee's personal and medical needs during the stay in the Schengen zone, and also for their return journey after the expiry of the visa. These stipulations can have a deterring effect particularly for smaller cultural institutions within the EU that have no prior experience in inviting guests from non-EU Mediterranean countries: such procedures thus prevent cultural exchange and intellectual mobility (Pace, 2006).

Storming relations between EU and Mediterranean partners have also related to the EMP's first basket objectives. Barcelona's first-pillar initial aims addressed issues of political governance, seeking to encourage democratic governance and respect for human rights throughout the Mediterranean, which are in turn linked to the objectives of the second and third baskets of the EMP.

But, regular references to shaky and/or undemocratic political systems, 'poor' governance, bad human rights records, regional conflicts and political violence as the order of the day in Mediterranean countries are not lacking in international media discourses, international reports and everyday political speeches. For example, although Lebanon signed up to several international agreements on human and civil rights including in 1997 the International Covenant on the rights of women, it refrained from signing the Agreement against torture. Following the arrest of anti-Syrian demonstrators in Beirut in August 2001, the EU expressed concern on human rights issues, passing of death sentences and lengthy prison sentences on journalists in Lebanon. Closure of MTV in the second half of 2002 was the subject of an EU démarche in Beirut. In its Resolution adopted on 16 January 2003, the European Parliament drew attention to the situation regarding human rights and democracy in Lebanon (Pace, 2005a). In 1997, the Islamic Action Front in Jordan boycotted that year's parliamentary elections. In August 2002, King Abdullah once again postponed the parliamentary elections (due in November 2001) to Spring 2003, without giving any new reasons (other than the instability in the 'region') to explain the new postponement. There have been several government reshuffles since the election of Ali Abul Ragheb's government from June 2000. In fact the average life span of Jordanian governments has been less than one year (since the country's existence) making this a destabilizing factor (although key ministers do keep their portfolios). Hence, a major constraint to political and economic reforms in Jordan has been the lack of continuity in governments. Algeria continues to be threatened by internal strife both from Islamic militants who have conducted a terror campaign since 1992, the Berber minority in eastern Algeria that has resorted to violence in search of greater autonomy, and the military who continue to exert considerable power. In July 2004, all 25 member states of the EU, in spite of intensive lobbying by Israel, supported a UN General Assembly Resolution, condemning Israel for its construction of the separation fence in the West Bank and demanding its immediate dismantlement. These are instances which created storming relations in EU and Mediterranean relations.

In terms of the second basket more specifically, this aims at promoting economic development through economic cooperation, based on the principle of free trade on a bilateral basis, mainly through association agreements with some partners having privileged arrangements such as a free trade area (Israel) and a customs union

(Turkey). Here, once again, storming relations have prevailed in Euro-Mediterranean dialogic encounters. Despite almost ten years of the Barcelona process, Mediterranean countries are still struggling with economic challenges including: state-controlled economies, underdeveloped infrastructures, small Foreign Direct Investment, low competitiveness, falling percentage of EU imports, deficit of the balance of payments, weak economic growth, high dependence on the EU market, low incomes, highly unequal distribution of incomes within the Mediterranean, high population growth, deficit in basic social services, high (youth) unemployment, high (illegal) emigration and environmental problems. Since 1995, only Lebanon experienced a fall in its population figure. The population of the majority of Mediterranean countries is relatively young. Young people are in turn most affected by unemployment. Egypt is by far the most populous country in the Arab world, and the rate at which the country's population is increasing remains quite high, at around 1.7 per cent annually. With an official unemployment rate of 9.5 per cent in 2002, the country faces a great challenge in providing sufficient employment for large groups of young people entering the workforce each year. Unemployment is fairly high in most of the MPCs. Although unemployment rates have fallen slowly in the Maghreb countries, since 2000, they are still among the highest in the region. In fact, from 1995, the rate of unemployment in the Mediterranean has been generally increasing – only Lebanon, Morocco and Tunisia experienced a slight decrease in unemployment since 1995. With a young population and an estimated 27.5 per cent unemployment rate, Algeria, like Egypt, urgently requires economic opportunities for its young. In Turkey, the government is facing a challenging test of its commitment to the reform programme of the agricultural sector that employs nearly 50 per cent of the workforce. With more than a quarter of the population already living below the poverty line, Turkey has yet to organize large-scale corporate farming to compete with the world's agricultural powers (Pace, 2005a).

Moreover, most Mediterranean partners have a trade deficit with the EU. Syria and Algeria are the only Mediterranean partners that regularly record a trade surplus with the EU. Algeria's resource base, its geographic location close to Europe, and the latter's endeavours to reduce the environmental impact of burning heavy hydrocarbons for heating and power generation, make pipeline deliveries of gas to the European energy market a feasible and highly demanded project. However, though the country possesses some of the larger proven natural gas reserves in the world, it is still considered as relatively under-explored. Its natural gas reserves of 160–200 trillion cubic feet put it in the world's top 10 gas resource holders (Economist Intelligence Unit, 2003). Hence, Algeria should theoretically have a positive future in terms of its potential as a growing supplier of gas to European markets for many years to come. Yet, the danger lies in its dependence on the agricultural and petroleum sectors, particularly in the context of the EU's protective Common Agricultural Policy. Although the EU is Israel's main trading partner in terms of overall trade (imports and exports), since 1997 Israel's deficit vis-à-vis the EU has been larger than its overall deficit (Israel imports far more than it exports to the EU). In Jordan, this trade deficit is partially offset by a surplus in services, mostly through tourism and remittances from Jordanians working abroad (Pace, 2005a).

Critics further argue that there is a lack of intra-Arab commercial trade. According to the Egyptian Businessmen's Association, there are a number of reasons contributing to limited intra-Arab trade including the instability of political relations between Arab countries, the high trade costs, with regard to trade financing, transport and communications, the big differences in individual incomes between Arab countries, the differences between consumption and buying behaviour in Arab countries, the competitive commercial structures, the differences in monetary and commercial policies and the fact that Arab producers are unable to compete with international producers in terms of price and quality, which makes it more attractive to import from non-Arab countries (Egyptian Businessmen Association, 2000). Hence, political differences between Arab leaders also affect Arab economic relations. In the political context, apart from the periodic crises the Arab world continues to suffer, leaders frequently undermine the mutual confidence between Arab countries and, as a result, a turbulent political atmosphere prevails (Pace and Schumacher, 2004).

Also uneven is the level of integration of the Mediterranean, mainly Arab, partners in the world economy (Escribano and Jordán, 1998). Besides the differences in natural resources and potential, this gap reflects the disparities between the economic policies of European and Arab governments and within Arab states. Up until the 1980s (even the 1990s in some cases), import substitution was the norm in the Arab partner states. The high tariffs applied converted import duties into a source of revenue that constituted a barrier to international trade. New export-oriented policies had to face up to the challenge of poorly diversified economies that relied heavily on oil exports. Morocco, Tunisia and to some extent Egypt were the exceptions while other Arab countries, like Jordan and Lebanon, made progress in services. Arab economies also encountered political difficulties, besides the economic ones. This led to a low inter-Arab economic integration. In 2002, Tunisia, Morocco, Egypt and Jordan decided to speed up the liberalization of trade between them through what was then the Agadir Initiative (Pace, 2005a). The Agadir Agreement provides for free trade between these four countries by 2006, and with the Commission of the European Union's provision of technical support for its implementation, there are some hopes that this initiative could move Euro-Mediterranean dialogue to a new phase. In Bakhtinian terms, although centripetal forces are at play in Euro-Mediterranean relations – where contestation is the language of their inter-action – centrifugal forces may also eventually emerge through these inter-changes between the two groups.

The above is but a glimpse of the ways in which Mediterranean and European partners often communicate with each other. While on the one hand, the EU talks of democracy, free trade areas and the creation of closer links between Euro-Mediterranean peoples, Mediterranean partners talk of their own domestic challenges including diverse political systems and structures, economic disparities, barriers to their peoples' mobility, explosive population growth rates, illiteracy. The storming phase in Euro-Mediterranean dialogic encounters is thus characterized by Mediterranean partners attempting to have their voices heard. At times, EU-Mediterranean relations in fact seem to be stuck in the storming phase albeit with short, brief episodes of norming and performing. What Euro-Mediterranean dialogism, à la Bakhtin, should aim for is therefore an orientation toward the interaction between the various languages of a speaker and the languages of a listener which may bring partners to the norming phase in their dialogic encounters.

The Norming Phase: Bakhtin's Heteroglossia in Euro-Mediterranean Relations

The solution to the Mediterranean partners' problems has been put forward in the Arab Human Development Report (HDR) of 2003. This complements the HDR 2003 in that it underlines the importance to Arab countries of education and knowledge as a powerful driver of economic growth through higher productivity. The said report asserts that an Arab educated society can achieve improved economic development (and thus the objectives of justice, human freedoms and dignity and good governance) through appropriate training of its youthful, albeit large, labour pool. This is an instance of true dialogue where, in Bakhtinian terms, Arab language coincides with the language of Europeans. In fact, this is the language of the UK's Presidency (from July 2005) whose vision of the EMP puts great emphasis on the importance of education at all levels in the South (UK Presidency, 2005). The remaining obstructions to development relate to defective structures, in particular political ones, but economic and social too (UNDP, 2003).

Although gaps persist, since 1970 many aspects of human development in the Mediterranean have improved thanks to higher incomes. Gender gaps in enrolment have been narrowing: in terms of gender equality in primary and secondary education, Mauritania led the group of poor countries through an increase in the ratio of girls to boys from 67 per cent to 93 per cent between 1990 and 1996. In Jordan, while not perfect, the democratization process has been regarded as one of the most advanced in the region. According to the UN's Human Development Report of 2003, during the 1990s, despite general economic stagnation, Lebanon and Tunisia grew by more than 3 per cent per year while Egypt realized the largest reduction in under-five mortality rates – from 10 per cent to 4 per cent (ibid.). It is not so easy to identify these positive developments as direct consequences of Euro-Mediterranean dialogic inter-actions but we could suggest that through heteroglossic interactions in which the diversity of voices in Euro-Mediterranean relations are allowed to flourish, group dynamics experience a socialization and learning process which impacts on their peoples' daily lives. Through such a process, all group members adopt new roles and one specific example of this outcome is the EMPA. At its first plenary session, 12–15 March 2005 in Cairo, the Euro-Mediterranean Parliamentary Assembly (inaugurated in Athens 22–23 March 2004) adopted various resolutions and Arab partners circulated a paper with their views in an attempt to exercise and reinforce the sense of joint ownership (European Commission, 2005). The Anna Lindh Foundation similarly creates a window of opportunity for Euro-Mediterranean relations to ensure an equitable climate for dialogue and a forum for debate.

Similar progress towards a truly Euro-Mediterranean dialogic encounter has also been made in addressing the challenge of joint ownership of the EMP process through co-chairmanship of sectoral ministerial meetings, closer consultations on the outcome of ministerial meetings and co-development of the Neighbourhood policy. The ENP's action plans are a step in the right direction if taken as a form of dialogue between the EU and Mediterranean partners on a bilateral basis. The dialogue envisioned in these action plans aims at a 'common' horizon where both groups make commitments and which, in practical terms, encourages Mediterranean partner governments to facilitate the activities of NGOs, such as to allow greater media freedom, while the European partners open up certain of their own policies and programmes to Mediterranean participation, including the internal market, police and judicial cooperation, border management, efforts to stem organized crime, money laundering and trafficking, energy and transport networks, exchange programmes and education, science and research initiatives (Leigh, 2005). One specific example of how a truly dialogic encounter between European and Mediterranean partners can develop was the international conference on the ENP organized by the Association for International Affairs and the Friedrich Ebert Stiftung in Prague, 20–21 May 2005. Participants included representatives from the Commission, the Council and the European Parliament, as well as southern and eastern representatives from civil society (including journalists, academics), political parties and opposition groups, and representatives from the Euro-Mediterranean Human Rights Network. Issues discussed included reform in the southern and eastern neighbouring countries, the EU's conditionality policies, EU's funding mechanisms, education, security and economic liberalization. Representatives of the EU took note of the suggestions made by southern and eastern partners for increasing the involvement of non-state actors and the necessity of co-ordination of all EU policies which address neighbouring states. In the context of the ENP, at the end of 2003, institutionalized or informal human rights dialogues have been initiated with several partners (European Commission, 2005). This is a good example of how European and Mediterranean partners are entering into a genuine dialogic relation with the others' ideas. Whereas, on the one hand, European representatives attempt to encompass their southern neighbours' multiplicity of languages (à la Bakhtin) and to include Mediterranean partners' ways of speaking, on the other hand, Mediterranean partners are also attempting to take in European ideas: at the same time, both groups are going through processes of reflection on the meanings conveyed by the other group. For instance, the commitments made between the EU and Mediterranean partners differ from one Mediterranean country to another, according to the particular needs and capacities and the respective country's relations with the EU (Leigh, 2005). Following the Arab Summit in Tunis in 2004 and the Algiers Summit in 2005, Arab partners reiterated 'The Drive for Development and Modernization in the Region' which will generate reforms from within their societies. The window of opportunity for a true dialogic encounter between European and Mediterranean partners seems to be opening towards a norming phase. This form of dialogue in Euro-Mediterranean relations can be enhanced if consultations with regards to action plans are also taken at the 'people' level.

The norming phase in Euro-Mediterranean relations has been further attempted, as mentioned briefly above, through the setting up of the Anna Lindh

Euro-Mediterranean Foundation for the Dialogue between Cultures. This is, significantly, the first *common* institution of the EMP financed with contributions from all the Partner countries as well as the Commission. The partners established 35 national networks, enhancing the role that civil society can play in the Euro-Mediterranean space. This initiative has been further supported by the setting up of a non-governmental Euro-Mediterranean Platform following the Civil Forum in Luxembourg early in 2005. The election of a representative board and the adoption of a charter help structure inter-actions of independent civil society actors. This also provides a connection with official EMP activities. Networking among civil societies both South–South and North–South has increased exchanges of people, particularly young people. The Euro-Mediterranean Youth Action Programme I has been particularly successful in this regard. Adopted at the end of 1998 and set up with the understanding that 'youth exchanges should be the means to prepare future generations for a closer cooperation between the Euro-Mediterranean partners' (European Commission, 1995), the first phase of the programme promoted mobility and non-formal educational activities for young people through youth exchanges, voluntary services and support measures. Since its launch, the programme has facilitated the participation and exchange of ideas between 20,000 young people across the Mediterranean. Following the conclusion of EuroMed Youth II, the Commission is now aiming at a new design for EuroMed Youth III with a new decentralized management (Pace and Schumacher, 2004; European Commission, 2001). Cooperation between groups such as NGOs, trade unions, business organizations, and Social and Economic Councils has also improved Euro-Mediterranean dialogic encounters in diverse areas such as human rights, the environment, sustainable development, cultural heritage and women's empowerment (Pace, 2005b).

These recent initiatives, especially the Euro-Mediterranean Parliamentary Assembly and the Anna Lindh Foundation, are newly created sites building on already existing signs for dialogue. They are workable instruments which have the potential for dialogic encounters between European and Mediterranean partners to flourish through equal participation under conditions of mutual recognition. Such initiatives offer the groundwork for Euro-Mediterranean group development to move towards the implementation of the objectives of the EMP, that is, the performing phase.

The Performing Phase: Bakhtin's Common Horizon of Euro-Mediterranean Relations

This stage in Euro-Mediterranean relations can only be attained when there is a move from EU rhetorical modes (monologia) to the integration of the concerns of the Mediterranean partner countries. The norming phase in Euro-Mediterranean relations has already kicked off some hope in this regard. Moreover, if the Agadir process takes effect, there is a prospect that most North African countries, possibly including Libya eventually, will progressively become more open. There is also another prospect that the third basket of the EMP gets off the ground and slowly works towards greater cross-cultural knowledge and mutual understanding and appreciation (heteroglossia), through the existing instruments of the Euro-Mediterranean Foundation and the Euro-Mediterranean Parliamentary Assembly. The former promises to build networks in spheres including archives, museums, libraries, school textbooks, book translations, comparative religion, migration studies, the press and the media, film-making and the performing arts (Frendo, 2005). The latter offers a context for dialogic inter-actions among parliamentarians – in particular among those from around the shores of the Mediterranean. It also offers an environment for the sharing of experiences that will encourage the integration of learning processes from each group (European as well as Mediterranean). European and Mediterranean partners need to be sensitive to the sense of boundedness, historicity and social determination inherent in dialogic notions of each other's languages. To enter into dialogue with each other, Europeans as well as Mediterranean partners need to attune to their own, as well as the Others', languages. Through dialogue, it is possible for Euro-Mediterranean partners to direct their speech acts towards possible responses of the Other. Through these dialogic processes both partners find more things to say, more ways to express things, so that the Other can understand the message(s). This diversity of voices in a truly dialogic relationship is the fundamental characteristic of heteroglossia. The recent Euro-Mediterranean initiatives have the potential to fulfil this imagined co-presence in Euro-Mediterranean dialogic relations. As Bakhtin reminds us, this stage of the dialogic process in Euro-Mediterranean relations is a long one and requires both partner groups to aim at achieving a 'common' horizon.

Conclusion: Is co-existence/co-presence of differences possible? Implications for Future Euro-Mediterranean Dialogic Relations

This analysis has outlined the theoretical and practical aspects of Euro-Mediterranean dialogue. It has sought to shed some new light on the process of dialogue in EU-Mediterranean relations and to apply the thinking of Bakhtin and Tuckman's stage model of group development to the practical reality that the EU and the Mediterranean partners find themselves in as they slowly attempt to move closer through dialogue.

It has argued that for a true dialogic encounter, Euro-Mediterranean partners need to find the space for critical self-reflection. Moving away from relations of domination, dialogue entails an overlap of the Self and the Other. Self-identity always owes a debt to alterity, and the Other always exists within as a source of internal difference. It is in the interest of both European and Mediterranean partners for the practice of dialogue to involve adapting to the language of the Other. Mediterranean partners need to acknowledge that the EU is going through some challenging times - the Constitutional debates, the next enlargement – while the EU partners need to adhere more to the concerns of their southern neighbours. The effectiveness of the EMP depends on the partners' capacity to 'read' each other's worlds. The more the effort at reading the Other's world, the less likely the unintended consequences of this special relationship (Inayatullah and Blaney,

2004). If we understand the Other, we are more likely to share with our partners local or global visions and to anticipate the behaviour and reactions of our partners. The opening up of spaces, in dialogic encounters, to the voices of the Other enables us to act effectively. This means some hard realities: Europeans have to face their own hegemonic practices while Mediterranean partners have to engage in more self-criticisms. The recognition of one's own participation in another's 'language' can create a bridge and a common horizon for dialogic interactions, or as Fabian describes a co-presence with the Other (Fabian, 1983). In so doing, each party to a dialogue has to move away from the idea that the Self and the values and norms it upholds are exclusive. For true dialogue and participation, recognition of one's particularities is one step toward the realization of the particularities of Others. Euro-Mediterranean dialogic relations must work towards establishing this overlap.

The artificial division between the three baskets of the EMP has thus far led to an excessive institutional complexity with a simultaneous gap in terms of involvement of social actors. As Iván Martín argued elsewhere, the biggest contradiction of the EMP is that it intends to promote democracy, bring about development and enhance mutual knowledge among the peoples of the Mediterranean by purely intergovernmental methods, without giving any say to the people affected. Thus, 'social consultation' with civil society, now confined to the third basket, should be extended to the *high politics* of economic and political issues currently handled in the first and second baskets. It follows that one of the major challenges for the future of the EMP will be establishing the procedures to make consultation with all the social actors involved, central to and part and parcel of the Barcelona process (Pace, 2005b and 2005c). The setting up of a Euro-Mediterranean Academy for Best Practices could potentially empower and activate wider civil society groups within the southern Mediterranean partners without creating conflict with their governments. Existing obstacles to increased mobility across the new EU boundaries, namely rigid visa regulations, should be ultimately removed or at least eased in the short to medium term.

While the EU's enlargement of May 2004 has added new challenges to the Partnership, the EMP remains, in Bakhtin's terminology, a creative force, a systematic and structured dialogic framework – not an empty vehicle for consensus building. It is a process which has the potential to develop into an inter-subjective, meaning formation and perpetual cognition mechanism for both partners – European as well as Mediterranean. As long as every partner has a voice, and as long as each party accepts the Other along this dialogic process, the integrationist logic of the EMP can provide for a truly dialogic encounter. What remains as a major challenge is the unity of the Self – both in Europe as well as in the Mediterranean areas: for true dialogue to come about, this is an urgent call. Euro-Mediterranean dialogic relations should aim at converging towards co-presence. The EMP should move away from being an inherently 'Western' praxis towards a EuroMed praxis paving the way for a true dialogic process. This dialogue mission therefore involves a dynamic interplay of Euro-Mediterranean cultures and communities between discourse (being) and practice (becoming).

Acknowledgements

I would like to thank participants at: the Roundtable on the Third Basket of the Euro-Mediterranean Partnership on Culture and Community in the EMP which took place in Alexandria, Egypt, 5–7 October 2003; the panel on the European Union and the Mediterranean: Theoretical Reflections, ECPR conference, University of Bologna, Bologna, 24–26 June, 2004; the International workshop on 'The Impact of European Union Involvement in Civil Society Structures in the Southern Mediterranean', Friedrich Ebert Stiftung, FES Maroc, Rabat, 4–5 December, 2004; and the Policy Brief discussion workshop on Bringing the Euro-Mediterranean Partnership Closer to the People: 35 Proposals to Engage Civil Society in the Barcelona Process, Friedrich Ebert Stiftung, FES Maroc, Rabat, 18–19 March, 2005 for thought-provoking debates on this topic as well as Tobias Schumacher, Sharon Pardo, Iván Martín, Nicola Smith and two anonymous referees for their constructive feedback.

Notes

[1] Adapted from Monar (1997).
[2] Communication between the author and Iver B. Neumann, September/October 2003. See Neumann (2003).
[3] See also Bakhtin (1984) and Clark (1984).

References

Arendt, H. (1961) *Between Past and Future: Six Exercises in Political Thought* (London: Faber).
Bakhtin, M. (1981) in: M. Holquist (Ed.) *The Dialogic Imagination: Four Essays*, trans. by C. Emerson and M. Holquist (Austin/London: University of Texas Press).
Bakhtin, M. (1984) in: C. Emerson (Ed.) *Problems of Dostoevsky's Poetics* (Manchester: Manchester University Press).
Clark, K. (1984) *Mikhail Bakhtin* (The Belknap Press of Harvard University Press: Cambridge, MA/London).
Collins (1987) *Cobuild English Language Dictionary* (London: Collins/The University of Birmingham).
Council of the European Union (2002) *New Neighbours Initiative*, Brussels, 14078/02, 12.11.2002.
Dallmayr, F. (2001) Conversation Across Boundaries: Political Theory and Global Diversity, *Millennium: Journal of International Studies*, 30(2), pp. 331–347.
Economist Intelligence Unit, Algeria Review (2003). Available at: http://www.eiu.com.
Egyptian Businessmen Association (2000) The World Trade Organisation and the Arab Countries. Communication to the 4th Forum of Arab Businessmen Society, Kuwait, May 2000, p. 6.
Escribano, G. & Jordán, J. M. (1998) Subregional Integration in the Southern Shore of the Mediterranean and the Euro-Mediterranean Free Trade Area, paper presented at the Valencia Forum on the Euro-Mediterranean Free Trade Area, organized by the Centro Español de Relaciones Internacionales, 20–21 November.
European Commission (1995) *Barcelona Declaration*. Adopted at the Euro-Mediterranean Conference, 27–28 November 1995. Barcelona.
European Commission (2001) Mid-term Evaluation of the Euromed-Youth programme, MEI/B7-4100/1B/0418, 24.08.2001.
European Commission (2003) Communication from the Commission to the Council and the European Parliament, Wider Europe-Neighbourhood: A New Framework for Relations with our Eastern and Southern Neighbours, Brussels, COM(2003) 104 final, 11.03.2003.
European Commission (2004) Communication from the Commission European Neighbourhood Policy, Strategy Paper, Brussels, COM(2004) 373 final, 12.05.2004.
European Commission (2005) Conclusions for the VIIth Euro-Mediterranean Conference of Ministers of Foreign Affairs, Luxembourg, 30–31 May, 2005. EuroMed Report (90), 1 June.
Frendo, H. (2005) Coexistence in Modernity: A Euromed Perspective, *The European Legacy*, 10(3), pp. 161–177.

Garton Ash, T. (2004a) Beyond the west, *The Guardian*, 10 June, 2004, available at: http://www.guardian.co.uk/print/0,3858,4943687-103677,00.html.
Garton Ash, T. (2004b) *Free World: Why a Crisis of the West Reveals the Opportunity of Our Time* (London: Penguin).
Guillaume, X. (2002) Foreign Policy and the Politics of Alterity: A Dialogical Understanding of International Relations, *Millennium: Journal of International Studies*, 31(1), pp. 1–26.
Habermas, J. (1971) *Towards a Rational Society: Student Protest, Science and Politics*, trans. by Jeremy J. Shapiro (London: Heinemann Educational).
Habermas, J. (1974) *Theory and Practice*, trans. (from German) by John Viertel (London: Heinemann).
Habermas, J. (1984) *Theory of Communicative Action*, trans. by Thomas McCarthy, Volume 1: Reason and the Rationalization of Society (Boston: Beacon Press).
Habermas, J. (1987) *Theory of Communicative Action*, trans. by Thomas McCarthy, Volume 2: Lifeworld and System: A Critique of Functionalist Reason (Cambridge: Polity).
Henk, G. (2002) Is the Notion of Intercultural Dialogue a Western Concept? (The Netherlands: University of Leiden). Article available at: http://sos-net.eu.org/red&s/dhdi/recherches/theoriedroit/articles/griffioen.htm (accessed on 20 May 2004).
Huntington, S. (1993) The Clash of Civilizations?, *Foreign Affairs*, 72(3), pp. 22–49.
Inayatullah, N. & Blaney, D. L. (2004) *International Relations and the Problem of Difference* (Routledge: London).
Joffé, G. (2005) The Status of The Euro-Mediterranean Partnership, EuroMeSCo working paper. Available at: http://www.euromesco.net/euromesco/artigo.asp?cod_artigo=117802.
Johannes, F. (1983) *Time and the Other: How Anthropology Makes Its Object* (New York: Columbia University Press).
Leigh, M. (2005) The EU's Neighbourhood Policy, in: E. Brimmer & S. Frohlich (Eds) *The Strategic Implications of EU Enlargement* (Washington DC: Center for Transatlantic Relations, Johns Hopkins University).
Martín, I. (Ed.) (2005) *Bringing the Euro-Mediterranean Partnership Closer to the People: 35 Proposals to Engage Civil Society in the Barcelona Process* (Rabat, Morocco: FES).
Monar, J. et al. (1997) Political Dialogue with Third Countries and Regional Political Groupings: The Fifteen as an Attractive Interlocutor, in: E. Regelsberger (Ed.) *Foreign Policy of the European Union: From EPC to CFSP and Beyond*, pp. 263–274 (London: Lynne Reinner).
Moré, I. (2004) The Economic Step Between Neighbours: The Case of Spain-Morocco, *Mediterranean Politics*, 9(2), pp. 165–200.
Neumann, I. (2003) International Relations as Emergent Bakhtinian Dialogue, in G. Hellmann (Ed.) Forum: Are Dialogue and Synthesis Possible in International Relations? *International Studies Review*, 5(1), pp. 137–140.
Pace, M. & Schumacher, T. (2004) Report: Culture and Community in the Euro-Mediterranean Partnership: A Roundtable on the Third Basket, Alexandria 5–7 October 2003, *Mediterranean Politics*, 9(1), pp. 122–126.
Pace, M. (2005a) *The Politics of Regional Identity: Meddling with the Mediterranean* (Oxford: Routledge, New IR Series).
Pace, M. (2005b) EMP cultural initiatives: what political relevance?, in: R. Youngs & H. A. Fernández (Eds) *The Barcelona Process Revisited* (Madrid: FRIDE and Real Instituto Elcano).
Pace, M. (2005c) Report: the impact of European Union involvement in civil society structures in the southern Mediterranean, *Mediterranean Politics*, 10(2), pp. 235–240.
Pace, M. (2006, forthcoming) People-to-people: education and culture, in: K. Weber, M. E. Smith & M. Baun (Eds) *Partners or Periphery? The European Union and the Governance of Wider Europe* (Cambridge: Cambridge University Press).
Todorov, T. (1984) *Mikhaïl Bakhtin: The Dialogical Principle* trans. by W. Godzich (Manchester: Manchester University Press).
Tuckman, B. W. (1965) Development sequence in small groups, *Psychological Bulletin*, 63(6), pp. 384–399.

Tully, J. (1995) *Strange Multiplicity: Constitutionalism in an Age of Diversity* (Cambridge/New York: Cambridge University Press).

Tully, J. (2004) Recognition and dialogue: the emergence of a new field, *Critical Review of International Social and Political Philosophy*, 7(3), pp. 84–106.

UK Presidency. *Achieving a Common Vision*: A *UK Contribution to the Future of the Barcelona Process*, position paper on British ideas on the EMP (2005).

UNDP Report (2003). Available at: http://www.undp.org/rbas/ahdr/english2003.html. Building a Knowledge Society (UN Publications: New York).

Wiener, A. (2005) The Dual Quality of Norms, paper presented at the workshop on Intersubjectivity and International Politics: Incentives from Jürgen Habermas's Work on International Relations and Political Theory, Johann Wolfgang Goethe-University Frankfurt, Campus Westend, 16–18 June 2005, R. 1.801.

Setting the (Cultural) Agenda: Concepts, Communities and Representation in Euro-Mediterranean Relations

RAFFAELLA A. DEL SARTO
European University Institute, Florence, Italy

Introduction

From the outset, the Euro-Mediterranean Partnership (EMP) addressed the issue of co-operation in cultural, social and (otherwise) human affairs under its so-called third 'basket'. However, during the first years of the EMP's existence, the third basket largely remained in the shadow of Euro-Mediterranean co-operation, for which there are three main reasons. First, while the whole idea of Euro-Mediterranean co-operation in the framework of the EMP was, *inter alia,* meant 'to prevent the emergence of a cultural rift' (Fahmy, 1997: 78), the relationship between the overall EMP project and its third basket remained undefined. Second, the three-basket structure of the EMP clearly separates between 'high politics' and economics on the one hand (dealt with in the first and second basket respectively), and 'low politics', constituting cultural and social affairs, on the other. Indeed, while government officials remained the key figures of Euro-Mediterranean co-operation within the first and the second baskets, the third was mainly left to civil society organizations and non-state actors. Third, and herewith related, very different areas of co-operation, which could not be accommodated within the 'political and security partnership' or within the realm of economics, were somewhat 'thrown' into the third basket. Thus, diverse issues such as human rights, health, sustainable development, environment protection, migration, youth, media, and inter-cultural dialogue were grouped within the EMP's third basket (Barcelona Declaration, 1995). In the best case, the issues dealt with under the third basket are disconnected from each other, thus considerably reducing the possibility of creating synergies. In the worst case, they may contradict each other. The objectives of promoting respect for cultural and religious diversity and of supporting universal principles of human rights – such as equality and women's rights for this matter – are a case in point.

While these structural problems related to the third basket have persisted, the importance given to inter-cultural dialogue dramatically increased in the aftermath of the events of 11 September 2001 – both within the EMP framework and beyond. Indeed, the number of events organized, under the headline of dialogue between cultures and religions, across the Euro-Mediterranean area (and beyond) have seen a dramatic increase ever since. Stressing that 'dialogue among cultures, civilizations and religions throughout the Mediterranean Region is more necessary than ever before in order to promote understanding among them' (Commission, 2002: 7), the EMP partners agreed, during the 5th Euro-Mediterranean conference of foreign ministers in Valencia in 2002, to establish a foundation that specifically deals with inter-cultural dialogue. Acting as co-ordinator between, and umbrella organization of, national civil society networks of the 35 EMP partners, the so-called Anna Lindh Euro-Mediterranean Foundation for the Dialogue between Cultures, with its headquarters in Alexandria, Egypt, became operational in the spring of 2005.

Against the background of the rising prominence of the 'clash of civilizations' discourse in the aftermath of 9/11, the objective of seeking to prevent such a clash by enhancing inter-cultural dialogue is certainly well intentioned. At the same time, it is undoubtedly imperative to address and fight against the dangerous phenomenon of global terrorism that justifies itself in terms of religion and hatred for 'the West'. In this context, it is also important to investigate the political and socio-economic sources of Islamist fundamentalism and terrorism as well as to counter-act the political exploitation of prejudices and misconceptions. The problem is, however, that the prescribed cure of establishing and strengthening an inter-cultural dialogue risks reproducing the same concepts and basic assumptions as the 'clash of civilizations' thesis. While challenging the predominant conception of world order (Adib-Moghaddam, 2002), Huntington's argument points to a paradigmatic shift in our understanding of international politics. Indeed, both Huntington's argument and the idea of inter-cultural dialogue presuppose the existence of distinct, and potentially incompatible, 'cultures' at the international level that may engage in conflict, or alternatively dialogue, with each other. From a *conceptual* point of view, this logic is, paradoxically, also reflected in the discourse of Islamist terrorism.

Against the background of the traditionally state-centred tradition of International Relations (IR) theory, the underlying assumptions of the 'clash of civilizations' thesis have important implications for the theory and practice of inter-cultural dialogue, as will be discussed in the first section of this essay. Combined with a number of insights from critical IR theory, the logic of the 'clash of civilizations' raises a number of conceptual issues that are crucial for our understanding of culture, community and dialogue. Taking into account the practice of inter-cultural dialogue in the Euro-Mediterranean area and beyond of the last couple of years, the second part of the essay will elaborate on these conceptual problems. They revolve, first, around dominating concepts and meanings within the so-called inter-cultural dialogue. How are 'cultures' and 'culture' defined, and how are meanings imposed? The second set of questions regards the issue of representation. Who represents the alleged 'cultures' or 'civilizations' within the inter-cultural dialogue, that is, 'who is speaking in the name of which culture'? The third consideration regards the concrete issue of agenda-setting. How do concepts, definitions and patterns of representations impact on the agenda of international politics in general, and Euro-Mediterranean relations in particular? And finally, how do definitions of boundaries between 'cultures' affect the sense of diversity and difference *between* and *within* the respective 'cultures', and why? Based on the findings of this investigation, the last section of this essay will briefly assess concepts, structures and programmes of the EMP's inter-cultural dialogue by focusing in particular on the recently established Anna Lindh Foundation. I conclude by stressing the necessity for redrawing the boundaries of difference and similarity in the Euro-Mediterranean context through the establishment of a trans-cultural dialogue along *thematic* lines.

The 'Civilizations Paradigm' between Theory and Discourse

In the post-9/11 era, the fame of Samuel Huntington's argument on the 'clash of civilizations', stipulating that in the post-cold war world the main source of conflicts would follow cultural and civilizational lines (Huntington, 1993: 25), is a puzzling phenomenon. Ever since Huntington published his 1993 article in *Foreign Affairs,* his clash of civilizations thesis has caused considerable academic debate (Foreign Affairs, 1996). Most scholarly responses, however, argued that the thesis was 'conceptually flawed and empirically unsustainable' (Welch, 1997: 198). The book-length, and slightly attenuated, elaboration of the argument (Huntington, 1996) did not substantially change the tenet of scholarly criticism. However, while Huntington's argument, which devotes considerable attention to a clash between 'Islam' and the 'West' in the immediate future (Huntington, 1993: 48), was refuted as a myth by many well-informed Middle Eastern scholars (for example Ajami, 1993; Halliday, 1996; Martín Muñoz, 1997), it did strike a chord in public debates. Particularly after the terrorist attacks in New York and Washington on 11 September 2001, the argument took hold of public discourses in many states of the so-called 'West', to the dismay of Muslim politicians and societies.

Thus, in a particularly unfortunate first reaction to the terrorist attacks of 9/11, US president George W. Bush called for a 'crusade' against (Islamist) terrorism

(*New York Times*, 17 September 2001: 2), and Italian prime minister Silvio Berlusconi publicly stressed the 'superiority of the Western civilization' (*Corriere della Sera*, 27 September 2001). These utterances went hand in hand with a general tendency of contrasting 'Islam' to the 'West' and providing *cultural* explanations for everything ranging from the lack of economic development and the persistence of authoritarianism to international terrorism. In the meantime, most politicians and public figures have become wary of explicitly depicting the phenomenon of Islamist terrorism as an issue of 'Islam' versus 'the West' – also because the subsequent attacks by Islamist terrorists in Bali, Djerba, Casablanca, Riyadh, Istanbul, Taba, and Cairo (among others) simply show the absurdity of such an argument. This restraint was also visible in the reaction of the European media and political elites to the events of '3/11', that is, the terrorist attacks in Madrid on 11 March 2004. It seems, however, that the 'civilizations logic' has trickled down to the minds of people. Thus, in public debates and in the media, the term 'Islamic world' is often used as an obvious, and unquestioned, concept (generally expressing difference to an equally unchallenged image of 'the West'). The question of whether 'Western' democracy is compatible with 'Islam' has been the argument of an impressive number of conferences and publications over recent years, as a quick search on any database reveals. There is also no doubt that over recent years the 'civilizations discourse' has, for instance, been resonating throughout the Italian media, whether public, 'government-owned' or independent. Thus, whether referring to religion, single states, individuals or terrorism, the adjective 'Islamic' (*Islamico*) has become predominant, replacing more differentiated (and more correct) terms, such as 'Muslims' when referring to persons or societies, and 'Islamist' when referring to political Islam.[1] The latter is, in itself, a heterogeneous phenomenon which would certainly necessitate further distinctions, such as between moderates, conservatives, liberals and, indeed, fundamentalists and terrorists (Ahmed, 2003; Al-Ashmawy, 1989). It was similarly striking that in his opposition to the US-led war on Iraq, the leader of the Italian communist party declared that 'we' are oppressing 'a civilization' in Iraq (*La Repubblica*, 12 April 2004). While political exponents of Italy's radical left certainly cannot be accused of adhering to Huntington's 'clash of civilizations' thesis and its predictions, the wording is nevertheless telling. Indeed, it shows that one does not have to agree with the clash of civilizations argument to be unconsciously drawn into its logic.

Certainly, dividing the world into allegedly clashing cultures, or civilizations, may be attractive as it provides simple black-and-white answers to very complex phenomena in world politics. In this vein, the prominence of Huntington's thesis may be interesting 'not because of what it says about the future of world politics, but because of what it says about *us* ... and how we see the world', as David Welch (1997: 199) has put it. Yet precisely because the clash of civilizations argument has implicitly or explicitly taken hold of many public discourses, in the 'West' and beyond, it is important to briefly revisit its particular set of ontological assumptions and implications for international relations. This is even more the case since it can be argued that the conceptualisation of the dialogue between cultures and civilizations implicitly or explicitly builds on what we may call the 'civilizations paradigm'. The questions 'what is the international system made of?' and 'what explains matters of peace and war?' are central to international relations theory. Considering that theorizing about world politics has witnessed a number of major developments over recent decades, does the clash of civilizations thesis constitute a paradigmatic shift within the study of world politics? And if so, in which way?

In traditional IR analyses, states undoubtedly stand at the centre of world politics. For most IR scholars, including for instance Waltz (1979) and Keohane ((ed.), 1986), states are the main actors in the international system, and – according to some – the only ones. Although the preoccupation with the process of foreign policy making shifted the focus of attention to domestic bureaucratic structures as well as to the psychology of individuals (Allison, 1971; Jervis, 1976), the propositions of this research stream were meant to *complement* the state-centred conceptualisation of world politics, not to replace it. From the 1980s onwards, research on international regimes (Krasner, 1982) and trans-national actors (Risse-Kappen, 1995) highlighted the importance of non-state actors in international politics. Certainly, within the clash of civilizations argument, Huntington himself affirms that 'states are and will remain the most important actors in world affairs' (Huntington, 1996: 36). Yet his prediction that the 'next world war, if there is one, will be a war between civilizations' (Huntington, 1993: 39) puts these 'civilizations' above states and their interests (Ajami, 1993: 9). In fact, the whole idea of clashing civilizations runs counter to any state-centred conceptualisation of international politics. Indeed, according to this world-view, states and even trans-national actors of world politics become subordinate entities within different civilizations, which are identified as the main units – and engines – of world politics. This point certainly marks a departure from common-sense international relations theory. More important, however, the lack of well-defined organizational and institutional structures makes it unclear how civilizations are supposed to act, let alone to engage in war.

The rise of the 'civilizations paradigm' somewhat reflected the growing preoccupation with questions of culture and identity that has marked IR theory since the end of the Cold War (Lapid and Kratochwil (eds.), 1996). Without refuting the contention that cultural factors matter in international relations, it is one thing to argue that culture and identity intervene at different levels in world politics and may determine outcome. It is quite another to depict civilizations and cultures as largely autonomous *agents* of international affairs, within which states are subordinate entities. Altogether, IR scholarship did not truly follow the paradigmatic shift that Huntington's thesis implies, most notably the challenge it poses to the role of the state in world politics.

However, the trendy phenomenon of organizing public events around inter-cultural and inter-civilizational dialogue after 9/11 further demonstrates that the interpretation of world politics in terms of fundamentally different, and potentially clashing, civilizations has gained currency among policy-makers, scholars and the media. In fact, the importance given to the dialogue between cultures and civilizations in recent years takes the distorted idea of civilizations as *agents* of international relations even further, as 'cultures' and 'civilizations' are now even regarded as capable of 'talking', that is, engaging in a dialogue with each other. Of course, we may dismiss this conceptualisation right away as pure nonsense. Civilizations and cultures do not communicate with each other, only individuals do. However, for the sake of the argument, let us assume that inter-cultural dialogue is possible and even useful in the current state of world affairs. But this assumption immediately raises a number of conceptual questions. First, what exactly are these 'cultures' that engage in dialogue? How are they defined, and, more importantly, *who* defines what these entities are? And second, who represents the respective cultures? Who speaks in the name of one culture or the other? Thus, rethinking the conceptualization of a 'dialogue between cultures' leads to an additional set of questions that, to a certain extent, is related to what has been termed 'the problem of communities in international relations' (Linklater, 1990).

In this context, critical approaches to IR theory provide a number of interesting insights, focusing on the stipulated dichotomy between international anarchy and the concept of community that corresponds to the nation-state. Stressing that the emergence, shaping, and survival of communities very much depends on closure and exclusion, critical theory has argued that the 'social construction of the "other" in different cultures and the significance of culturally defined differences between insiders and outsiders for the conduct of external relations are the key to the whole exercise' (Linklater, 1990: 146). Put differently, defining communities in international politics is a largely *arbitrary* process that includes some groups or individuals while *necessarily* excluding others. The nation-state logic of community, thus, stands in contrast to the idea of a global society and the universality of the rights of *human beings* (Walker, 1993). Moreover, the process of inclusion and exclusion follows the preferences of powerful interest groups, which thus succeed in imposing a specific interpretation of world affairs over possible others. To what extent are these insights useful in assessing the currently fashionable phenomenon of inter-cultural dialogue? By considering the practice of inter-cultural dialogue in the Euro-Mediterranean area and beyond, of the last couple of years, the next section will elaborate on these aspects.

Inter-cultural Dialogue and the Question of Community and Representation

Attempts to apply the insights of critical theory to the phenomenon of inter-cultural dialogue must start with the question of how 'cultures' in our context are defined. Similarly, what are the implications of these definitions for international politics, particularly in light of the 'clash of civilizations paradigm'? In fact, a central point of criticism of Huntington's thesis pointed to the conceptual flaws of defining the concept of civilization (Welch, 1997; *Foreign Affairs*, 1996). What, exactly, is a civilization? Considering that civilizations and cultures mix and overlap, as Huntington himself recognizes (Huntington, 1993: 24), the idea of clashing civilizations indeed poses a number of analytical difficulties. Moreover, if *change* is the essence of civilizations in a historical context, as Robert Cox (2000: 220) has argued, any prediction on the question of how and when civilizations may clash becomes a futile exercise.

The idea of inter-cultural dialogue faces the same conceptual problems. It not only presupposes that 'culture' is quantifiable or at least assessable, which is far from being the case (Jepperson and Swidler, 1994), but it also assumes that cultural *entities* can be identified. Indeed, every event organized in the framework of inter-cultural dialogue must start with an *at least implicit* definition of what these different 'cultures' are. In practice, it is true that many of the inter-cultural dialogue events of recent years have operated with a multiplicity of possible definitions. At the international level, for instance, UNESCO's inter-cultural dialogue programme has been organizing a large number of symposia and conferences that revolve around very different topics and regions, thus juxtaposing a large array of possible 'cultures' that are to engage in a dialogue with each other.[2] Amongst the events of UNESCO's inter-cultural dialogue programme, only a few reflected the 'civilizations paradigm', such as, for instance, the conference on the 'Dialogue between Civilizations' that specifically focused on the subject of 'Islam' and 'the West', held in May 2005 in Canada. Similarly, the activities of the Council of Europe typically concentrate on cultural co-operation, and in this framework, conceptualise inter-cultural dialogue as cutting across states and religions.[3]

Within the context of the Euro-Mediterranean, however, the available categories of inter-cultural dialogue are much narrower. Typically they trace a boundary between 'Europe' and 'the Arab world' or focus on the dialogue between the monotheistic religions in the Euro-Mediterranean area. In fact, after 9/11 *inter-faith* dialogue and the theme of religion have attracted an increasing attention in this context (Melasuo, 2002: 124-5). The EU-hosted international symposium on Intercultural Dialogue that took place in March 2002 in Brussels is a concrete example of the dominant concepts and narrow categories of Euro-Mediterranean inter-cultural dialogue. Indeed, reflections on the *conceptual framework* of intercultural dialogue raised the question of how to interpret the *differences* between the cultures of the Mediterranean, how to find common ground, and how to calm the tensions between them (Kaelble, 2002). Another keynote speaker, commenting on the conceptual framework of Euro-Mediterranean inter-cultural dialogue, focused on different discourses and practices of modernity (Eisenstadt, 2002), while a third speaker framed the inter-cultural dialogue in terms of the dichotomy between 'Europe' on the one side, and 'the Maghreb and the Arab world' and 'Islam' on the other (Chebel, 2002). Although other participants were far more critical regarding these pre-given categories (for example Stråth, 2002), the conceptualisations and categories mentioned above usually serve as implicit *starting point* of any critical reconsideration. Other examples include the Intercultural Dialogue Platform, a Turkish initiative,[4] which mainly deals with inter-faith dialogue, or the meeting between different *religious* leaders organized by the Euro-Mediterranean Parliamentary Forum in December 2001. Similarly, under the title 'Is the Dialogue between Cultures Possible?', the Royal Academy of Morocco organized a conference in December 2003 that juxtaposed 'the West' with 'Arab culture' and 'Islam'.[5] And the almost annual conferences on dialogue between cultures and civilizations of ISESCO, the Islamic Educational, Scientific and Cultural Organization based in Fez, regularly articulates the dichotomy between 'Islam' and 'the West'.[6] While two conferences on inter-cultural dialogue organized (or funded) by the EU's DG for Education and Culture represent a notable exception,[7] these categories and conceptualisations have dominated a large number of inter-cultural dialogue conferences and seminars in the Euro-Mediterranean area over the last years. The various events at the regional, national or local level are indeed too numerous to mention.

While cultural diversity is undoubtedly a reality in the Euro-Mediterranean area and beyond, there is, however, nothing obvious about the definitions of 'cultures' that underpinned the above-mentioned events. The first argument here is that the dominant concepts of 'cultures' in the Euro-Mediterranean context (and beyond) are conspicuously very heterogeneous *within*, and many states are characterized by internal fragmentation in terms of political identity, culture and values (Del Sarto, forthcoming). Similarly, there is no doubt that 'the West' entails very different political entities (which may be states, regions or other political entities), and it comprises a multiplicity of different cultures and sub-cultures. The same considerations apply to the concept of 'Europe' (Malmborg and Stråth (eds.), 2002; Christiansen et al. (eds.), 2001). Similarly, the idea of a more or less culturally homogeneous 'Arab world' is more imaginary than real, as any serious Middle Eastern scholar will convincingly demonstrate, and political rivalries among Arab states are not a new phenomenon either (Kerr, 1971; Sela, 1989). As far as the notion of 'Islam' is concerned, it is well known that there are many different schools, streams and 'sects' *within* Islam. The struggle between liberal, conservative and fundamentalist versions of Islam and their supporters demonstrates this most clearly (Al-Ashmawy, 1989; Ahmed, 2003; Fuller, 2003) – not to mention the current sectarian conflicts between Shia and Sunni Muslims in Iraq.

To put it differently, there are many different ways of defining similarities and differences, and thus to trace the boundaries between different communities and 'cultural' groups. Of course we may define the religions of Islam, Christianity, and Judaism as representing three different 'cultures'. But we may also consider a 'religious culture' in opposition to a 'secularist culture'. Such a conceptualisation would produce a completely different alignment of states and domestic groups across the Euro-Mediterranean area, underlining that defenders of secular and liberal values in, say Italy, Morocco, France and Turkey, have more in common with each other than with their respective religious-conservative co-nationals. Similarly, why not promote a dialogue between a 'culture of patriarchy' and an 'egalitarian culture' across the Euro-Mediterranean region? Why not establish a dialogue between conservative, reactionary and progressive 'cultures'? What these suggestions show is that alternative definitions of 'culture' produce coalitions and alignments that cut across the easily assumed divide between 'Islam' and the 'West', as well as the 'North–South' dichotomy. Moreover, these examples also demonstrate that the way different 'cultures' are defined in the framework of an inter-cultural dialogue impacts on our conceptualisation of similarities and differences in international politics. Thus, defining different 'cultures' that are to engage in a dialogue clearly entails a process of imposing – or cementing – *inter-subjective meanings,* and with it, of giving preference to one particular interpretation of reality over possible others (Searle, 1995). At the same time, defining 'cultures' according to a stipulated 'West-Islam' and 'North-South' dichotomy follows what Linklater (1990: 147) has described as 'the logics of ... exclusion, which perpetuate or revive culture closure'.

This aspect becomes even more conspicuous if we consider that in order to engage in dialogue, 'cultures' must be represented by specific individuals. Yet the designation of who speaks in the name of a certain 'culture' cannot be separated from the actual definition of these 'cultures', including the designation of their dominating features, boundaries, and counter-part(s). It can be observed that in the framework of high-profile inter-cultural events, such as UNESCO's Intercultural Dialogue Programme or the events organized by ISESCO, heads of state or prime ministers regularly participate as representatives of 'cultures', along with intellectuals and religious leaders. Implicitly, the combination of politicians and religious leaders in the realm of representation already traces the boundaries between 'the West' and the 'Arabic-Islamic world'. More than that, from a conceptual point of view, it is of course not self-evident at all that a head of state, or a government official, shall represent a 'culture' – particularly since in authoritarian states, political leaders cannot even claim to speak in the name of their own citizens. It could also be argued that the representation of a 'culture' by political leaders at high-level events gives governments (once more) the opportunity to define what 'culture' is. This is a problematic move, and not only in authoritarian states, where regimes already have a monopoly over the definition of political and cultural values. In fact, seeking to limit the emergence of sub-national and trans-national patterns of identity and solidarity among citizens corresponds to the logic of the territorial nation-state from the outset (Linklater, 1990: 149), mainly because these trans-national patterns potentially undermine the legitimacy of the 'nation-state' and of state authority. Another problematic aspect of having heads of state and government officials speak in the name of a 'culture' is that, instead of representing a 'culture', government officials are more likely to speak in the name of the state and government they represent, thus seeking to promote specific interests and policies in the international arena. In combination with the 'civilizations paradigm', the representation of 'cultures' by political actors within any inter-cultural dialogue also implies that states position themselves within a broader and culturally defined *community of states*, in defiance of both intra-state and inter-state divergences and differences. Thus, while serving as just another tool to strengthen state authority and to promote government policies, the inter-cultural dialogue becomes politicised, thus failing to address the objectives it was meant to address in the first place.

The representation of 'cultures' by religious leaders is similarly problematic, as it plainly ignores that there are very different streams within every religion – with only the different Christian denominations tending towards a clear hierarchic institutional order. In this vein, engaging religious leaders in an inter-cultural dialogue ignores the fervent debates over the 'right' meaning of religion that characterize most religions. Similarly, the religious representation of 'cultures' plainly disregards the domestic conflicts over the role of religion in public life that are taking place in many states – and not only in the Middle East, but also in 'the West'.[8] Related herewith, the representation of a 'culture' by religious leaders implicitly entails that secular forces are not part of that 'culture', or at least, that they are not relevant enough to deserve representation. Thus, framing inter-cultural dialogue in religious terms through the representative function corresponds to the marginalization process of groups and 'cultures' that critical scholars have described (Linklater, 1990; Walker, 1993). In practical terms, it should also be taken into consideration that clerics who engage in inter-cultural dialogue will most probably belong to the moderate or even modernist streams of the respective religion. While the real challenge probably consists of engaging the fundamentalist streams within each religion in a dialogue, it would clearly be absurd to concede the *representative function* to radicals and fundamentalists in the framework of any inter-cultural dialogue. A final aspect in the context of representation regards the question of those groups that fall in between the delineated categories. Thus, in the context of the generally assumed cultural difference between the 'West' and 'Islam', which 'culture' would a Turkish head of state represent, for instance? And who would represent the millions of Muslim citizens of Europe (or the US, for that matter)?

Thus, deliberately tracing boundaries in the definition of 'cultures' and assigning the representation of that 'culture' to specific individuals (but not to others) are two inter-related aspects of how inter-cultural dialogue potentially contributes to the inter-subjective process of imposing meanings. The third aspect, related to the previous two, regards the issue of agenda-setting. Indeed, it is important to acknowledge that the definition of 'cultures', and their representatives, impacts on the question of which issues are deemed as particularly important and which ones are not. Thus, religious leaders may discuss the issue of tolerance and respect for other religions, while affirming the importance of faith and moral principles. These issues may well be important, but they may not be the most pressing issues. For instance, promoting tolerance of and respect between religious and *secular* individuals, and debating the issue of how religion is to relate to politics, may have a far greater political relevance. It is not likely, however, that inter-religious dialogue will tackle these types of questions and problems. In general, inter-cultural dialogue, by definition, deals with cultural diversity, stereotypes, values and other cultural phenomena. While it is certainly important to give attention to common values, and to promote the understanding between peoples, it may be much more pertinent to address *socio-economic* and *political* issues for improving the current state of Euro-Mediterranean relations, or, for that matter, global affairs. Thus, the agenda-setting function of inter-cultural dialogue is a reflection of supporting hegemony in the Gramscian sense, defined as the process by which dominant groups are conceded additional powers in order to present their particular interests as universally valid, while forging the consensus of those groups that are dominated (Gramsci, 1977).

Finally, although the dynamics between different social groups or communities – once defined – are very complex (Hogg and Abrams, 1998), it is important to keep in mind that in-group and out-group perceptions tend to be profoundly biased. This bias entails, for instance, the tendency to have a more negative image of members of the other group, or 'culture' in our context, than of members of your own 'group'. Another important aspect of the so-called in-group/out-group bias is that the delineation of different groups forges the conviction that the members of your own group share a much stronger similarity than is actually the case (Sherif, 1966: 41). To put it differently, in the process of interacting with other social groups, or 'cultures', members of the in-group will act together to preserve, defend and enhance what they came to perceive as their common features (Bloom, 1990: 26), even if these allegedly shared characteristics are exaggerated or even invented

(Anderson, 1991). While situations of conflict between groups or 'cultures' undoubtedly reinforce the sense of solidarity and similarity within each group (Sherif, 1966: 81), any type of interaction, including dialogue, contributes to these dynamics. In our context, then, an inter-cultural dialogue across the Euro-Mediterranean area that depicts 'the Arab-Islamic world' versus 'Europe' and 'the West' as potentially antagonistic 'cultures' in fact tends to increase the perception of homogeneity *within* the respective 'culture', while cementing the perception of difference vis-à-vis the respective other 'culture'. This, however, stands in direct opposition to the objective of enhancing understanding between peoples and cultures that inter-cultural dialogue activities are intended to facilitate.

Thus, from a conceptual point of view, the inter-cultural dialogue in the post-9/11 era follows Huntington's 'civilizations paradigm' which it explicitly intends to counter, while it also largely reinforces questionable categories and interpretations of world politics. In this context, Fred Halliday (2001: 46) criticized the dialogue between faiths and civilizations as a 'well-intentioned project of recent years ... but as soon as you admit the fundamental difference and legitimacy of cultures, and implicitly of those, usually bearded old men, who interpret them, you are caught in a spider's web.' Moreover, with regard to Huntington's thesis, Welch (1997: 205–6) made the important point that 'Although it may make some abstract sense to distinguish the West from Islam, this distinction will only be relevant ... in the presence of a meaningful stake over which the parties contend *qua* Westerners and Muslims.' Yet the establishment of an inter-cultural dialogue – even in the broader sense – is simply another area in which different parties face each other *qua* their previously defined *differences*. Finally, our discussion stressed that inter-cultural dialogue is a means of setting the agenda, imposing hegemony, defining priorities, and deviating the attention from other, far more pressing issues and problems, such as state-society relations or poverty. With regard to the EMP's recently launched initiative of enhancing the 'dialogue between cultures' and the establishment of the Anna Lindh Foundation, we should ask, then, whether this initiative reflects the conceptual flaws of the inter-cultural dialogue practice discussed so far. How likely is it that the EMP's 'dialogue between cultures' will contribute to its stipulated objectives?

Inter-cultural Dialogue in the EMP Context

By stressing the supreme importance and urgency of inter-cultural dialogue after 9/11, the Valencia Action Plan, which stipulated the establishment of the Anna Lindh Foundation (Commission, 2002), undoubtedly reproduced the logic of the 'clash of civilizations' argument. Moreover, unlike previous EMP documents, the Valencia Action Plan specifically stresses the need to foster dialogue between religions. However, the 2003 report of the so-called *Groupe des Sages* (Commission, 2003), which considerably influenced the principles and planned programmes of the Anna Lindh Foundation, took a far more critical stance – if not necessarily conceptually, then at least in terms of practical recommendations. While the report underlines that the 'dialogue of civilizations' 'unfortunately shares the same logic' as the 'clash of civilizations' (Commission, 2003: 12), it does not challenge the idea of a dialogue between civilizations and cultures *per* se. In fact, although it pointedly remarked that the 'clashes of ignorances' (16) is a much more dangerous phenomenon than any 'clash of civilizations', the report actually affirms that '*it is paradoxically between "civilisations" that dialogue is easiest*' (Commission, 2003: 12, emphases in the original). With it, the report does not explicitly address the problem of conceding civilizations a predominant role in world politics, defining communities, along with questions of representation and agenda-setting. It does, however, stress the diversity within any type of culture, for instance by observing that 'Different visions of modernity very often find expression *within* a single culture, whatever that culture may be' (6, emphasis in the original). In this context, the report recommends, for instance, that the 'south must urgently enter into an inter- and intracultural dialogue with itself' (13).

In its propositions regarding which issues should be tackled within the Euro-Mediterranean dialogue between peoples and cultures the report clearly departs from the government-dominated and/or religiously-oriented events which have characterized the Euro-Mediterranean dialogue so far. While adopting a broad conceptualization of culture that includes 'all the practical and day-to-day features of living cultures' (2), such as education, role of women, place and image of immigrant populations, it draws attention to a number of pressing socio-economic and political issues across the Euro-Mediterranean area. Thus, education, mobility, youth and the media are singled out as the most important vehicles for promoting the dialogue between cultures.

Largely following this line of thought, the Anna Lindh Foundation defines its mission as the strengthening of 'intellectual co-operation and capacity-building in fields such as human rights, democratic citizenship, sustainable development, learning, knowledge and information society, gender and youth' (Anna Lindh Foundation, 2005). While identifying youth as a main target group and defending an understanding of culture that includes 'all aspects of human life', the foundation defines six major fields of actions, namely 'education, science, culture and communication, human rights, sustainable development, and women empowerment' (Anna Lindh Foundation, 2005). Thus, by drawing attention to far more relevant issues in the context of Euro-Mediterranean relations, inter-cultural dialogue as conceptualized by the Anna Lindh Foundation in the framework of the EMP notably differs from the practice of inter-cultural dialogue that has characterized recent years. Theoretically, it also departs from the problematic conceptualization of communities and how they are represented, as discussed above. Indeed, 'culture' is defined in a broad and multiple manner, and civil society actors are meant to be the representatives as well as the principle actors of the 'dialogue between cultures'.

Although this is undoubtedly a positive development, the organizational structure of the foundation remains problematic. While the role of the foundation does not include the funding of specific events, but is limited to the co-ordination of activities of national networks, it is regrettable that many of the national networks of the 35 member states are headed, or heavily influenced by, national ministries (usually the foreign ministry or the ministry of culture and education). Interestingly, this also applies to the national networks in some EU member states, which points somewhat to the general trend towards politicizing culture, or, alternatively, the 'over-culturisation of Euro-Mediterranean relations' (Melasuo, 2002: 133). With it, government interests and hegemonic visions of 'culture', 'cultures', and their representatives, are likely to enter the EMP's inter-cultural dialogue through the back-door. In a similar way, the national networks that engage in dialogue are, indeed, organized along *national* lines, and not around themes and issues. This organizational principle may have been necessary from both a political and a logistical point of view, but it potentially prevents the dialogue among and between different 'cultures' that are represented *within* the same state. At the same time, it may hinder the theory and practice of *trans-cultural* dialogue (Stråth, 2002), which seems of pressing concern considering the current state of world affairs. Indeed, a truly trans-cultural dialogue would imply the redrawing of the cognitive boundaries that have so far dominated Euro-Mediterranean politics in particular, and world politics in general, by stressing the similarities of groups and actors *across* the Euro-Mediterranean.

Altogether, however, one is left wondering why such crucial issues of Euro-Mediterranean relations as sustainable development, human rights and education are subordinated to the realm of the 'dialogue between cultures'. There is no doubt that Euro-Mediterranean cultural co-operation is important, and the involvement of non-state actors and civil society, within the EMP and beyond, is certainly crucial. On both accounts, however, there already are important structures and activities in the framework of Euro-Mediterranean relations. Thus, there are different foundations, networks, and projects that focus on culture and cultural co-operation, both within the EMP framework and outside of it (Melasuo, 2002). These structures and activities, however, are usually framed not in terms of inter-cultural dialogue, but simply as co-operation on cultural issues. Similarly, the more or less independent involvement of civil society actors in Euro-Mediterranean relations and their co-operation started with the establishment of the Euro-Med Civil Forum in 1995, held in parallel to the ministerial meeting that constituted the Barcelona Process. Co-operation on cultural issues is one among the many themes of the Euro-Med Civil Forum platform, along with human rights, women's rights, sustainable development, migration, tourism, university co-operation and others.

It is unquestionable that education, the promotion of political freedom and human rights, and sustainable development, lie at the heart of the political and economic malaise of most southern EMP countries (UNDP, 2005). Hence, effectively addressing these issues should be the key priority of the EU's Mediterranean policy. By focusing on these themes, the Anna Lindh Foundation certainly provides greater visibility to, and increases the profile of, these important challenges. But it is highly questionable whether nationally grouped civil society actors have the appropriate tools for effectively promoting education, sustainable development, and human rights – whether co-ordinated by foreign ministries or not. It seems that rather than increasing the profile of these issues through the establishment of a foundation, more funds are needed in general for addressing these topics, along with adequate (EU) policies. Moreover, conceptually linking these issues to the phenomenon of inter-cultural dialogue in the Euro-Mediterranean area, which has so far contributed to the cementing of a particular interpretation of states, societies, and world politics, may simply be counter-productive.

Conclusions

Many of the events organized under the headline of inter-cultural dialogue have, thus far, at least implicitly adopted the conceptual underpinnings of the 'clash of civilizations' argument. In the Euro-Mediterranean context and beyond, 'the West', or alternatively 'Europe', has thus generally been contrasted with 'the Arab world' and 'Islam', and these definitions of 'cultures' have served as the starting point for the promotion of dialogue. More often than not, political leaders and clerics represented these 'cultures' in the inter-cultural dialogue, which, in turn, also impacted on the subjects and themes of the dialogue. Revisiting the clash of civilizations argument, this contribution has argued that it is not only absurd to concede to 'cultures' and civilizations the status of *agents* in international relations, to which states are subordinated entities, but that the practice of inter-cultural dialogue framed in these terms contributes to the imposing, or cementing, of questionable interpretations of regional and international politics. More importantly, by defining 'cultures' and their representatives according to the fashionable 'Islam-West' and 'North-South' dichotomy, the theory and practice of inter-cultural dialogue in the Euro-Mediterranean context and beyond potentially increases the power and legitimacy of political and religious elites in imposing their hegemonic vision of culture and politics. While ignoring difference and diversity within and among states, and forging at least questionable concepts of community and difference in world politics, inter-cultural dialogue that remains embedded in the civilization logic is also a means of setting the agenda and defining priorities. With it, the attention is diverted from far more urgent problems in international relations in general, and Euro-Mediterranean relations in particular, such as poverty, sustainable development, human rights and education.

The recently established Anna Lindh Euro-Mediterranean Foundation for the Dialogue between Cultures has adopted a different conceptual framework, in which cultures are defined in a broad and multiple manner. The foundation has also placed crucial issues of Euro-Mediterranean relations, such as education, sustainable development and human rights, at the top of its agenda. While this approach is certainly laudable, the structure of the foundation and its activities remain problematic. The national networks of civil society actors, that the foundation aims at co-ordinating, are not likely to produce a truly trans-cultural dialogue on different issues, that is, a dialogue that builds on similar interests and sets of values of groups and individuals *across* states, regions and societies. Moreover, many of the networks are under the direct influence of the respective governments. Altogether, a notable increase of available (EU) funds in these issue areas would make a far greater difference than the establishment of a prestigious foundation that has only co-ordinating functions. Moreover, given the importance of these issue areas, it is counter-productive to frame the activities of civil society actors in promoting human rights, sustainable development and education as a *dialogue between cultures*.

In fact, it would be helpful to analytically distinguish between co-operation on cultural issues on the one hand, and promoting human rights, sustainable development and education on the other. Of course, education towards tolerance remains a crucial tool to enhance understanding between individuals and groups with different backgrounds, values and aspirations within and across Europe and the Mediterranean. But education, socio-economic development and human rights are crucial developmental objectives *per se,* irrespective of culture and cultural co-operation. In fact, associating these issues with 'culture', and thus 'low politics', in the context of Euro-Mediterranean relations does more harm than good.

Finally, preventing, or counter-acting, a possible clash of civilizations, which is the conspicuous aim of any inter-cultural dialogue, cannot succeed if we operate with the same categories, concepts and cognitive boundaries as the 'civilizations paradigm' – which *conceptually* resembles the rhetoric of the *al-Qaeda* terrorists. This is not to say that arguments related to cultural diversity and tolerance should not be discussed among clerics, secularists, teachers, journalists, academics, NGO activists, cultural actors, politicians and so on. The framing, however, should radically depart from what has so far dominated inter-cultural dialogue events, characterized by high-profile political events, narrow concepts, restricted patterns of representation and a questionable agenda. While keeping in mind that categories of 'cultures' and their boundaries are largely arbitrary social constructions that, hence, can be changed, a re-conceptualization of difference and similarity across the Euro-Mediterranean and beyond is necessary. In order to achieve this aim, the establishment of a truly trans-cultural dialogue that builds on *the common values and interest of groups and individuals across states and regions* may be the most appropriate starting point. At this stage, and given the problematic organizational principles, it remains to be seen whether the Anna Lindh Foundation will be able to support such a development.

Notes

[1] There are too many examples to mention. To give at least one example, in the very popular talk show *Otto e mezzo* on the Italian Channel 7 (*La 7*) of 22 September 2004 on the issue of 'Islam and democracy', the talk show host, Giuliano Ferrara, affirmed that 'Islamic countries are not democratic', which provoked a debate on whether 'Islam' is compatible with 'democracy'. The question of what an 'Islamic' country is, and whether the term 'Islamic' refers to the predominance of *shariah* law or simply to the fact that the majority of its citizens are Muslims, was not even addressed. In the case of the latter, one wonders where Turkey fits in, while the question also arises of whether, by analogy, secular France, for instance, should be considered a 'Christian' country.

[2] For further information on UNESCO's Intercultural Dialogue Programme, see http://www.unesco.org/dialogue2001 (accessed 27 May 2005).

[3] Information on the activities on cultural co-operation and intercultural dialogue of the Council of Europe is available at http://www.coe.int (accessed 4 June 2005).

[4] Information on the Intercultural Dialogue Platform is available at http://www.cul-dialogue.org (accessed 28 May 2005).

[5] The programme of the conference is available at the website of the Moroccan Ministry of Communication at http://www.minculture.gov.ma/fr/en-nadwa.htm#2 (accessed 1 June 2005).

[6] Information on the regular conferences of ISESCO is available at http://www.isesco.org.ma (accessed 30 April 2005).

[7] Two conferences on inter-cultural dialogue, organized (or funded) by the EU's DG Education and Culture in March 2002 and May 2004, adopted a much broader concept of 'culture' and departed from the 'classical' categories and concepts. Information on these events is available at http://europa.eu.int/comm/culture/portal/action/dialogue/dial_en.htm (accessed 4 June 2005).

[8] Regarding the role of religion in public life in European countries, the debates about in-vitro fertilization in Italy before the June 2005 referendum that witnessed the massive intervention of the Catholic church, the fervently contested issue of abortion in the US, and the heated discussions in a number of European countries about the compatibility between the 'secular state' and the displaying of religious symbols in public institutions are cases in point.

References

Adib-Moghaddam, A. (2002) Global Intifadah? September 11th and the struggle within Islam, *Cambridge Review of International Affairs*, 15(2), pp. 203–216.

Ahmed, A. S. (2003) *Islam under Siege: Living Dangerously in a Post-Honor World* (Cambridge: Polity).

Ajami, Fouad (1993) The summoning, *Foreign Affairs*, 72(4), pp. 2–9.

Al-Ashmawy, M. S. (1989) *L'Islamisme contre l'Islam* (Paris/Cairo: La Découverte and Al-Fikr).

Allison, G. T. (1971) *Essence of Decision: Explaining the Cuban Missile Crisis* (Boston: Little, Brown & Co).

Anderson, B. (1991) *Imagined Communities: Reflections on the Origins and Spread of Nationalism*, 2nd edition (London: Verso).

Anna Lindh Foundation (2005) Website, at http://www.euromedalex.org (accessed 4 June 2005).

Barcelona Declaration Adopted at the Euro-Mediterranean Conference, 27–28 November 1995, Barcelona, 28 November 1995, Final Version.

Bin, A. (Ed.) (1996) *Co-operation and Security in the Mediterranean: Prospects after Barcelona* (Malta: The Mediterranean Academy of Diplomatic Studies).

Bloom, W. (1990) *Personal Identity National Identity and International Relations* (Cambridge: Cambridge University Press).

Chebel, M. M. (2002) Colloque 'Dialogue intercultural', *presented at the International Symposium on Intercultural Dialogue*, Brussels, 20–21 March 2002, available at http://www.ecsanet.org/dialogue/contributions.htm (accessed 23 May 2005).

Christiansen, T., Jorgensen, K. E. & Wiener, A. (Eds) (2001) *The Social Construction of Europe* (London: Sage).

Commission of the European Communities (2002) Vth Euro-Mediterranean Conference of Foreign Ministers, Valencia, 22–23 April 2002, Presidency Conclusions, Valencia 23 April 2002, 8254/02 (Presse 112).

Commission of the European Communities, High Level Advisory Group (2003) Dialogue between Peoples and Cultures in the Euro-Mediterranean Area: Report of the High-Level Advisory Group Established at the Initiative of President of the European Commission, *Euromed Report*, 68, 2 December 2003.

Cox, R. W. (2000) Thinking about civilizations, *Review of International Studies*, 26(5), pp. 215–234.

Del Sarto, R. A. (forthcoming) *Contested State Identities and Regional Security in the Euro-Mediterranean Area* (New York: Palgrave).

Eisenstadt, S. N. (2002) The dialogue between cultures or between cultural interpretations of modernity: multiple modernities on the contemporary scene, available at http://www.ecsanet.org/dialogue/contributions.htm (accessed 23 May 2005).

Fahmy, N. (1996) After Madrid and Barcelona: prospects for Mediterranean security, in: A. Bin (Ed.) *Co-operation and Security in the Mediterranean: Prospects after Barcelona* (Malta: The Mediterranean Academy of Diplomatic Studies).
Foreign Affairs (Ed.) (1996) *The Clash of Civilizations? The Debate* (New York: Council on Foreign Relations).
Fuller, G. (2003) *The Future of Political Islam* (New York: Palgrave Macmillan).
Gramsci, A. (1977) *Quaderni dal carcere* (Torino: Einaudi).
Halliday, F. (1996) *Islam and the Myth of Confrontation: Religion and Politics in the Middle East* (London: IB Tauris).
Halliday, F. (2001) *Two Hours that Shook the World: September 11, 2001, Causes and Consequences* (London: Saqi).
Hogg, M. A. & Abrams, D. (1988) *Social Identifications: A Social Psychology of Intergroup Relations and Group Processes* (London: Routledge).
Huldt, B., Engman, M. & Davidson, E. (Eds) (2002) *Euro-Mediterranean Security and the Barcelona Process* (Stockholm: The Swedish National Defence College).
Huntington, S. P. (1993) The clash of civilizations?, *Foreign Affairs*, 72(3), pp. 22–49.
Huntington, S. P. (1996) *The Clash of Civilizations and the Remaking of World Order* (New York: Simon & Schuster).
Jepperson, R. L. & Swidler, A. (1994) What properties of culture should we measure?, *Poetics*, 22, pp. 359–371.
Jervis, R. (1976) *Perception and Misperception in International Politics* (Princeton: Princeton University Press).
Kaelble, H. (2002) Colloque sur 'Le dialogue interculturel' à Bruxelles le 20 et 21 mars 2002 organisé par la Commission européenne, available at http://www.ecsanet.org/dialogue/contributions.htm (accessed 23 May 2005).
Keohane, R. O. (Ed.) (1986) *Neorealism and Its Critics* (New York: Columbia University Press).
Kerr, M. H. (1971) *The Arab Cold War: Gamal Abd al-Nasir and his Rivals*, 3rd edition (London: The Royal Institute of International Affairs and Oxford University Press).
Krasner, S. D. (1982) Structural causes and regime consequences: regimes as intervening variables, *International Organization*, 36(2), pp. 185–205.
Lapid, Y. & Kratochwil, F. (Eds) (1996) *The Return of Culture and Identity in IR Theory* (Boulder, Co: Lynne Rienner).
Linklater, A. (1990) The problem of community in international relations, *Alternatives*, 15, pp. 135–153.
Malmborg, M. & Stråth, B. (Eds) (2002) *The Meaning of Europe: Variety and Contention within and among Nations* (Oxford/New York: Berg).
Martín Muñoz, G. (1997) Razon en contra del la confrontacíon Islam/Occidente, in: M. A. Roque (Ed.) *Identitades y conflicte de valores: Diversidada y mutacíon en el Mediterráneo* (Barcelona: Institut Català de la Mediterrània d'Estudis i Cooperació).
Melasuo, T. (2002) Cultural relations and co-operation in the Mediterranean, in: B. Huldt, M. Engman & E. Davidson (Eds) *Euro-Mediterranean Security and the Barcelona Process* (Stockholm: The Swedish National Defence College).
Risse-Kappen, T. (Ed.) (1995) *Bringing Transnational Relations Back In: Non-state Actors, Domestic Structures, and International Institutions* (Cambridge: Cambridge University Press).
Roque, M. A. (Ed.) (1997) *Identitades y conflicte de valores: Diversidada y mutacíon en el Mediterráneo* (Barcelona: Institut Català de la Mediterrània d'Estudis i Cooperació).
Searle, J. R. (1995) *The Construction of Social Reality* (London: Penguin Books).
Sela, A. (1998) *The Decline of the Arab-Israeli Conflict: Middle East Politics and the Quest for Regional Order* (Albany: State University of New York Press).
Sherif, M. (1966) *In Common Predicament: Social Psychology of Intergroup Conflict and Cooperation* (Boston: Houghton Mifflin).
Stråth, B. (2002) Outline of the session 'Images of Europe in the World', Intercultural Dialogue Conference Brussels 20–21 March 2002, available at http://www.ecsanet.org/dialogue/contributions.htm (accessed 23 May 2005).

UNDP (United Nations Development Programme) (2005) *Arab Human Development Report 2004: Towards Freedom in the Arab World* (Amman: National Press).

Walker, R. B. J. (1993) *Inside/Outside: International Relations as Political Theory* (Cambridge: Cambridge University Press).

Waltz, K. N. (1979) *Theory of International Politics* (Reading: Addison-Wesley).

Welch, D. A. (1997) The 'clash of civilizations' thesis as an argument and as a phenomenon, *Security Studies*, 6(4), pp. 197–216.

The Politics of De-Paradoxification in Euro-Mediterranean Relations: Semantics and Structures of 'Cultural Dialogue'

STEPHAN STETTER
University of Bielefeld, Germany

Introduction

This essay analyses, from a systems theoretical perspective, 'cultural dialogue' in the framework of the Euro-Mediterranean Partnership (EMP). It thereby focuses in particular on the construction of identity discourses in Euro-Mediterranean relations and shows how such semantics of identity impact on 'cultural dialogue' in the context of the EMP. The overall aim of the study is to provide a theoretically informed discussion on the concept of 'cultural dialogue' in Euro-Mediterranean relations.

The first two sections look at the semantics of 'culture' in the context of the EMP. First, it is argued that the concept of 'cultural dialogue', as it becomes institutionalized in the EMP, rests upon the observation and problematization of 'identity' as a primary differential reference point – a symbolic border – between the EU and the southern Mediterranean countries. Based on an analysis of Self/Other distinctions in Euro-Mediterranean relations, it is argued that on the EU-side of the border patterns of collective identities are associated with a peaceful and harmonious co-existence of difference. In contrast, collective identity patterns in the southern Mediterranean are problematized and based on the observation of contradictory and conflictual discourses of difference.

Second, the continuous observation of these differences in regional identity patterns thereafter takes on a powerful political role in Euro-Mediterranean relations since it leads to a 'semantic sedimentation' of these identity constructions. In other words, the observation in the EMP of different regional identity patterns on both sides of the Mediterranean fosters the semantic construction of 'culture' as a prime differential category between North and South. As a result, 'culture' becomes a hegemonic semantic reference point in Euro-Mediterranean relations.

Such an argument requires, thirdly, an analysis of the way in which these semantics of culture relate to the structures of dialogue that become institutionalized in the context of the third basket of the EMP. The article argues that the role which 'culture' has acquired in Euro-Mediterranean relations directs attention to the paradoxes of 'cultural dialogue'. Based on a systems theoretical analysis of 'culture', it is argued here that, notwithstanding the goodwill inherent in the concept of 'cultural dialogue', its institutionalization is problematic. Thus, 'cultural dialogue' is presented as a paradoxical and conflictual operation. It depends on 'culture' as a differential unit while at the same time advocating the overcoming of this fundamental distinction. Due to the conflictual disposition of 'cultural dialogue', which is nurtured by underlying threat-perceptions, the institutionalization of 'cultural dialogue' is analysed here as a useful example of the politics of de-paradoxification, i.e. the political significance of 'cultural dialogue' can be found in the invisibilized conflictual foundations inherent in this concept.

Based on the observation that due to these semantic and structural reasons, 'cultural dialogue' is a problematic institutional form for bilateral (as well as multilateral) relations, the final section looks for alternative ways through which collective identity patterns in the Euro-Mediterranean area could be forged. It thereby proposes three different alleys. First, integration – in a more orthodox reading of systems theory – can be provided for through less emphasis on normatively inclined concepts, such as 'cultural dialogue'. Seen from that perspective, 'cultural dialogue' is not only a paradoxical but also quite a problematic operation, since the thematization of 'culture' bears potential for conflict because of pre-conceived views and valorizations of 'culture'. Second, rather than observing allegedly *divergent* 'cultures', the EU and the southern Mediterranean countries could focus on the *shared* world societal reference point of their political relations – which is, however, a different notion from a shared identity. Third, the divergent and cross-cutting debordering processes that characterize Euro-Mediterranean relations on various levels should be more coherently addressed.

Before elaborating further on these arguments, some introductory remarks on modern systems theory as far as they are relevant for the purpose of this article might be helpful for those readers less familiar with this theory (see Luhmann, 1995b; 2000; Stichweh, 2000). Modern systems theory is a general theory of society that starts from similar assumptions as other constructivist theories that have followed the linguistic turn in the social sciences. All societal operations are, hence, constituted by communication only. In other words, there is no *social* reality outside communication. The main function of communication is to produce distinctions – distinctions between what is communicated and what is not communicated. Society then becomes possible through the continuous connection of communications. What matters here is that communications are always contingent artefacts, that is, what is expressed could always be expressed differently. On this basis, one of the most central distinctions in modern systems theory is the distinction between system and environment. A system is a communicatively upheld structure that operates and reproduces itself on the basis of system-specific communication codes. On the basis of these codes, systems can be distinguished from the societal environment. While systems are thus operatively autonomous from their environment, both are at the same time co-constitutive because systems continuously observe their environment and 'translate' inputs from the environment into the operations of the respective system.

While modern systems theory conforms with post-structuralist approaches on the contingency and hence the paradoxes (or 'madness' in post-structuralist terms) of communications, it offers a different outlook and transcends the mere 'celebration of paradoxes' in post-structuralism (Stäheli, 2000: 16). Thus, modern systems theory focuses on the connectability of communications and how this process generates social forms. Social distinctions, structures and borders emerge because of – rather than in spite of – the ever-present contingency of how they are drawn. In a nutshell, society is the continuous and paradoxical transformation of unlikely (contingent) into likely (form-specific) operations on the basis of communication. But how can these distinctions, structures and borders of society be conceived of? Since (almost) all communications on the globe are in principle connectable with each other, today's society must be understood as a single world society. Yet, world society is not a normative or integrative concept. Quite the opposite: world society is characterized by many fractures, borders (the most important one being borders between different functional systems such as politics, law, economy, science, arts) and various forms of inclusion and exclusion. However, what matters in this context is that all these distinctions are *internal* distinctions within world society rather than between different (territorially differentiated) societies. As the following sections of this article aim to demonstrate, some of these communicatively produced distinctions in world society then acquire over time a more stable meaning which can therefore be repeatedly referred to in communications. This is when specific 'semantics' emerge that stand in correlation with societal 'structures'.

Semantics of Identity: Self/Other Distinctions in Euro-Mediterranean Relations

When talking about 'cultural dialogue' in the context of the third basket of the EMP, the suitability of 'culture' and 'dialogue' as useful reference points for the study of political relations at the non-state level is often assumed, both amongst practitioners and academics (on the cultural dimension in the EMP see Peresso, 1998; High-Level Advisory Group, 2003; Pace & Saurette, 2000; Pace, 2005). This essay does not suggest that this centrality of 'culture' in Euro-Mediterranean relations is from the outset unwarranted. However, what it tries to do is to take the discussion one step backwards. Thus, it offers a theoretical reading from the perspective of modern systems theory on the fundamental conditions which underlie the choice of 'cultural dialogue' as a differential category of Euro-Mediterranean relations (see also with a different perspective Soysa & Zervakis, 2002). In other words, how is 'culture' constructed as a differential unit in Euro-Mediterranean relations and what are the political implications of institutionalizing a 'cultural dialogue'?

As this and the following section aim to show, the rhetoric of 'cultural' difference between both sides of the Mediterranean rests on certain semantic strategies that are far from being given (see Braudel, 1986; for an alternative conceptualization see also Aliboni, 2004). As is argued here, a deconstruction of these semantics of 'culture' also brings to the fore the conflictual aspects in using 'culture' as a code of observing Euro-Mediterranean relations. The study, hence, argues that there is a conflictual disposition at the heart of this semantic operation. More precisely, the emergence of 'culture' as a code, which structures political relations in the context of the third basket of the EMP, relies on three contingent semantic operations. It depends, first, on a symbolic bordering process between both sides of the Mediterranean, which ascribes different patterns of regional collective identity relations to each unit. Second, this binary coding of European versus southern Mediterranean identity relations, which is analysed here on the basis of different modes of Self/Other distinctions, is then supplemented by value attributions for each side of this distinction. While semantics on collective identity patterns on the European side primarily observe their peaceful and co-operative dynamics, semantics on collective identity patterns in the southern Mediterranean are problematized, thereby stressing the conflictual and violent dynamics in this region. While these two semantic operations will be discussed in this section, the next section will then show how this problematization of identity shapes the discourse of different 'cultures' in Euro-Mediterranean relations.

As all social artefacts, the emergence of 'culture' as a differential unit of Euro-Mediterranean relations is also a communicatively generated construction, in other words the marking of an unlikely and contingent distinction (see Luhmann, 1997, 2002). Thus, it is a precondition of 'cultural dialogue' between both sides of the Mediterranean that a line is drawn between the North and the South in the first place. Otherwise, a formalized *dia-logue* between two distinct 'subjects' cannot be established.[1] But how does such a drawing of a line in the context of the EMP materialize and to what types of borders does it relate (Marchart, 2002)? A useful starting point for answering these questions is to discuss the different types of borders that characterize world society (see from a non-systems theoretical perspective Brown, 2001; Newman, 2003). Thus, the primary form of internal differentiation in world society is located on the functional level (Luhmann, 1995b; Stichweh, 2000; for an International Relations perspective see World Society

Research Group, 2000; Albert & Hilkermeier, 2004). Functional borders refer to those social borders that separate different functional systems, such as politics, economy, religion, law, science, sports or arts, from each other. Within this context of functional differentiation, however, other forms of internal differentiation of world society exist, and it is on this level that territorial borders gain prominence. This is the case, for example, with regards to the political system of world society, within which territorial borders are still an important structural feature. Territorial borders of the world political system relate mainly to either national or regional borders, that structure the political system internally into different states and, increasingly, regional political clusters (Albert, 2002). A third type of borders in world society are, then, symbolic borders, that is borders that differentiate between identities on the basis of collective ascriptions of Self/Other differences. These symbolic borders structure, for example, ethnic, national, political or religious identities (see Bonacker, 2004: 15). What is important to emphasize here is that these three types of borders are all social borders. Thus, they are all constituted by communication only and, accordingly, their social reproduction depends on their continuous re-articulation (see from a non-systems theoretical perspective Rajaram, 2004). In other words, neither functional nor territorial nor symbolic borders are exogenously given. Hence, they do not exist outside communication and must all be understood as dynamic and discursive processes rather than static structures.

As far as the EMP is concerned, the 'rhetoric of cultural dialogue' – which ascribes a differential 'cultural' status to each side of the Mediterranean – draws such a symbolic border within the Euro-Mediterranean area (Librett, 2000). This is because the ascription of 'cultural' status depends on a previous communicative bordering process which constructs a distinct collective status, and therefore a distinct identity, for each side of the symbolic distinction. To pick up on an argument by Eisenstadt and Giesen, it can thus be argued that, as a precondition for 'cultural dialogue' in the EMP, 'collective identity is produced by the social construction of [symbolic] boundaries' between Europe and the southern Mediterranean (Eisenstadt and Giesen, 1995: 75). Symbolic bordering in the context of the third basket of the EMP is, however, a more complex process than this definition might initially suggest. Thus, while symbolic bordering with regard to 'cultural dialogue' does create two sides – the EU, on the one hand, and the southern Mediterranean countries, on the other – none of these sides is internally characterized by a strong sense of shared collective identity, despite rudimentary forms of a single European identity in the EU or the integrative function of Islam in most countries of the South. Since 'primordial' or 'civil codes' of identity construction are only weakly developed on both sides, the question arises as to how the symbolic bordering process of two separate, but internally highly fragmented units is semantically produced and sustained (Albert, 2002: 104–5).[2] From a similar perspective, some authors have thus argued that as far as EU-identity is concerned, the establishment of a symbolic border that separates the EU from the 'non-EU' depends on communicative processes of 'Othering' (Neumann & Welsh, 1991; Houtum & Naerssen, 2002; Rumelili, 2004; Diez, 2004). 'Othering' then means that collective 'identities are always constructed against the difference of an other'

(Diez, 2004: 321).[3] As far as the collective identity of the EU is concerned, such 'Othering' processes relate either to a temporal or a spatial dimension. In the former case, the construction of a collective EU-identity becomes possible by contrasting the Self against the background of the war-torn European past up and until the Second World War – Europe's own history thus becomes its 'Other'. In the latter case, 'Othering' relates to a spatially represented 'Other', be it the religion of Islam or states such as Turkey, Russia or the United States (ibid.: 328). It can thus be summarized that from the perspective of modern systems theory – but also poststructuralist approaches – all processes of collective identity formation depend on the discursive construction and distinction between the 'Self' and the 'Other'.

As already indicated, there are different ways in which such symbolic bordering processes operate. Hence, what matters is the question as to which discursive field the Self/Other coding of collective identities is embedded. For example, the collective identity of a 'Self' can be distinguished from the 'Other' through positive or negative value attributions (or none of these); the 'Other' can thus be represented as a partner or as being a threat (or simply, as being different). At first glance, 'cultural dialogue' in the EMP relates to the first category. Thus, it draws a symbolic border between both sides of the Mediterranean but it equally emphasizes that both sides relate to each other on the basis of co-existence, mutual respect, increasing co-operation and partnership. Or, in the words of practitioners of EMP-cultural dialogue, 'culture is by nature egalitarian, giving equal weight to all its forms: it is therefore both the basis of and the vehicle for an equitable relationship' in the Euro-Mediterranean area (High-Level Advisory Group, 2003: 3). However, this standard evocation of equality and shared values is supplemented – in the context of the EMP – by the parallel observation of specific threats to 'cultural dialogue' such as 'extremism, radicalisation and incitement' as well as a lack of 'freedom and initiative' on the other (Council of the European Union, 2004). As is argued here, the coding of the Self/Other distinction in Euro-Mediterranean relations is, thus, not entirely neutral but takes on a specific value dimension, that is, a coding of the form good/bad.[4] Sharing some of the suspicions held by students of 'Othering' processes by the EU, this article argues that the symbolic bordering process on which Euro-Mediterranean 'cultural dialogue' relies is underpinned by such a value dimension. Thus, value attributions become intermingled with Self/Other distinctions. More precisely, most of the aforementioned threats are attributed to one side of the symbolic border, the southern Mediterranean. Thus, this latter side is represented as the negative value of the Self/Other distinction, an area of threat, instability and conflict. In contrast, the EU is constructed as the positive value, an area of co-operation and peace.[5] It is, hence, no surprise that the aforementioned objectives of 'cultural dialogue' closely mirror the very objectives of the European integration project, as a project that allows regional identities to co-exist in a peaceful and co-operative manner. In more Habermasian terms, the goal of 'cultural dialogue' is, therefore, an extension of European 'values' to the entire Mediterranean basin rather than a 'reasoned consensus' between both sides (Habermas, 1992).

These arguments on the observation of areas of co-operation and conflict, which supplement the symbolic bordering process of 'cultural dialogue' with a specific value dimension, thus turn the spotlight on how these two units are internally constructed. This is also interesting from a theoretical perspective, since by definition both conflict and co-operation depend on specific forms of symbolic bordering below the level of a larger collective unit. In both instances it takes at least two to tango. Thus, when identifying areas of co-operation and conflict, which result from a symbolic bordering process, the question is how collective identities within these regional blocs are observed. The focus on areas of co-operation already indicates that the 'Other' must thus not necessarily be constructed in a 'negative' way (Rumelili, 2004; Stetter, 2004). The observation of the EU as an area of co-operation thus stresses the co-operative interplay between different collective identities *within* the EU. This 'positive' form of Self-Other observation has indeed a prominent role in the social construction of identities in the EU. As Thomas Risse has argued, this positive coding in Europe takes on different forms. For example, European 'identities can be nested, conceived of as concentric circles or Russian Matruska dolls, one inside the next' or they could be embedded in 'the "marble cake" model of multiple identities' (2004: 168). What matters here is that in all these cases the collective identity at the aggregated level – the EU – is underpinned by a positive evaluation of the interrelationship between collective identities at one or more of the lower level(s) – mainly the national. In a similar way, regional collective identity patterns within the EU are discursively represented as cases of positive 'Othering' and, hence, serve as a semantic orientation for a more peaceful future in the Euro-Mediterranean area. This is, of course, not to argue that there are no conflicts in Europe. What matters for the purpose of this article is rather the argument, that in the context of symbolic bordering in Euro-Mediterranean relations, the collective identity of the EU is constructed as the conglomeration of nested/multiple identities that relate to each other in a 'positive' and co-operative manner. At the same time, the manifold conflictual relations between these identities become the blind spot of this internal symbolic bordering process.

In the context of the EMP, the observation of regional collective identity patterns in the southern Mediterranean is quite different from such positive evaluations. Thus, it is in particular the disruptive and conflictual relationship between collective identities in the South that is observed. This dynamic then also renders the southern Mediterranean the 'negative' side of the symbolic bordering process advanced through 'cultural dialogue'. One of the functions of this symbolic bordering process is that the reasons for the aforementioned threat perceptions can more easily be accounted for. They can now be linked to concrete actor constellations, thereby observing regional identity patterns in the South on the basis of 'contested domestic identities' on the national, ethnic or religious levels (Del Sarto, 2005; UNDP, 2005). Or, to use a classical International Relations terminology, it is the 'valorization' of the symbolic bordering process in Euro-Mediterranean relations, which results from a linkage between threat perceptions and ascriptions of collective identities, through which the 'cultural dialogue' between both sides becomes securitized (see Buzan, Wæver & de Wilde, 1998). This argument also elucidates how reference to the European experience serves as the horizon of a threat-less shared future in the Euro-Mediterranean basin, since the valorization of regional collective identity patterns allows representation of one side of the distinction as a positive model. As has already been outlined above, the argument here is not that the southern Mediterranean is primarily characterized by conflictual identity relations. In fact, nested or multiple identities can also be found in this region, but they in turn become the blind spot in the observation of areas of co-operation and conflict in the context of Euro-Mediterranean relations.

Semantics of Culture: Memories and the Problematization of Difference

This observation of different regional identity patterns for each side of the symbolic border and the problematization of only one side then underpins the emergence of a discourse of two distinct 'cultures'. While 'most scholars working on collective identities today have abandoned essentialist conceptualizations of social identities', the problematization of regional identity patterns fosters the observation of such categorical difference between Europe and the southern Mediterranean in the context of the EMP (Risse, 2004: 167). More precisely, the construction of 'culture' as a differential category of Euro-Mediterranean relations is the result of a semantic 'sedimentation' of the identity-related Self/Other distinction, which has been discussed in the previous section. This sedimentation, thus the memorizing of this specific distinction as a categorical differentiation (and the forgetting of other possible distinctions), is, however, far from being neutral since it leads to the ascription of a quasi-ontological status of these 'cultures', including the aforementioned valorization (see also Saurette, 2000).[6] The European and the southern Mediterranean 'cultures' are hence no longer observed as 'imagined communities' but rather as essentialist units (Anderson, 1991). As this and the following section argue, these semantics of 'culture' are problematic for several reasons. Not only do they take the a priori existence of two distinct sides as a given – which is problematic from any communication theoretical perspective. In addition, this semantic sedimentation turns 'culture' into a hegemonic semantic reference point of Euro-Mediterranean relations, including the underlying perceptions of threat that shape the Self/Other distinction.

Such an argument requires further clarification on how 'identity' and 'culture' differ. As Mathias Albert has argued, 'it would be wrong to equate "culture" and "collective identity"' (Albert, 2002: 108).[7] Thus, identity refers to the processes through which symbolic borders are drawn and the 'symbolic codes of distinction' become substantially defined (ibid: 104). In contrast, culture is not primarily characterized by such bordering and symbolic demarcation processes. This argument might at first sight be surprising, given the quasi-ontological status which many authors ascribe to 'culture', Samuel Huntington's thesis of a 'clash of civilizations' only being one of the most simplistic (Huntington, 1993). However, as the previous section has argued more peaceful conceptualizations of culture, as they are intended through 'cultural dialogue' in Euro-Mediterranean relations, are also based on the understanding that 'cultures' are characterized by clear-cut borders that separate the Self from the Other.

In order to elaborate on the differences between identity and culture, it might thus be worthwhile to recall Luhmann's argument that 'culture is ... the memory of social systems' (Luhmann, 1995a: 47). More specifically, culture is the unity of the difference between remembering and forgetting and as such also serves a specific function. It is facilitating in so far as social systems have to continuously select from an overwhelming amount of possibilities. 'It is the result of this highly selective remembering, that [the system] only remembers what it repeatedly requires' and this process of remembering allows the system to 'define ... its own character' (ibid). Culture is, thus, the communicative 'condensation of identities', which enables a system to remember and observe itself and, on the operative level, to rely on previously established practices' (ibid.). However, at the same time 'culture' is a paradoxical operation, since it 'formulates a problem of "identity" which it cannot solve by itself – and which it hence problematizes' (ibid.: 42). Thus, 'culture' remembers previous selection processes, but tries to make the contingency of these previous selections invisible by translating them into a distinct character or identity of the system.

At the same time, however, this invisibilization always remains incomplete, since by comparing previous and current selections it also has to remember the contingency of all these selections. The linkage – but also the differences – between identity and culture now becomes clear. While identity relates to the dynamic processes of both symbolic bordering between a Self and an Other and marking of the substantive identities of both sides, culture refers to the memory of previous selections by the Self. While identities are, hence, characterized by the symbolic bordering that separates a specific identity from a temporal or spatial 'Other', the same cannot be said for cultures. Thus, cultures compare an actual situation with what has been memorized – the 'Other' of culture are those parts of the 'Self' that have been forgotten. The bordering process with regard to cultures is, thus, not located between these cultures, but rather within each culture, that is the distinction between the marked space of what is memorized, the unmarked state of what is forgotten. It is hence 'not meaningful to draw a precise border between cultures' (Albert, 2002: 108).

This distinction between 'identity' and 'culture' is also of relevance to the study of 'cultural dialogue' in Euro-Mediterranean relations. It first of all allows disentanglement of these two concepts. While identity – thus the process of bordering and marking – relates to the distinction between a Self and an Other, culture addresses the paradox of the Self, that is the invisibilization of previous contingent selections by the 'Self' that the 'Self' has forgotten. In the context of Euro-Mediterranean relations, the strong reference to 'cultures' leads to a semantic sedimentation of the symbolic borders that draws a distinction between Europe and the southern Mediterranean. What is henceforth remembered, in other words what becomes the culture of Euro-Mediterranean relations, is the observation of distinct cultures. This 'culture of culturalization' already indicates the paradoxical character of 'cultural dialogue', since it has to continuously make the contingency of this selection invisible. This might not be a problem if it were not for the assumption of a clear-cut separation between 'cultures', which emphasizes the need for dialogue but at the same time carries an essentialist notion and problematization of difference.

What matters here is that this 'culture of culturalization' is a process of hegemonic self-description of Euro-Mediterranean relations, in which the selection of other possibilities becomes structurally disadvantaged. Following Urs Stäheli, it can thus be argued that the notion of 'cultural dialogue' in Euro-Mediterranean relations, which is underpinned by the observation of antagonistic identity patterns as outlined in the previous section, is a political act of de-paradoxification. While this argument will be further elaborated in the following section, it can now be summarized that in Euro-Mediterranean relations culture has become a 'hegemonic self-description' (Stäheli, 2002). Thus, 'culture' has turned from one amongst many possible 'particular semantics' into a 'serious (and therefore) hegemonic semantic' (ibid.: 222). The transformation of culture into a hegemonic semantic of Euro-Mediterranean relations requires the invisibilization of alternatives; its institution as the dominant self-description is ultimately a political act. Consequently, culture becomes the main semantic reference point for societal relations in Euro-Mediterranean for a; the symbolic bordering of identities can henceforth be represented in a quasi-ontological binary sense. This process is hegemonic at three levels. First, it neglects other possibilities, in particular other possible processes of symbolic bordering. Second, one side of the border is remembered as the problematic one, the other side as the preferred one. Third, through the form of a 'culture of culturalization' it consciously remembers difference and it forgets sameness. Of course, this process does not remain unchallenged. Indeed, many political initiatives and academic writings stress equality between both sides (Pace & Schumacher, 2004; Partenariat Euromed, 2003). Hegemony always rests on shaky grounds. Alternative bordering processes can be invoked – such as through recourse to the heritage of the Roman Empire, to a Mediterranean culture, to the Monotheistic tradition or to shared interests, habits or values – but all these alternatives have to be voiced under the shadow of the observation of two distinct 'cultures', which shapes the 'cultural dialogue' of Euro-Mediterranean relations.

Structures of 'Cultural Dialogue': The Politics of De-paradoxification

What are the consequences of the institutionalization of the semantics of culture in Euro-Mediterranean 'dialogue' (see also contributions by Michelle Pace in this volume)? As has already been argued, this Euro-Mediterranean 'cultural dialogue' is an institutionalization of difference on the basis of a prior symbolic bordering process. There is no doubt that this institutionalization of difference is guided by goodwill. Thus, both sides aim to reassure the other of their respect and both sides emphasize that they share basic values (High Level Advisory Group, 2003).[8] However, the semantics of two distinct cultures also means that they primarily memorize the difference, while the memory of shared characteristics is structurally dis-preferred. In other words, the difference becomes emphasized – regardless of the reference to shared symbols – and problematized. The paradoxical nature of 'cultural dialogue' then is that it aims to overcome or at least to bridge differences between two sides, but fails to see that it creates difference in the first place. In more theoretical terms, 'the politics of de-paradoxification is based on the construction of a paradox, which it then aims to undo' (Stäheli, 2002: 272).[9] The institutionalization of 'cultural dialogue' in Euro-Mediterranean relations, therefore, ensures the continuation of the observation of difference as well as its underlying assumptions. It is a politicization of culture in so far as it rests on a prior semantic problematization, that is the valorization of each side of the symbolic border. Hence, 'cultural dialogue' uses the observation of cultures of co-operation and conflict in order to reinscribe its own distinction into political discourses, which in turn allows the attribution of threats and conflicts to one side only. From a theoretical perspective, these conflictual foundations of 'cultural dialogue' closely relate to the argument that 'the politics of de-paradoxification are antagonistic and, hence, use the form of conflicts' (ibid.).

This argument requires further clarification on the conflictual foundations of 'cultural dialogue'. As a starting point, it seems useful to trace the 'conflictual moment of a decision for a specific distinction and the marking of both sides', hence the moment in which the de-paradoxification inherent in the institutionalization of 'cultural dialogue' becomes political (ibid.: 273).[10] It is in fact a de-paradoxification, since the semantics of culture, which are inscribed in Euro-Mediterranean relations, aim to make the contingency of this distinction invisible. It is political, since its establishment relates to an underlying conflictual disposition of this relationship. In summarizing such a paradoxical operation, Luhmann argues that it is 'only those questions that are in principle undecidable, on which we can decide' (Luhmann, 1994: 22). In the context of 'cultural dialogue', these undecidable questions are located at the level of symbolic bordering processes. However, once the cultural code has been established, other possible distinctions become structurally dis-preferred. Thus, 'distinctions must be proposed, which take the place of the paradox, in order to make it invisible and to construct instead connective identities' (Luhmann, 2000: 265). To follow that argument, there is no external justification for the operation of this code; it reproduces itself communicatively through reference to itself. Hence, 'the fundaments of the code are the secret of its own success and, based on that, of the irresolvable violence of its institutionalization' (Stäheli, 2002: 253; see also Baecker, 1996). The rhetoric of 'dialogue' in Euro-Mediterranean relations underlines this logic of reasoning. Thus, dialogue becomes itself a de-paradoxification, since it aims to make the impossibility of inter-subjective understanding invisible. This invisibilization can then also have a conflictual and violent dimension since 'the reciprocal exchange of hermeneutic dialogue will always simply redouble and perpetuate the violence of misunderstanding of the other' (Librett, 2002: xvii). The good intentions of 'cultural dialogue' are then only a weak consolidation. 'The resultant mutual violence may be that of counterbalancing forces, a violence which holds itself in check or fails to appear as such, and it may seem or be, in a given instance, a violence of extremely small proportions producing negligible effects, but it is not less a matter of violence merely because it can appear in micrological or minimal ways' (ibid.: xvii–xviii).

These views on the politics of de-paradoxification of 'cultural dialogue' can now be made fruitful for the study of the 'conflictual moment' which precedes the institutionalization of 'cultural dialogue' in Euro-Mediterranean relations. Where precisely is this 'conflictive moment', the 'violence' in the institutionalization of 'cultural dialogue', located? A historical perspective might be helpful in tracing this conflictual structural disposition of 'cultural dialogue'. Thus, it is interesting to note that the link between the notion of distinct 'cultures', including the underlying valorization of difference as a key differential unit and its subsequent institutionalization in Euro-Mediterranean relations, is relatively new.[11] Thus, the politicization of culture can, in particular, be traced since the mid-1990s. As Schumacher has outlined, it was the Barcelona Declaration that explicitly linked the observation of 'culture(s)' with the observation of (in)security and conflict in the context of Euro-Mediterranean relations (Schumacher, 2005: 331). Thus, the third basket of the EMP has, from the outset, been divided into two parts. While the first part addresses both cultural differences and co-operation between 'cultures', the second part deals with all possible threats, such as 'illegal immigration, terrorism, drug trafficking as well as international crime and corruption' (ibid.). However, these two parts do not stand in isolation from each other but, as the first section of this article has already argued, have become connected. It is then one side of the symbolic border – the southern Mediterranean – that becomes associated with these threats. This attribution of responsibility becomes particularly obvious when EU-statements that do not directly address 'cultural dialogue' are taken into perspective. To quote but one example, the EU security strategy observes that 'the Mediterranean area generally [sic!] continues to undergo serious problems of economic stagnation, social unrest and unresolved conflict' (European Council, 2003). It is then the role of Europe, which 'has never been so prosperous, so secure nor so free' as in this 'period of peace and stability' to assist the southern Mediterranean countries to develop in a similar way (ibid.). The rhetoric of 'cultural dialogue' thus becomes underpinned by an attribution of responsibility and, hence, a conflictive moment in Euro-Mediterranean relations in which negative attributions in the form of an identity conflict structure 'cultural dialogue' (Diez, Stetter & Albert, 2004; Messmer, 2003).

It is important to reiterate that this securitization of culture (see Malmvig in this volume) does not follow a Huntingtonian logic: in this way, the horizon of co-operation and sameness is not lost out of sight. Notwithstanding this argument, the conflictual moment in the institutionalization of 'cultural dialogue' in Euro-Mediterranean relations can now well be traced. Political conflicts emanating from the southern Mediterranean become problematized and through symbolic bordering processes can then be attributed to one side. The aforementioned horizon of a shared identity, which might lead to a disappearance of these two distinct 'cultures', also builds on this conflictual understanding. This is due to the equation of a peaceful *shared* future with the current fundaments of collective *European* identity patterns.

The observation of two distinct cultures, a European culture of co-operation and a southern Mediterranean culture of conflict, allows for an 'explanation' of the origins of the aforementioned threats (see also Ahmed, 2003). But there are also other dimensions on which this form of observation has a significant impact. Thus, the rhetoric of distinct cultures is a powerful semantic source of undermining democratic reforms or conflict settlement in the South, where political leaders can always refer to their different cultural dispositions in order to justify autocratic policies or political measures in conflict situations (see also Soler i Lecha, 2003). As a word of caution it should, however, be emphasized that this argument does not propose a simplistic rationalistic understanding of this institutionalization of difference through 'cultural dialogue'. Thus, it is the de-paradoxification of inscribing culture into Euro-Mediterranean relations that ensures the reproduction of this distinction, rather than the de-contextualized interests of specific actors. In contrast to such actor-centred perspectives, this process can thus be understood as the 'construction of imagined unity of the system' by the system itself, while this construction always rests on shaky grounds, since it relies on the continued invisibilization of its foundational paradoxes (Stäheli, 2002: 281). Notwithstanding this argument, the unity of cultural dialogue is based on a categorical distinction between two separate entities which relate to each other in the form of an antagonistic relationship. And herein lies the political significance of the inscription of 'cultures' into Euro-Mediterranean relations.

Euro-Mediterranean Relations and World Society: Bordering and Debordering Processes

The critique of the semantics and structures of 'cultural dialogue' in Euro-Mediterranean relations, which this essay has developed in the previous three sections, should not be read as a blunt attack on the underlying symbolic bordering processes. This would be too simplistic. As has been mentioned above, *all* communicative operations and, hence, all social structures depend on the production of difference. For that reason, difference itself cannot be held responsible for the emergence of conflicts (Stetter, 2004). As Stäheli has put it, 'an antagonistic articulation of the system requires a radicalization of the negation: the external is what the system is not, but this negation is now articulated as a threat to the system' (2002: 298). Based on the arguments of the previous section, what matters therefore is to analyse the de-paradoxification and the conflictual moment of 'cultural dialogue' and, in a second step, to move beyond the horizon which this distinction aims to make invisible in order to overcome this specific conflictual disposition. Accordingly, it is not the construction of difference in Euro-Mediterranean relations that is the focus of critique here. Rather, it is the specific way of the de-paradoxification in the rhetoric of 'cultural dialogue' in Euro-Mediterranean relations that is criticized.

This final section argues that what 'cultural dialogue' makes invisible is the shared world societal reference point of collective identities in both the EU and the southern Mediterranean. This allows a conceptualization of the contours of a de-problematization of the symbolic border of Euro-Mediterranean 'cultural dialogue' (on de-problematization see Prozorov, 2004). The discussion in this section proceeds in three steps. Based on the understanding that symbolic bordering processes are a structural feature of world society's internal differentiation, it argues that the character of symbolic bordering has to be addressed. In the context of Euro-Mediterranean relations, this relates in particular to the valorization of this distinction, where one side is represented as a model, the other as a threat. This coding shapes the antagonistic fundaments of 'cultural dialogue', and it is insufficiently dealt with. Moreover, rather than observing allegedly distinct 'cultures', the shared world societal reference point for the EU and the southern Mediterranean could be more clearly elaborated. Finally, this requires an attempt to address the relationship between symbolic (de-)bordering processes, on the one hand, and (de-)bordering processes on other dimensions, such as functional and territorial borders, on the other. Again, the argument of this section is not that borders should disappear – borders are a necessary element of all communication and, hence, of world society's internal differentiation – but rather challenges the way with which these borders are institutionalized in the context of the EMP, including 'cultural dialogue'.

As has been argued above, the Self/Other distinction of symbolic bordering in 'cultural dialogue' is supplemented by two specific features: first, a semantic sedimentation in the observation of regional identity patterns, which fosters the observation of two distinct 'cultures'; in a second step, these cultures become coded on the basis of value attributions. Thus, one side – the EU – is associated with good [sic!] governance, peace and harmonious regional identity patterns. The other side, the southern Mediterranean is represented as a potential threat characterized by conflictual regional identity patterns. It is this secondary coding which shapes the antagonistic features of 'cultural dialogue' and hence its conflictual structural disposition.[12] To be fair, it must be emphasized that this critique of 'cultural dialogue' must be put into perspective. Thus, cultural dialogue is at the same time shaped by a horizon of sameness with regard to a shared heritage and a shared future, as all official documents related to 'cultural dialogue' emphasize. Yet, what the notion of two distinct cultures fails to address is the shared *present*, also on the dimension of symbolic borders. As it stands, the present is problematized and is also read in the context of difference and conflict.

This directs attention to the shared world societal reference point of Europe and the southern Mediterranean. Addressing the world societal dimension does not question the process of symbolic bordering as such. As indicated above, world society is not a homogenous unit that can be represented in terms of a single 'world culture' or a disappearance of difference. World society is not characterized by normative integration but rather by the connectability of communications, that produces difference (but see also Albert & Brock, 2001). Thus, it stresses the internal fragmentation of world society. This also relates to collective identities that result from symbolic bordering practices, since the occurrence of different collective identities and 'cultures' *within* world society point to the shared world societal horizon of all identity related communications. However, this shared world societal context is not sufficiently addressed in Euro-Mediterranean relations, and a stronger focus would require a discussion of instances of symbolic bordering in a more detailed manner. This not only relates to the assumption of a clear-cut border between 'cultures', but in particular to a de-valorization of difference in Euro-Mediterranean relations.[13]

This argument does not suggest that the goal is the construction of a shared identity – which cannot be planned anyway. To reiterate, world society is characterized by manifold internal bordering processes, also on the symbolic level, and *per se* bordering is not of a conflictual nature. It would, however, require giving up the notion of regions as 'cultural containers', i.e. an attribution of categorical features to contingent spaces, that are represented as functionally, territorially and symbolically homogenous. This can be achieved by addressing (de-)bordering processes on other levels – such as with regard to functional or territorial borders – and relating these processes to symbolic borders (see also Albert & Brock, 2000). This would, first, direct attention to the manifold cross-cutting features of these various types of borders, that tend not to converge. Second, it would also render the valorization of symbolic bordering processes and, thus, its potentially conflictual disposition, more difficult. To summarize, a greater focus on constant processes of (de-)bordering with regard to various types of borders would be a more useful platform for Euro-Mediterranean relations than the ontologization of 'culture' as this has been constructed in Euro-Mediterranean relations since the beginning of the Barcelona process.

Conclusion

The critique of 'cultural dialogue' in this essay should not be misread. It is not the construction of difference *per se* in 'cultural dialogue' that is criticized here. What this analysis has rather attempted to do is to observe the blind spots of 'cultural dialogue'. Thus, the argument is not that symbolic bordering processes must come to an end. Why should they? This essay has instead attempted to elaborate on how 'cultural dialogue' in Euro-Mediterranean relations is based on a prior problematization of collective identities which appear as quasi-ontological units (cultures) and which relate to a specific conflictual structural disposition. As it stands, 'cultural dialogue' has strong features of an antagonistic concept even in those cases in which it is approached in good faith. This is not to argue that new inscriptions would be unproblematic. A distinction has always to be drawn, and only then do we know to what extent these new distinctions are based on a conflictual disposition. However, while any new distinction will also draw symbolic borders, the concrete form of its de-paradoxification might be less structured on the basis of a valorization of difference. This can be read as a plea for greater awareness of difference, one which is less inclined to observe homogenous units and one which pays greater attention to constant processes of debordering and rebordering, not least in the Euro-Mediterranean area.

Notes

[1] Emphasis is here on the syllable 'dia' which stems from the Greek word for 'two'.
[2] All translations from German originals are made by the author.
[3] On similarities – and differences – between constructivist, post-structuralist and systems theoretical approaches see also Åkerstrøm Andersen (2003); Stäheli & Stichweh (2002).
[4] It should be emphasized that the 'Self' can be the EU or the southern Mediterranean. The same applies to the 'Other'.
[5] See on this 'peace-assumption' Diez, Stetter & Albert (2004).
[6] This ontologization of regional units is, for example, reflected in the common reference to an 'Arab world', as if the Arab region could be understood without reference to its world societal embeddedness. See also UNDP (2005).

[7] See also Jacques Derrida's argument that 'le propre d'une culture, c'est de n'être pas identique à elle-même', quoted in Luhmann (1995a: 42).

[8] This emphasis on shared values, such as peace or humanity, has become a prominent rhetorical element of relations between western states or organizations, such as the EU or the US, and non-western regions, in particular since the Iraq war. Reference to these shared values is used as 'proof' that conflicts in which western powers are involved are not clashes of cultures but rather clashes between those in the West and other regions which value human rights, and those who do not.

[9] It should be emphasized here that this conceptualization of 'politics' differs from the classical systems' theoretical concept developed by Luhmann (2000). However, it might be possible in further research to find out how the politics of de-paradoxification can be linked with the systems theoretical understanding of politics as a functional sub-system of world society. This would be particularly useful in order to relate this wider reading of politics to the form-specific features of political communication as they have been analysed by systems theory. I am grateful to Jochen Walter for this comment.

[10] As already argued, such a definition of 'politics' is somewhat wider than the more limited approach suggested by Luhmann (2000). See also Guzzini (2004) for contours of a wider approach.

[11] Of course, notions of ontological difference have existed prior to this period. Edward Said's work on 'Orientalism' is still a seminal illustration of such dynamics (1978). But they lacked an institutionalization similar to 'cultural dialogue' in the EMP.

[12] Some authors argue that the notion of 'cultural dialogue' is in itself conflictual. See Librett (2000).

[13] Thus, one might ask, should patterns of conflicts in Europe and patterns of cooperation in the southern Mediterranean not be addressed to a greater degree?

References

Ahmed, A. S. (2003) *Islam under Siege: Living Dangerously in a Post-Honor World* (Cambridge: Polity).

Åkerstrøm Andersen, N. (2003) *Discursive Analytical Strategies: Understanding Foucault, Koselleck, Laclau, Luhmann* (Bristol: Policy Press).

Albert, M. (2002) *Zur Politik der Weltgesellschaft: Identität und Recht im Kontext internationaler Vergesellschaftung* (Weilerswist: Velbrück).

Albert, M. & Brock, L. (2000) Debordering the world of states: new spaces in international relations, in: M. Albert, L. Brock & K. D. Wolf (Eds) *Civilizing World Politics: Society and Community Beyond the State* (Oxford: Rowman & Littlefield).

Albert, M. & Brock, L. (2001) What keeps Westphalia together? Normative differentiation in the modern system of states, in: M. Albert, D. Jacobsen & Y. Lapid (Eds) *Identities, Borders, Orders: Rethinking International Relations Theory* (Minneapolis: University of Minnesota Press).

Albert, M. & Hilkermeier, L. (Eds) (2004) *Observing International Relations: Niklas Luhmann and World Politics* (London: Routledge).

Aliboni, R. (2004) Inventing a cooperative identity, *bitterlemons-international.org*, 4, 2, http://www.bitterlemons-international.org/previous.php?opt=1&id=25.

Anderson, B. (1991) *Imagined Communities* (London: Verso).

Baecker, D. (1996) Gewalt im System, *Soziale Welt*, 1, pp. 93–109.

Bonacker, T. (2004) Krieg und die Theorie der Weltgesellschaft: Auf dem Weg zu einer Konflikttheorie der Weltgesellschaft, unpublished manuscript.

Braudel, F. (1986) *La Méditerranée et le monde méditerranéen à l'époque de Philippe II* (Paris: Armand Colin).

Brown, C. (2001) Borders and identity in international political theory, in: M. Albert, D. Jacobsen & Y. Lapid (Eds) *Identities, Borders, Orders: Rethinking International Relations Theory* (Minneapolis: University of Minnesota Press).

Buzan, B., Wæver, O. & de Wilde, J. (1998) *Security: A New Framework for Analysis* (Boulder: Lynne Rienner).

Council of the European Union (2004) Presidency Conclusion of the Euro-Mediterranean Meeting of Ministers of Foreign Affairs, The Hague, 29–30 November 2004, 14869 (04) (Presse 331).

Del Sarto, R. (2005 forthcoming) *State-Identity and Regional Security in the Euro-Mediterranean* (New York: Palgrave).
Diez, T., Stetter, S. & Albert, M. (2004) The European Union and the Transformation of Border Conflicts: Theorising the Impact of Integration and Association, Working Papers Series in EU Border Conflicts Studies (Birmingham: University of Birmingham).
Diez, T. (2004) Europe's other and the return of geopolitics, *Cambridge Review of International Affairs*, 17(2), pp. 319–355.
Eisenstadt, S. N. & Giesen, B. (1995) The construction of collective identities, *Archive Européenne de Sociologie*, 36, pp. 75–102.
European Council (2003) A secure Europe in a better world, European Security Strategy, 12 December 2003, Brussels, http://ue.eu.int/uedocs/cmsUpload/78367.pdf.
Guzzini, S. (2004) Constructivism and international relations: an analysis of Luhmann's conceptualization of power, in: M. Albert & L. Hilkermeier (Eds) *Observing International Relations: Niklas Luhmann and World Politics* (London: Routledge).
Habermas, J. (1992) *Faktizität und Geltung: Beiträge zur Diskurstheorie des Rechts und des demokratischen Rechtsstaats* (Frankfurt: Suhrkamp).
High-Level Advisory Group (2003) *Dialogue Between Peoples and Cultures in the Euro-Mediterranean Area* (Brussels: European Commission).
Houtum, H. V. & Naerssen, T. V. (2002) Bordering, ordering and othering, *Tijdschrift voor Economische en Social Geografie*, 93(2), pp. 125–136.
Huntington, S. (1993) The clash of civilizations?, *Foreign Affairs*, 72(3), pp. 22–49.
Librett, J. S. (2000) *The Rhetoric of Cultural Dialogue: Jews and Germans from Moses Mendelssohn to Richard Wagner and Beyond* (Stanford: Stanford University Press).
Luhmann, N. (1994) Die Paradoxie des Entscheidens, *Nummer 1*, 1, pp. 22–32.
Luhmann, N. (1995a) Kultur als historischer Begriff, in ibid *Gesellschaftsstruktur und Semantik: Studien zur Wissenssoziologie der modernen Gesellschaft, Band 4* (Frankfurt: Suhrkamp).
Luhmann, N. (1995b) *Social Systems* (Stanford: Stanford University Press).
Luhmann, N. (1997) *Die Gesellschaft der Gesellschaft* (Frankfurt: Suhrkamp).
Luhmann, N. (2000) *Die Politik der Gesellschaft* (Frankfurt: Suhrkamp).
Luhmann, N. (2002) *Theories of Distinction: Redescribing the Descriptions of Modernity* (Stanford: Stanford University Press).
Marchart, O. (2002) On drawing a line: politics and the significatory logics of inclusion/exclusion, *Soziale Systeme: Zeitschrift für soziologische Theorie*, 8(1), pp. 69–87.
Messmer, H. (2003) *Der soziale Konflikt: Kommunikative Emergenz und systemische Reproduktion* (Stuttgart: Lucius & Lucius).
Neumann, I. B. & Welsh, J. M. (1991) The other in European self-definition: an addendum to the literature on international society, *Review of International Studies*, 17, pp. 327–348.
Newman, D. (2003) On borders and power: a theoretical framework, *Journal of Borderland Studies*, 18(1), pp. 13–25.
Pace, M. & Schumacher, T. (2004) Report: culture and community in the Euro-Mediterranean Partnership: a roundtable on the third basket, Alexandria 5–7 October 2003, *Mediterranean Politics*, 9(1), pp. 122–126.
Pace, M. (2005) Euro-Mediterranean Partnership cultural initiatives: what political relevance?, in: R. Youngs & F. Haizam Amirah (Eds) *The Barcelona Process Revisited* (Madrid: FRIDE and Real Instituto Elcano).
Partenariat Euromed (2003) Euro-Mediterranean Foundation for a Dialogue of Cultures, 57/03 REV2[EN], 12 November 2003.
Peresso, E. M. (1998) Euro-Mediterranean cultural cooperation, *European Foreign Affairs Review*, 3, pp. 135–156.
Prozorov, S. (2004) The Logic of Deproblematisation in Border Conflicts: Euregio Karelia as a Model of Border Transformation, conference paper presented at the Fifth Pan–European meeting of the Standing Group on International Relations of the European Consortium for Political Research, The Hague, 9–11 September 2004.

Rajaram, P. K. (2004) Disruptive writing and a critique of territoriality, *Review of International Studies*, 30, pp. 201–228.
Risse, T. (2004) Social constructivism and European integration, in: A. Wiener & T. Diez (Eds) *European Integration Theory* (Oxford: Oxford University Press).
Rumelili, B. (2004) Constructing identity and relating to difference: understanding the EU's mode of differentiation, *Review of International Studies*, 30, pp. 27–47.
Said, E. W. (1978) *Orientalism* (New York: Penguin).
Saurette, P. (2000) International relations: image of thought: collective identity, desire and Deluzian ethology, *The International Journal of Peace Studies*, 5(1), pp. 39–59.
Schumacher, T. (2005) *Die Europäische Union als internationaler Akteur im südlichen Mittelmeerraum: 'Actor Capability' und EU-Mittelmeerpolitik* (Baden-Baden: Nomos).
Soler i Lecha, E. (2003) The external dimension of sub-national government: dealing with human rights at the Barcelona and Valencia Euromed civil fora, *Mediterranean Politics*, 8(2–3), pp. 112–132.
Soysa, I. & Zervakis, P. (Eds) (2002) Does Culture Matter? The Relevance of Culture in Politics and Governance in the Euro-Mediterranean Zone, ZEI Discussion Papers C 111.
Stäheli, U. (2000) *Sinnzusammenbrüche: Eine dekonstruktive Lektüre von Niklas Luhmanns Systemtheorie* (Weilerswist: Velbrück).
Stäheli, U. & Stichweh, R. (2002) Inclusion/exclusion – systems theoretical and poststructuralist perspectives, *Soziale Systeme: Zeitschrift für soziologische Theorie*, 8(1), pp. 3–7.
Stetter, S. (2004) The Study of Conflicts and Modern Systems Theory: Reflections on the Distinction between Difference and Disaccord, conference paper presented at the Fifth Pan–European meeting of the Standing Group on International Relations of the European Consortium for Political Research, The Hague, 9–11 September 2004.
Stichweh, R. (2000) *Die Weltgesellschaft: Soziologische Analysen* (Frankfurt: Suhrkamp).
UNDP (2005) *The Arab Human Development Report 2004: Towards Freedom in the Arab World* (New York: UNDP).
World Society Research Group (2000) Introduction: world society, in: M. Albert, L. Brock & K. D. Wolf (Eds) *Civilizing World Politics: Society and Community Beyond the State* (Oxford: Rowman & Littlefield).

Security through Intercultural Dialogue? Implications of the Securitization of Euro-Mediterranean Dialogue between Cultures

HELLE MALMVIG
Danish Institute for International Studies, Copenhagen, Denmark

After years of neglect, the human and cultural dimension of the Euro-Mediterranean Partnership has now become a centre of attention. Enhancing civil society exchanges in the Euro-Mediterranean area is to bring new life and visibility to the Barcelona Process, and it is hoped to help circumvent the stalemate and crisis of the first basket. Hence, at the Valencia conference in 2002 it was agreed to take full advantage of the possibilities offered in the third basket. The flagship initiative became the Euro-Mediterranean Foundation for a Dialogue between Cultures; officially inaugurated in Alexandria in April 2005.[1]

The renewed interest in the third basket is, however, also a response to a changing security environment. In the aftermath of September 11 and the US Administration's war on terror, the EU has been looking for alternative ways to approach radical extremism and ever increasing mutual mistrust; ways which do not rest on scenarios of inevitable clashes of civilizations (see Gillespie, 2004a: 22–4, 2004b). Intercultural dialogue was here seen as a vital instrument to further mutual understanding and knowledge, and as a way to combat tendencies of xenophobia and stereotyping on both shores of the Mediterranean.

The increasing importance attributed to intercultural dialogue has also been reflected in various new bilateral and multilateral initiatives, such as the UN's 'Year of Dialogue among civilizations' and the German initiative for a 'Dialogue with the Islamic world', as well as in recent International Relations (IR) literature. Drawing on Critical Theory, in particular Habermas, IR theorists have, for some time, argued that a genuine and open dialogue between cultures constitutes a forceful alternative – and even remedy – to war and confrontation (Dallmyer, 2002; Tehranian & Chappell, 2002; Lynch, 2005; Linklater, 2005).

This essay will, however, focus on the *consequences* of turning intercultural dialogue into a means for avoiding war and conflict – or, in other words, into a means of security. More specifically, it will show *how* intercultural dialogue is represented as a means to security and *what* the implications are of this representation. It will suggest that the new initiative for a Dialogue between Cultures to a great extent is inspired by Habermasian ideals of dialogue, but that these ideals are difficult – if not impossible – to apply in practice given that this Dialogue has become framed within a context of security. The main argument is that the *securitization* of the 'Dialogue' has paradoxically served to provide it with extraordinary legitimacy and urgency, while at the same time compromising the very conditions of possibility for a dialogue along Habermasian lines.

The study is structured into three main parts. The first part briefly spells out Habermas' understanding of the main preconditions for *communicative action*, and shows how these requirements are also echoed in the Euro-Mediterranean initiative for a Dialogue between Cultures. On the basis of the Copenhagen School's conceptualization of security, the second part will analyse how the reasoning behind, and justifications for, intercultural dialogue securitize the very purpose and logic of dialogue. The third part will discuss the specific implications of securitization, demonstrating how the Dialogue has in practice become an object of extreme politicization and tight governmental control.

Habermasian Understanding of Dialogue

> 'When actors engage in truth-seeking discourse, they must be prepared to change their own views of the world, their interest and sometimes even their identities' (Risse, 2000: 2)

Habermas' theory of communicative action has a normative rather than descriptive purpose. Its primary objective is to advance mutual understanding through intersubjective dialogue, in which dialogical exchanges should be free from relations of power and exclusion (Diez & Stean, 2005; Linklater, 2005). In order to engage in this type of dialogue, which Habermas also terms as 'the ideal speech situation', several preconditions have to be satisfied. These conditions cover what could be called the 'mindset' and motivations of the participating actors as well as the 'rules' of interaction.

First, the ideal speech situation requires that the participants share certain common traits such as a common language, culture or history. They have to share what Habermas calls a 'common lifeworld' allowing them to communicate and refer back to shared experiences or value systems. It also requires that dialogue is open and inclusive. Everyone affected by the issues and decisions of dialogue should ideally have equal access to participate in the dialogue, and they are, moreover, to be recognized as equal partners.

Secondly, communicative action demands a certain mindset or predispositions of the interlocutors. They have to be prepared to change their own views of the world, their interest and even their identities. This implies that neither party is to strive for a predefined outcome or a certain result when engaging in dialogue, and that parties cannot be driven by egoistic notions or strategic thinking. Instead, the participants need to be able to take the position of their interlocutors (see Pace in this volume). They need to be empathetic listeners, who are able to see the world from the others' point of view and ready to change their own predefined perceptions.

The interlocutors are, however, not only to seek a mere understanding of the others' worldviews; they are ultimately to reach a new and shared consensus of views. They have to be prepared to be convinced by the better argument, which requires that the participating actors are willing to set interest and beliefs aside in order to construct a new common ground. As Thomas Risse argues: 'In this sense, relationships of power, force and coercion are assumed absent when argumentative consensus is sought' (Risse, 2000: 11). Consensus, it is assumed, can be reached through *reasoned* deliberation, and the participants are accordingly presumed to know what the better argument is, independently from the power or prestige of the argument's advocate (Habermas, 1984).

These ideal conditions are to a large extent reflected in the declarations and documents concerning the Euro-Mediterranean Dialogue between Cultures.[2] As we will see below, these documents – in particular the High-Level Report – operate with a very similar understanding of what makes a dialogue authentic and effective.

The Preconditions for a Dialogue between Cultures

The Dialogue between Cultures promises to be an authentic dialogue, as is emphasized in the Crete declaration (Crete, 2003, Annex 1). But what does 'an authentic' dialogue mean, and how does it depart from, for instance, everyday conversation or normal diplomatic exchanges? As Habermas would argue, this is answered by reference to a set of preconditions or guiding principles that have to be met in order for dialogue to be authentic.

The basic principles are: respect, equality and understanding of the Other. The participating actors are expected to be open to and to learn from the Other. They are to respect the Other's cultural and religious diversity, and not to try to change the Other in accordance with specific values or beliefs. The interlocutors are to meet one another with curious minds, striving to reach a better understanding and knowledge of each other, rather than trying to persuade each other to accept the superiority of certain values or identities. Moreover, dialogue is to be based on openness and equality. The participants are to be recognized as equals, and they are to have equal access to dialogue, assuring that the Dialogue is inclusive and broadly based (See in particular, Valencia, 2002: 14; Crete, 2003: Annex 1; Naples, 2003: 12; Schoefthaler, 2004).

These requirements for an authentic dialogue are discussed in more detail in the so-called High-Level Report on *Dialogue between peoples and cultures in the Euro-Mediterranean area*. Commissioned by the then President of the EU Commission, Romano Prodi in 2002, the High-Level Report was written by a group of intellectuals and academics from both shores of the Mediterranean. This group was to make recommendations on the envisioned Foundation for a Dialogue between Cultures and to provide input for the final decisions on the Foundation's working principles and priorities (Naples, 2003: 12, High-Level Advisory Group, 2004).

In the report, the Group argues that in order to achieve the goals of the Dialogue and to make it 'an authentic dialogue', the participating actors have to share and continuously comply with a number of fundamental principles. They are not mere ideal conditions but are to be observed *in practice* (High-Level Advisory Group, 2004: 29).

The principles, which the report outlines, equally revolve around notions of equality, respect, openness, and absence of coercion and power (see in particular 29–32). The report especially stresses the importance of the principles of equality and freedom. Equality is taken to mean that the participating actors have both an equal 'status' in and an equal 'access' to the dialogue. In other words, no actors are to have a privileged voice or representation in the dialogue. 'Proposals and ideas (should) be judged only on their respective merits and not according to the power and strength (economic, financial, military or other) of their advocates' (High-Level Advisory Group, 2004: 31). Again, echoing Habermas' notion of 'the better argument', it is demanded that deliberations take place on the basis of reason and merit rather than on the basis of power and strength. The precondition of equality is also related to the principle of freedom (or to the absence of coercion and power). The dialogue, it is argued, is to take place 'in absolute freedom and without restrictions of any kind' (High-Level Advisory Group, 2004: 30). No topic is to be excluded beforehand, neither are predefined ideas or values to be imposed.

Although the dialogue is to be based on 'total respect for the other' – and hence on a respect for differences and diversity – it is at the same time stressed that the dialogue is to develop a 'shared destiny' and feeling of belonging among the participants (High-Level Advisory Group, 2004: 27). Through dialogical interaction 'a common understanding and convergence of cultures' is to emerge (see also Statute 104/04 REV 4, 12.11.2004, Article II). Ultimately, the aim of the dialogue is to create a new and common identity which reaches beyond current differences. It is to construct what is called 'a common civilisation' (7). The participants are accordingly not only to respect and cherish different worldviews and values; they are also to 'create conditions favorable to the harmonious combination of cultural and religious diversity' (High-Level Advisory Group, 2004: 8): ultimately constructing new common reference points and ways of being. Hence, convergence, consensus, and harmony are given precedence over divergence, disagreement, and conflict.

In sum, the stipulated requirements for 'an authentic' Dialogue between Cultures very much resemble Habermas' understanding of the ideal speech situation. Yet, this gives rise to pertinent questions in terms of the possibility – or even desirability – of applying these ideal conditions in practice.

The Difficulties of a Habermasian Dialogue

The theory of communicative action has been challenged from different theoretical perspectives ranging from rational choice theory to poststructuralism.[3] The latter has, in particular, questioned Habermas' reliance on Western notions of rationality and truth, and his quest for harmony and consensus (see, for example, Derrida, 1978; Foucault, 1984; Hutchings, 2005; Simons, 1995; Diez & Stean, 2005; Connolly, 2001; Neumann, 2003).[4] In the context of this essay, two of the most important points of critique concern the presumptions of the possibility to engage in a dialogue free from relations of power and the readiness of the participating actors to engage in this type of ideal dialogue – two presumptions which, as we have seen, also run through the new Dialogue between Cultures.

In terms of the assumption of the absence of power, it has frequently been pointed out that this is a highly problematic assumption (see e.g. Risse, 2000; Lynch, 2005; Diez & Stean, 2005; Neumann, 2003; Pace, 2004). In international politics, it is argued, relations will rarely – if ever – be characterized by an absence of power, and the participating actors in dialogue can seldom be considered as equals.

The question of asymmetrical relations is addressed in the High-Level Report. Here, it is stressed that the imbalances between the North (EU) and the South (the Mediterranean partners) need to be tackled in order for a real dialogue to take place. The North and South are structurally unequal partners in terms of economic, political and social power. These inequalities are further compounded by the fact that the EU is able to act as a unitary and coherent whole, in contrast to the southern partners who are torn by regional conflicts and divisions. The dialogue cannot therefore reach its full potential or 'take on the same role and scope' for the southern partners as for the northern, as long as these structural inequalities remain (High-Level Report, 17–21).[5]

However, the critique of the possibility of a power-free dialogue goes beyond the question of whether the participants are actually equal, or how much power they possess relative to one another. As Foucault has argued, any 'dialogue' is always already imbued with power relations. Power is not a 'thing' which the participating actors possess prior to engaging in dialogue or hold externally to the dialogue. Rather, Foucault asserts, dialogue is power. Any dialogue – or discourse, in Foucault's terminology – has certain internal rules for what counts as legitimate or valid statements, who can authoritatively make such statements, who has access to making such statements, and what these statements can be about. For Foucault, the interesting question is not, as critical theory would have it, how we can minimize the workings of power or construct a dialogue free from power relations – since this is an impossible task – but rather, how discourse and power empirically interact and construct the conditions of possibility of a certain discourse or dialogue (see, for example, Foucault, 1972, 1980).

The second point of critique against a Habermasian understanding of dialogue concerns the disposition of the interlocutors to engage in a dialogue where they have to set aside self-interest, ultimately challenging their identity and perceptions of the world. As Chris Brown argues:

> The problem is that (Habermas) presupposes a prior willingness to engage in moral debate, that parties desire reasonable agreement.... Yet to engage in this kind of dialogue is to undertake a re-evaluation of one's values that inevitably will be painful and with no guarantee that the eventual outcome will be agreeable. Why would those who are comfortable with their values, as will often be the case, ... enter into this process in the absence of some compelling reason to think that their situation is untenable?" (Brown, 2000: 208).

A number of recent books and articles have sought answers to this question. Arguing for the relevance of critical theory in IR, several scholars have suggested that a Habermasian 'dialogue of cultures' is needed more than ever, and that there are indeed compelling reasons to engage in this kind of dialogue (Dallmyer, 2002; Tehranian & Chappell, 2002; Lynch, 2005; Linklater, 2005). Why is this so? These works point, in particular, to two factors: (1) the need to formulate an alternative to the prophesy of an inevitable clash between civilizations, (2) the terrorist attacks of September 11 and others that followed in other world capitals.

Mark Lynch in fact directly answers Brown's question by arguing that 'terrorism has supplied such a compelling reason' (Lynch, 2005: 9). September 11 and the US's militaristic response to the terrorist attacks has led to increasing levels of mistrust and violence between the West and the Muslim world. Yet, it has also led to an increasing awareness and public debate of the need for dialogue. Dialogue now constitutes, according to Lynch, the only viable alternative to extremism and violence, and hence to refuse dialogue is to 'grant victory to terrorists, whose violence pointedly aims to destroy trust and spread fear of the other' (Lynch, 2005: 11). Dialogue can change political opinions and identities and can embolden moderates, whereas refusals to engage in dialogue will only strengthen the position of radicals and their worldviews; ultimately leading to self-fulfilling prophesies of clashes of civilizations (Lynch, 2005: 27). In short, dialogue is seen as a necessary response to heightened tension and extremism, because the alternative is growing radicalization, fear and insecurity.

This line of justification for intercultural dialogue also runs through official EU documents and the High-Level Report, as will be shown below. However, this form of legitimation is not without problems. Although it provides a persuasive and mobilizing answer for engaging in dialogical interaction along Habermasian lines, by making security concerns the driving force of dialogue, it securitizes the very purpose of intercultural dialogue.

Legitimizing the Urgency of a Dialogue between Cultures

'The clash of civilisations is for the moment just a fiction manipulated by some and hoped for by others, if it is to remain this way – despite the worrying portents of the international scene – *we must act now*" (High-Level Advisory Group, 2004: 52, italics added).

This section will analyse how the need for a dialogue is established through acts of securitization. Drawing on the Copenhagen School's conceptualization of securitization (Wæver, 1995), it will be demonstrated how the very justifications and reasoning behind the Dialogue construct a situation of urgency and imminent conflict, effectively moving the dialogue within the realm of security concerns.

According to the Copenhagen School, security can be analysed as a discursive practice – a speech act – by which a certain issue or development is turned into a security problem. Security is a social construction which brings something into being, rather than 'an objective representation of a threatening reality' (Hansen, 1998: 35). As Ole Wæver explains: 'Security is not of interest as a sign that refers to something more real; the utterance *itself* is the act. By saying it, something is done (as in betting, giving a promise or naming a ship). By uttering "security" a state-representative moves a particular development into a specific area, and thereby claims a special right to use whatever means are necessary to block it' (Wæver, 1995: 55). This area is a specific realm in which extraordinary means can be used; a realm, which denotes that 'we' need to act now, if a certain threatening scenario is not to materialize. Securitization does not necessarily mean that the word 'security' is used, but that an imminent danger is constructed, that a threatening future is invoked, which demands urgent attention. Securitization is about dramatizing and bringing urgency to a certain matter, because it threatens the world as we know it.

Three Indications of Securitization

How do the legitimations of the Dialogue then work to securitize the dialogue? Three indications can be pointed out: (1) the articulation of an alternative analysis of the root causes of conflict between cultures, constructed in stark opposition to Huntington's analysis of a clash of civilizations, (2) the articulation of dialogue as an urgent necessity, (3) the articulation of a threatening future in the absence of dialogue.[6]

Huntington's (in)famous proposition of an emerging clash of civilizations is used as a continuous point of reference in the High-Level Report (High-Level Advisory Group, 2004: see in particular 8, 19, 25, 52). Yet, Huntington's analysis is surely not accepted. Rather, it is used as a basis for constructing an alternative explanation of conflict and as a forceful example of how ignorance and misperceptions can lead to dangerous and self-fulfilling prophesies. To see how this is done, let us first look briefly at the main elements of Huntington's analysis.

In his *Foreign Affairs* article from 1993, Huntington proposes that in the post-cold war era confrontation and conflict will run along civilizational lines. The sources of conflict will no longer be economic, political or ideological differences, but differences between civilizations. Divergent religious and cultural values will result in an inevitable and possibly violent clash of cultures. According to Huntington, especially Islamic and Western civilizations are prone to clash. Quoting Bernard Lewis, Huntington claims that the next violent confrontation will be between Islam and the West (Lewis, 1990: 60). The West will seek worldwide expansion and challenge 'our Judeo-Christian heritage (and) our secular present'. This bleak analysis of an emerging clash of civilizations leads Huntington to formulate several policy recommendations, among which that the West should maintain its technological and military superiority over other civilizations, and that the West should especially concentrate on limiting the expansion of the Islamic civilization by using the well-known tactic of 'divide and rule' thereby exploiting differences between Islamic states (Huntington, 1993).

In stark opposition to this hypothesis, the High-Level Report argues that Huntington's analysis is not only flawed but also dangerous due to its stereotyping and belligerent reading of what culture is and how cultures interact. What is at stake is not an imminent clash of civilizations, but a clash of ignorance, the report stresses:

> Dialogue is now more than ever a necessity – not to align ourselves on the ideology of the clash of civilisations ... but to thwart ignorance, of which the idea of the clash of civilisations is one of the most harmful forms. For the problem is rather the **clash of ignorance**, which is much more destructive (High-Level Advisory Group, 2004: 25. Bold in original).

The root causes of conflict and tension are not placed within any essentialist differences among cultures, but are instead seen as a result of ignorance and misperceptions – Huntington's thesis being a prime exponent of such ignorance.

Although Huntington's thesis, in this way, plays an important role in the report, the authors are very cautious of not implicitly aligning themselves with the underlying logic of Huntington's argument, for instance by proposing that a dialogue should be undertaken in order to avoid a clash of civilizations.

> The dialogue of civilisations derives from the polemical, not to say warmongering, concept of the "clash of civilisations" and while it may be intended as a counterblast, it unfortunately shares the same logic in spite of itself, giving credence to the idea that the whole question is thrashed out between blocks distinguished by quasi-ontological differences. (ibid.: 19).

This important note of caution – of the dangers of unconsciously reproducing Huntington's basic line of analysis, although trying to do the opposite[7] – may also account for the changing names of the Dialogue. In the Valencia and Create declarations, the dialogue was called a 'Dialogue between cultures and civilisations'. It was later named a 'Dialogue between peoples and cultures', and now it is simply a 'Dialogue between cultures'.

However, the attempts to escape Huntington's analysis do not succeed completely. It is arguably the case that by situating the causes of conflict at the level of ignorance and misperception, a very different response than that of Huntington's realist power politics emerges. The promotion of dialogue is to disseminate (real) knowledge about the Other; it is to challenge our predefined views, and to alleviate the tendency to construct easy stereotypes about the Other's identity, values and beliefs, thereby tackling the proposed root causes of conflict. This guides us towards a very different direction than Huntington's self-assured notions of superiority and the policies of divide and rule. Yet, it does not deny that a conflict or clash may be in the making. Huntington's clash of civilizations is seen as a 'false conflict', but it is substituted with another conflict – that of a clash of ignorance.

Thus, although the root causes of tensions and conflict are taken to rest on the absence of knowledge and misconceived perceptions – being open to change and correction – the basic notion that conflict is under way is not evaded but in fact reproduced. Conflict is seen as imminent if 'we' do not act: 'The clash of civilisations is for the moment just a fiction manipulated by some and hoped for by others. If it is to remain this way – despite the worrying portents on the international scene – we must act now' (High-Level Advisory Group, 2004: 52).

This call for immediate action is closely related to the second indication of securitization: that of urgency. When legitimizing the need for dialogue, urgency, expediency and necessity are frequently invoked. The dialogue needs to begin now, it is stressed. 'They expressed their concern and eagerness to confront violence and hatred by addressing the very causes of violence, terrorism and dehumanisation ... there is an *urgent need* to go further ... and to promote all those initiatives which can be premises of dialogue' (Crete, italics added). 'For this is a matter of urgency, and by urgency we mean starting tomorrow and not stopping the day after tomorrow' (High-Level Report: 49). 'Dialogue is more than ever a necessity' (25). 'There is an immediate need to engage in renewed dialogue ... there is an urgency in all the sectors of activities concerned' (37).

These calls for immediate action are, as the theory of securitization points out, not simply innocent enunciations. They infuse the call for dialogue with a sense of alert and urgency and construct a situation where it is seemingly almost too late to act. The appeals to urgency and need for action point to 'an immediate future' where something of existential and devastating consequence will happen, if action (that is, dialogue) is not undertaken.

What does this frightening scenario consist of, and what will happen in the absence of dialogical interaction? This question concerns the third indication of securitization, and is closely related to the former two. Here, the basic premise is that if dialogue is not undertaken, misperceptions and stereotypes are allowed to prevail and these will foster radicalism and violence. As the High-Level Report argues 'closed minds (who are) locked in their political and religious certainties ... can produce terrifying examples of deviancy – terrifying in the true sense of inspiring terror by setting off a chain of unstoppable collective reactions which produce fanaticism and ultimately violence' (50). In fact, the report argues, 'what is at stake is nothing less than peace itself' (49). The reverse logic is hence that if dialogue is not pursued, war and conflict will erupt.

In a similar, yet less explicit, manner, the Valencia and Crete documents stress that dialogue and exchanges between civilizations are to 'remove the threats to peace' (Crete, 2003). 'Against the highest levels of tensions in the region, the ministers stressed the need for an increased dialogue ... and understanding between cultures and civilisations' (Valencia, 2002). In other words, it is presumed that in the absence of authentic dialogue, extremism and xenophobia are allowed to take root. This will spur a vicious spiral of further radicalization leading potentially to (more) terrorism and war. Dialogue between cultures is hence seen as 'an efficient means of conflict prevention' (Crete, 2003). In fact, the President of the High-Level group refers to dialogue as a weapon. Intercultural dialogue 'provide real weapons for the purpose of anticipating, defusing, averting and resolving conflicts ... it should therefore ... not be an end in its own right, but rather a modus operandi for defusing aggressiveness' (Alaoui, 2004: 222, italics added).

Articulating intercultural dialogue in these terms of war and weapons effectively securitizes the goals and intentions of dialogue. Within this logic of securitization, intercultural dialogue, it seems, is not to be promoted in order to strengthen culture, but culture is to strengthen security. Intercultural dialogue becomes a means to a higher end; that end being security.

Implications of Securitization

What are the consequences of these securitization practices? What are the implications of turning intercultural dialogue into a security instrument, imbuing it with notions of urgency and fearful scenarios of the future? In the first instance, the consequence is of course that 'we' indeed are provided with 'a compelling reason' to engage in Habermasian dialogue, as argued by Mark Lynch. Feelings of vulnerability and insecurity serve to mobilize and make 'us' support actions which we perhaps normally would not have undertaken (Lynch, 2005: 9). This positive aspect of securitization is also emphasized by the Copenhagen School. Securitization, it is argued, 'has an enormous power as an instrument of social and political mobilization. Putting something on the security agenda persuades us of the need to furnish urgent and unprecedented responses; it signals imminent danger and is therefore given a high priority' (Wæver, 1995: 63). Securitization, in short, works as a rallying cry: as a forceful way of attracting resources and political attention.

However, the increased attention comes with a price. Security is not unquestionably positive, à la 'the more security the better' (Hansen, 1998: 36). There may, in fact, be many issues that are better dealt with by not being represented as matters of security (Wæver, 1995: 57). This is primarily because securitization is an extreme form of politicization. It is an act which brings heightened sensitivity and constraints to a political process, compelling the securitizing actors to seek tight control and monitoring over the decision-making process. This often means that it becomes more difficult for non-governmental or non-elite groups to influence the terms and framing of the debate, or even to take part in the process

(Hansen, 1998: 37; Edkins, 1999: 11). Securitization brings closure and hypersensitivity to an issue and constructs a restrained situation where governmental actors are overtly conscious of maintaining control.

This obviously creates a situation very far from the Habermasian ideals of openness and equality. Although securitization creates exactly that kind of 'untenable situation' that Brown calls for in order to be persuaded to engage in dialogical interaction, it also brings exclusion and extreme politicization. Indeed, as will be spelt out below, indications of extreme politicization and strict governmental control are already visible in the initiative for a Dialogue between Cultures.

The Extreme Politization of the Dialogue

In particular, three issues illustrate how the Dialogue between Cultures has become an object of tight governmental control and extreme politicization. These concern (1) the question of who has access to dialogical interaction, (2) who decides which actors are granted access, and (3) which topics and themes can be debated in the dialogue.[8]

First, as discussed above, one of the preconditions of 'an authentic dialogue' is openness both in terms of the themes that can be discussed and the actors that can participate. Yet, participation in the Dialogue has in fact from the beginning been severely restricted. The National Networks and Heads of National Networks – who are supposed to represent independent voices and coordinate the activities of civil society – have all been appointed and approved by their respective governments. Several of the Heads of the National Networks are also either directly involved in government or working in organizations closely associated with their respective governments, such as national libraries or cultural institutes. Seven of the 35 national networks are placed in either the Ministry of Foreign Affairs or in the Ministry of Cultural Affairs (51/05, 10.05.05, Secretariat ALF). Moreover, for at least the next three years the Board of Governors is composed of the members of the Euromed Committee. This board is the effective decision-making body, which awards grants, adopts the annual work programme and decides the exact guidelines of the Foundations (104/04REV 4,12.11.04). Thus, Euro-Mediterranean governments have effectively gained firm control over the kinds of civil society organizations that have been given access to the Dialogue.

These mechanisms of control over the access and participation of civil society groups are also reflected in the way the scope of the Dialogue has been amended. In the first documents and declarations concerning the establishment of the Dialogue between Cultures, it is repeatedly pointed out that the Dialogue should be inclusive, involving actors outside of cultural and governmental elite circles. For example, in the Valencia action plan it is stated that the Dialogue should involve 'the general population', and in Naples it was further specified that the Dialogue should involve 'cultural circles outside official diplomatic and cultural forums' (Valencia, 2002: 14; Naples, 2003: 12). In the first draft to the Statutes of the Foundation, it is similarly established that a main objective of the Dialogue is 'to hold a close and regular dialogue between cultural circles often kept outside the main diplomatic and cultural exchanges' (57/03, 12.11.2003). However, in the revised statutes from 2004, these paragraphs have been completely removed (104/04 REV 4, 12.11.2004). The original objective of promoting a broadly based dialogue which could reach beyond exchanges between cosmopolitan elites seems to have disappeared. Those groups outside of governmental circles who may be regarded as controversial, oppositional or outright dangerous can easily be excluded, and the possibilities of including, for instance, moderate Islamist groups are therefore remote (see also Gillespie, 2004: 234).

Secondly, the Dialogue has been confined not only in terms of access but also in terms of its themes and activities. The Euro-Mediterranean Committee and the Foreign Ministers, prior to the actual launch of the Dialogue, have already adopted a working programme specifying priority areas, target groups and projects for the next three years.[9] The thematic focus of the Dialogue has therefore been predetermined by Euro-Mediterranean governments, inhibiting civil society networks from formulating their own goals and priorities. The point is not that such decisions on themes and priority areas could or should be avoided, but that they are inherently political in the sense that they exclude some themes while including others.

This 'political element' is particularly visible with respect to the work programme's focus on so-called 'capacity building'. Here, the Dialogue is envisioned to build capacities within the fields of human rights, democratic citizenship and empowerment of women, among others (137/04, 29.11.2004). Equally, in the statutes of the Foundation, one of the four tasks identified is to 'promote the consolidation of the rule of law and basic freedoms' (104/04 REV 4, 12.11.2004). This is a highly political and sensitive element, since it seems to take the Dialogue beyond the goals of mutual, intercultural understanding and knowledge and into the realm of the democracy promotion agenda (see also Gillespie, 2004: 234).[10]

This not only confines the 'thematic openness' of the Dialogue, but it may also reinforce the tendency of Euro-Mediterranean governments to seek close monitoring and control over the projects and activities of the national networks. Whereas the EU sees a strengthening of the democratic potentials of civil society in the southern Mediterranean as a means of creating long-term stability and security, the authoritarian governments in the South make the exact opposite analysis. Enhancing the role and democratic awareness of civil society is seen as a threat to their continued survival and hold on political power, as a potentially de-stabilizing rather than stabilizing force. Given this, Mediterranean governments may politicize the Dialogue even further, trying to maintain control over who participates in the Dialogue and which specific activities are promoted.

In sum, there are already indications of the fact that the securitization of the Dialogue between Cultures has led to processes of exclusion and tightened governmental control. This is particularly clear with respect to both the prioritized fields of activities and the selection of civil society groups given access to the Dialogue. Arguably, this not only brings the Dialogue far away from the ideal world of Habermasian dialogue but also, perhaps more importantly, points to the paradox of using security concerns as a legitimizing strategy. Securitization, on the one hand, serves as a powerful justification for engaging in an ambitious and challenging dialogue, yet on the other hand it also threatens to compromise the ideal conditions of dialogue by bringing extreme politicization and increased attempts of governmental control. This in turn leads to policies of exclusion and limits the participation of a plurality of civil society groups, those very groups who were intended to be the driving forces and engines of the dialogue.[11]

Conclusion

The Dialogue between Cultures was envisioned as an alternative and non-confrontational response to the US-led war on terror following September 11. Faced with a looming war in Iraq and mounting scenarios of an imminent clash of civilizations, it was decided to enhance the third basket by creating a Foundation for Dialogue between Cultures.

However, being framed within a context of security has from the outset compromised those Habermasian ideal conditions on which the Dialogue is based. As this analysis has shown, the securitization of the Dialogue paradoxically both served to provide a compelling reason for engaging in dialogical interaction and at the same time seriously restricted the very conditions of possibilities for an authentic dialogue. Securitization moved the Dialogue into a specific realm where intercultural dialogue was articulated no longer as a goal in itself but instead as a means – or even a weapon – to a higher end, that end being security.

Scholars who are arguing for the urgent need and relevance of a Habermasian-inspired dialogue often neglect this problematic side of securitization. By making references to September 11 and imminent clashes of civilizations – be they real or imagined – they place the need for intercultural dialogue firmly within a logic of security. Legitimizing intercultural dialogue in this way, however, is a double-edged sword. As this study has shown, securitization serves to mobilize people; it draws political attention, and it brings urgency to a certain matter. But it also brings closure, extreme politicization and governmental control.

Some of these problematic implications have already become visible with respect to the Dialogue between Cultures. As indicated, the Dialogue has already become extremely politicized and an object of tight governmental control. In particular, Euro-Mediterranean governments have confined the Dialogue in terms of prioritized themes and selected civil society groups. This not only has inhibited civil society groups from formulating their own goals and priorities but it has also compromised the Dialogue's original preconditions of openness and inclusiveness.

These restraints may ultimately risk jeopardizing the original visions of the initiative and reducing its impact. Without an inclusive approach to dialogue, where controversial, divergent and diverse voices can be heard, the prospects for promoting new perceptions and breaking down stereotypes seem bleak. The Dialogue risks being confined to intellectual exchanges and conferences rallying cosmopolitan elites who are reinforcing their (similar) worldviews and values, leaving little impact on the general population. Such an outcome would of course run counter to the very ideals and objectives of the Dialogue. It is therefore crucial that efforts be made to influence the start of the Dialogue towards a more open and inclusive direction, both in terms of actors and themes.

Arguably, this will be a very difficult task. Given the fact that the third basket has increasingly emerged as a substitute for the first, the securitization of the Dialogue will be hard to escape. For the foreseeable future it is therefore more likely that the Dialogue will continue to be an object of difficult and highly politicized bargaining between the Euro-Mediterranean governments, thus restraining the influence of civil society groups in the process.

Notes

[1] The full name of the dialogue is the 'Anna Lindh Foundation for the Euro-Mediterranean Dialogue between Cultures'. For the remainder of the essay it will be referred to as the Dialogue between Cultures or for short, the Dialogue.

[2] Here, it should be emphasized that given the fact that the Dialogue between Cultures is a new initiative, there are relatively few official EU documents which address the content of the initiative in detail. The most elaborate document is the High-Level Report, on which the following analysis will particularly rely.

[3] For an overview of these critiques within IRT, see for example Linklater (1996, 2005) or Risse (2000).

[4] For instance, Connolly has argued that Habermas' quest for consensus comes to absorb difference, hence undermining the ideal of respecting and cherishing plurality (Connolly, 2001). Foucault has equally argued that 'the search for a form of morality acceptable to everyone in the sense that everyone would have to submit to it, seems catastrophic to me' (quoted in Linklater, 1996: 290).

[5] In other words, the southern partners' commitment to the dialogue and their sense of co-ownership of the initiative is in practice deeply affected by the asymmetrical relationship. As the High-Level Report points out: 'Culture and dialogue cannot have the same role and scope as they do for the ageing and world-wise populations of the northern Mediterranean' (18).

[6] Here, the point is not that these securitizing moves are undertaken deliberately or for strategic reasons. The idea is not to show how, for example, EU representatives or the High-Level group manipulatively appeal to security in order to persuade a certain audience, but rather how the legitimations of the dialogue – perhaps despite their good intentions – come to rest on and produce a logic of security.

[7] This point is particularly worth stressing since it is often the case that calls for civilizational dialogue – albeit unwillingly – seem to embrace Huntington's argument. For example Dallmayr emphasizes the need for dialogue the following way: 'In my view the significance of 2001 is not diminished but rather intensified by September 11 and its aftermath: the attacks and the ensuing military clashes precisely underscore the urgent need to strengthen goodwill and dialogue among peoples and civilizations around the globe, *as a preventive antidote to civilizational conflict*' (Dallmyer, 2002: x, italics added).

[8] Gillespie has equally pointed out that the Dialogue was highly politicized from its very beginning, in particular over issues of location, funding and organizational structure of the Foundation (Gillespie, 2004b: 234, see also Pace, 2005). Yet, a debate over such issues can be seen as an expression of a relatively normal political process, whereas the extreme politization of the Dialogue concerns the very terms or preconditions of the dialogue.

[9] This has occurred in cooperation with the Executive Director of the Foundation.

[10] According to a member of the Euromed Committee, one of the ideas of the initiative is exactly to try to influence the southern partners in the direction of democracy and greater respect for human rights through the enhancement of civil society exchanges (Interview in connection with the launch of the Foundation in Alexandria, 18–20 April 2005).

[11] However, on the basis of the Foucauldian critique of Habermas, here it may be argued that these confines on the dialogue in terms of actors and themes are unavoidable, given that any dialogue is political and enmeshed with power relations. Any dialogue will be restricted in terms of the subjects who are given access to speak and the objects and concepts that can be discussed. The point is, however, that although any dialogue in this sense is political, securitization brings an extreme form of politization – and hence governmental restrictions – to the dialogue.

References

Alaoui, B.A. (2004) The high-level advisory group: a living illustration of dialogue between peoples and cultures in the (intercultural) Euro-Mediterranean area, *IEMed Yearbook 2003*, Barcelona.
Anna Lindh Euro-Mediterranean Foundation for the Dialogue between Cultures (2004) *Three Years Programme 2005-2007*, 29.11.2004, 137/04.
Brown, C. (2000) Cultural diversity and international political theory: from the *Requirement* to 'mutual respect'?, *Review of International Studies*, 26, pp. 199-213.
Commission/Council Secretariat (2004) 12.11.2004, Draft Statute, 104/04 REV 4.
Connolly, W. (2001) Cross-state citizen networks: a response to Dallmayr, *Millennium: Journal of International Studies*, 30(2), pp. 348-355.
Diez, T. & Stean, J. (2005) A useful dialogue? Habermas and international relations, *Review of International Studies*, 31, pp. 127-140.
Edkins, J. (1999) *Poststructuralism and International Relations: Bringing the Political Back In* (Boulder/London: Lynne Rienner).
Euro-Mediterranean Foundation for a Dialogue between Cultures (2003) 12.11.2003, 57/03 REV 2.
Euromed (Interne) Draft Statute (2004) 21.10.2004, 61/04 REV 1.
Euromed Draft Statute (2004) 12.11.2004, 104/04 REV 4.
Foucault, M. (1972) *The Archaeology of Knowledge & the Discourse on Language* (New York: Pantheon).
Foucault, M. (1980) *Power/Knowledge: Selected Interviews and Other Writings 1972-1977* (New York: Pantheon).
Gillespie, R. (2004a) Culture, community and the Euro-Mediterranean foundation, *IEMed Yearbook 2003*, Barcelona.
Gillespie, R. (2004b) Reshaping the agenda? The internal politics of the Barcelona Process in the aftermath of September 11, in: A. Jünemann (Ed.) *Euro-Mediterranean Relations after September 11* (London: Frank Cass).
Habermas, J. (1984) *A Theory of Communicative Action, Parts I & II* (Cambridge: Polity Press).
Hansen, Lene (1998) Western Villains or Balkan Barbarism? Representations and Responsibility in the Debate over Bosnia, PhD Thesis, University of Copenhagen.
High-Level Advisory Group (2004) *Group of Policy Advisors*, Dialogue between Peoples and Cultures in the Euro-Mediterranean Area, Brussels.
Huntington, S. (1993) The clash of civilizations, *Foreign Affairs*, 72(3), pp. 22-49.
Jünemann, A. (2004) Security-building in the Mediterranean after September 11, in: A. Jünemann (Ed.) *Euro-Mediterranean Relations after September 11* (London: Frank Cass).
Köchler, Hans (1997) Philosophical Foundations of Civilizational Dialogue: The Hermeneutics of Cultural Self-Comprehension versus the Pradigm of Civilizational Conflict, unpublished article, http://i-p-o.org/civ-dial.htm.
Lewis, B. (1990) The roots of Muslim rage, *The Atlantic Monthly*, 266.
Linklater, A. (1996) The achievements of critical theory, in: S. Smith, Ken Booth & M. Zalewski (Eds) *International Theory: Positivism & Beyond* (Cambridge: Cambridge University Press).
Linklater, A. (2005) Dialogical politics and the civilising process, *Review of International Studies*, 31, pp. 141-154.
Lynch, M. (2005) Transnational dialogie in an age of terror, *Global Society*, 19(1), pp. 5-28.
Neumann, I. (2003) International relations as emergent Bakhtinian dialogue, *International Studies Review*, 5, pp. 137-140.
Pace, M. & Schumacher, T. (2004) Report: culture and community in the Euro-Mediterranean Partnership: a roundtable on the third basket, Alexandria 5-7 October 2003, *Mediterranean Politics*, 9(1), pp. 122-126.
Pace, M. (2004), The Role of Political Dialogue: A Dialogical Understanding of European-Mediterranean Relations, Second Pan-European Conference Standing Group on EU Politics, Bologna, 24-26 June 2004.
Pace, M. (2005) Euro-Mediterranean Partnership cultural initiatives: what political relevance?, in: R Youngs & F. Haizam Amirah (Eds) *The Barcelona Process Revisited* (Madrid: FRIDE and Real Instituto Elcano).

Presidency Conclusions (2003) Mid-Term Euro-Mediterranean Conference, Crete, 26–27 May 2003.
Presidency Conclusions (2003) Euro-Mediterranean Conference of Ministers of Foreign Affairs, Naples, 2–3 December 2003.
Presidency Conclusions. Euro-Mediterranean Conference of Foreign Ministers, Valencia, 22–23 April 2002.
Risse, T. (2000) Let's argue! Communicative action in world politics, *International Organization*, 54(1), pp. 1–39.
Said, E. (2001) The clash of ignorance, *The Nation*, October 22.
Schoefthaler, Traugott (2005) The first steps of establishing the Anna Lindh Euro-Mediterranean Foundation for the Dialogue between Cultures, *IEMed Mediterranean Yearbook 2004*, Barcelona.
Wæver, O. (1995) Securitization and desecuritization, in: R. Lipschutz (Ed.) *On Security* (New York: Columbia University Press).

Global Civil Society Across the Mediterranean: The Case of Human Rights

LAURA FELIU
Universitat Autònoma de Barcelona (UAB), Barcelona, Spain

Introduction

This essay applies the concept of global civil society to the Mediterranean and, more specifically, to everything to do with pro-human rights activism. To this end, as a first step, global civil society and other related concepts are analysed, while as a second step the networks created in recent years in the field of human rights in the Mediterranean are reviewed. What are these networks, and what are their main features? To what extent are these networks exponents of the emergence of an alleged global civil society? Alongside analysis of these aspects, the essay includes a number of reflections on the capacity of groups and associations in civil society which seek the democratization of political systems and respect for human rights to produce substantive changes in their respective countries. It then goes on to assess the contribution of networking on the promotion of a culture of dialogue and its limitations in the Mediterranean region.

The study analyses the general theoretical and practical framework without analysing specific cases. A subsequent task of verifying or refuting some of the general arguments presented in this article is yet to be performed.

Democracy and Liberalization in the Mediterranean

The problem of democratization of the countries of the southern and eastern Mediterranean has rarely been approached by democratic theory or by studies related to comparative politics.[1] Works that have had the greatest influence on the theory of democratization have totally overlooked this group of countries.[2] In fact, up to the mid-1990s, the scant studies on this matter from a comparative perspective distinguished 'the exceptional nature of the Arab world'; the Arab world does not fit into analysis models designed primarily for Europe or the Americas. American armed intervention in Afghanistan and Iraq, where the U.S. administration has used the argument of the need for democratization in the Middle East, together with others, to justify actions lacking all legitimacy, and legality, in Iraq, have sparked greater interest in the matter among academic circles. These questions, as we will see, are directly related to the possibility of the existence of an active transnational network advocating the defence of human rights in the Mediterranean.

Application of Concepts to the Region

More than a decade ago, the publication in 1991 of S.P. Huntington's work, *The Third Wave,* spurred the search by different authors for proof of the expansion of democratic values around the globe, with a view to confirming the neo-liberal theses that reformulate the principles of the democratic peace rooted in the Kantian doctrine. Democratization is understood in general to mean the spread and extension of political participation, as well as the fact that broader sectors of the respective societies can exert a certain control over public policy. But the concept of democracy, like the grand concepts of Social Sciences, is used with a wide variety of meanings. The holding of elections lies at the core of most definitions. This minimum Schumpeterian definition focuses the concept around calling transparent elections with a wide voting base. The definitions are broadened from this initial electoralism to include the enjoyment of public liberties and the effective capability of the government that is elected to govern. The increase in the requisites, from the more procedural definitions, continues with the list of specificities of industrial democracies and their political, economic and social characteristics, before finally reaching maximalist views that aspire to social and economic equality or the people's participation at all decision-making levels (Collier and Levitsky, 1997).

Applying the concept of political participation to the Arab world involves certain difficulties. Political systems based on traditional structures, where different groups exert a certain influence over political decision-makers through very diverse means, have been little studied by contemporary political scientists. The dominant model of the democratic system, the model whose export is being attempted, is associated with the forming of modern, stable political parties, the regular holding of elections, and the peaceful transfer of government power.

The use of the term democracy is usually associated with respect for human rights and public liberties. This field of liberalization can be understood to mean the spreading and extension of the public space. Liberalization is related to a greater freedom of speech and of organization which are at the core of public liberties. It is important to note that liberalization by no means equals democratization. Though a clear link exists between freedom and democracy, there is no mechanical relationship between the two concepts.

The authors involved in addressing the question of democratization wonder whether western-style concepts can be applied to societies with such different traditions (Salamé, 1994). Faced with these major methodological dilemmas, most of the still scant literature that analyses this matter in the region prefers to describe the main features of Arab societies, their traditional power structures linked to tribalism, their religious beliefs (where Islam occupies a central place), and then goes on to assess their compatibility with the democratic ideal. As was already indicated, in general most studies on the subject find numerous arguments to justify this lack of will – and even the impossibility – to democratize. The studies by Salamé (Salamé, 1994), Khader (Khader, 1997), or Brynen, Korany and Noble (Brynen, Korany and Noble (eds.), 1997) thoroughly review the arguments (and key authors). Two stand out among them: cultural aspects, sometimes analysed from a simplistic and reductionist perspective, and the economic field.

Transitions that Never Arrive

Although the arguments concerning the 'Arab exception' continue to have a strong presence (and the events of 9/11 triggered a surge in references to the matter), in recent years a number of authors have underscored the existence of timid liberalization processes in these countries, even to the point of talking of a 'mini-wave' of democratization (Ibrahim, 1995: 27). The American position, that identifies the promotion of democracy as one of the objectives of its foreign policy in the Middle East, has also contributed to the search for evidence that progress is indeed taking place.[3] This liberalization appears to be the effect of a series of factors that have coincided. These can be seen primarily as: greater presence and effectiveness of socio-economic formations, a clearly expanding civil society (both elements linked to the mass education drive and the appearance of new middle classes) and an external action driven both by large intergovernmental organizations (IGOs) and nongovernmental organizations (NGOs), as well as by some western states.

Be that as it may, although the late-1980s were identified as the period when the definitive shift in the Arab world toward the democratic option should have occurred (not coincidentally, corresponding with the end of the Cold War), subsequent events put a dampener on such hopes. Regrettably, by the mid-1990s, democracy continued to be absent from the region, and liberalization processes had shown their limitations, with some notable reversals, the clearest case in the 1990s being Algeria.

At present, although some signs of liberalization can be identified in specific countries, power structures remain essentially unaltered. In a recent study, Daniel Brumberg (2003) reviews the political systems in the Arab world and groups them into dictatorships or full autocracies and liberalized autocracies. In the latter, although a minority controls the country's economic resources by rule of force, a 'partial inclusion' of broader sectors of the population has occurred. According to the author, the former group includes countries like Syria, Tunisia, Libya, Iraq and Saudi Arabia, and the latter includes Morocco, Kuwait, Jordan, Yemen, Algeria or Egypt (Brumberg, 2003: 3).

Civil Society in the Mediterranean

Civil society is, without doubt, one of the concepts that has attracted the greatest research efforts in recent years. Dozens of books have been devoted to analysing, above all, the emergence of all kinds of associations, particularly those most closely related to politics and devoted to 'just causes.[4] As the global civil society concept constitutes a continuation and extension of the civil society concept on a transnational scale, it is necessary to analyse some of the circumstances surrounding its construction.

Within various political spheres it has been suggested that the path towards democratization by authoritarian regimes is inevitably linked to the existence of a strong civil society. This has led western countries to seek and identify potential major players, on whom most of the hopes (and burdens) of becoming key players in future democratization processes are placed. This exercise most often results from a lack of will to exert direct pressure on regimes with which close ties have been built, as it is less risky to rely on gradual, long-term transformations through a 'change of mentality' (political culture) towards which civil society plays a crucial role.

The Concept

The concept of civil society has evolved significantly in the last few decades. Its initial links to the State were diluted by the strong influence of the political experiences of the 1960s when a series of political and social players confronted an omnipresent and dictatorial state, particularly in Latin America. These experiences, in which certain groups demanded greater public freedom through demonstrations, strikes and other forms of mobilization, led to an intensification of its prescriptive and ideologized side, and contributed to presenting those movements as the panacea of democratization.

The view of civil society as a third sector that is opposed primarily to a first sector comprised by the State and its administration, is reinforced by the rise of the neo-liberal ideology, which grants central value to the actions of the individual and natural market laws.[5] The experiences of Czechoslovakia or Poland in the 1990s had a decisive influence on papers that were written on the subject too,[6] and introduced certain biases into the analysis of civil society. Consequently, it is necessary to recover a conceptualization focusing on the classic distinction between the citizen, the prince and the merchant. Civil society falls within the sphere of the citizens – individuals who, grouped freely, associate to further their interests and objectives. It is a matter of the private versus the public. Civil society, in its modern sense, should be linked to the problems deriving from industrialization processes and the effects of the expansion of capitalism and an increasingly omnipresent state.

The term civil society is highly informative with regard to the creation of social networks, the addition and visibility of interests, the complexity of flows between official agents and interest groups. The concept, therefore, should be used above all from an organizational and relational approach. Civil society is a form of organization and, at the same time, of relationship between political and social players; it is more a dynamic relationship than an intermediate space.

The Human Rights Movement in the Mediterranean

In keeping with the greater interest on the part of academic studies in democratic issues lying outside the western-centric outlook, in the 1990s authors from both within and outside the Arab world took an interest in analysing the 'health' of civil society in these countries. As was already mentioned, the study of civil society is interpreted as an important indicator of the stage at which the respective political system stands with regard to its 'progress toward democracy'.

Both Arab and western literature coincide in highlighting the weakness of civil society in countries of the southern and eastern Mediterranean. The main problems found include the difficulty that groups have in terms of creating structures beyond the most essential links, on the one hand, and the control exerted by the state, on the other hand. After reading Arab texts, M.K. Al-Sayyid (1995: 134) deduces that most authors reach the conclusion that there is no 'genuine' civil society as such. That is, there are signs of an activity of this kind, but the 'abnormalities' are so prevalent that certain social players could hardly be qualified as exponents of civil society. But most of the works point to the formation of civil society institutions, driven primarily by socio-economic changes (Norton, 1995: 22).

The characteristics of civil society in different Arab countries differ significantly, but their vigour can be measured on the basis of common elements. Based on different indicators, studies on the matter distinguish between groups of states depending on the vigour of their societies in direct relation to the degree of political liberalization.[7]

The presence and characteristics of human-rights advocacy groups vary greatly depending on whether the country has a liberalized or a full autocracy. This is logical, given the absence of space for organization and criticism in the case of the latter. In this way, a large number of the self-proclaimed human rights associations in full autocracies are controlled (and in some cases even created) by the regimes in power, which use them both to improve their image abroad and to control certain political sectors inside the country. The few activists and groups who seek action free from the authorities are doomed to a fate of prison, exile or even physical elimination.

Only in liberalized autocracies can human rights associations with stable structure, continued activity and a certain independence be found. However, they must overcome tremendous obstacles. It is in these countries where three different phases (or 'generations') in the understanding of pro-human rights activism and its insertion in the socio-political context exist. Yet, while in cases such as Morocco or Turkey it is possible to find all three generations, in others one or more of these phases are missing. In general, the three moments are more developed in countries that have gone further down the road toward liberalization. These three conceptions occur rapidly over time and operate like communicating vessels that provide fuel for the experiences which follow.

In the first generation, the associations are linked to political parties and depend on them. In the second, the associations break away from the mother parties and seek to transcend them, taking the fight to the state with a universalized human rights discourse. In the third, the associations are highly professionalized and specialized; they exert influence over the definition and application of public policy; their work follows its own cycle, which is almost independent from the political context and has important connections abroad. Nowadays, these three models subsist and overlap.

In the first generation, the concept of human rights used by the association faces numerous obstacles that strip it of its universal nature. With the appearance of the second generation of organizations (in general in the late-1980s), the demand for civil and political rights, linked to the democratic ideal, became the centre of the discourse. Ideological positions could no longer disregard the defence of human dignity, or convert rights into the exclusive property of specific sectors. This emergence of the individual and the citizen evidences the profound transformations that are taking place in the midst of society. The third generation confirms the acquisition and assimilation of a new, highly legalized and technical language, a somewhat aseptic jargon that moves away from the political side of the action to equate it to reality in many other parts of the world.

In the first generation, associations live in almost virtual isolation in their own milieu, with little funds and very limited actions, basically circumscribed to the most pressing problems of militancy in the ranks of the opposition, fulfilling a highly rudimentary task of denouncement.

The second generation involves the development of 'independent' sectors, citizens with a developed political and social conscience who work with the associations on an individual basis. The objective of independent action, whether real or not, and whether achieved or not, becomes the *Leitmotiv* of the discourse of many organizations. The professionalization of the human rights movement which evolved throughout the 1990s implies a number of decisive changes in the management of resources and in their transformation. In addition to more human resources, the associations receive increasing sums from external donors and materialize their equity.

The third generation has been able to emerge thanks to increased liberalization in the political field, and is driven by factors as diverse as the accumulation of knowledge, the new tasks which these associations had to deal with, and the influence of international organizations that fund projects. The third generation is, therefore, more a trend than a given, and its characteristics were not fully developed; rather, they began to emerge as the 1990s came to a close, albeit imperfectly. The blocking of the democratization process surely played a fundamental circumstantial role in the difficulty in confirming this, but the lack of material and human resources, as well as the slowness of the transformation process of the political culture, also played a significant role.

The profile of the third generation has a number of distinguishing features, one of which is the desire to go beyond the work that, until then, had been the top priority – namely denunciation – and contributes more 'constructively' to the creation of a new democratic and modern state. Associations begin to design policies and, if necessary, contribute to their management. The state, the administration and certain elites are the privileged interlocutors, not only as the passive recipients of a vision, but also as allies in the introduction of reforms. Action is geared toward influencing institutions and elites. Though broader strata of the population can be recipients of the movement's action, these are conceived more as indirect beneficiaries than as agents of transformation. The mass action that appears in the bylaws of some of these associations is more a formula than a programme. In practice, there is a transformation of the priorities, and these are dictated by strategic matters and by the search for resources.

Inevitably, the bridges built through these practices moderate the discourse of the players. Lobbying is especially important, and overlaps with (and in some cases takes precedence over) the more traditional methods of denouncing, raising awareness or education. Associations are in direct contact with ministries of, for example, Education, Justice or Human Rights, participate in their Committees, and propose and monitor their policies.

In addition, associations specialize in specific areas of civil and political rights. This process takes place in parallel with the creation of a large group of NGOs that deals with development and socio-economic issues in general, particularly in the rural milieu.

External inflows are determining factors in this process. The bridge was, basically, the arrival of a major contingent of foreign aid from the European Union (e.g. the MEDA-Democracy programs), western states through direct bilateral aid, or private or semi-public foundations from Germany, the U.S. or Canada.[8] Many of these associations also participate in international networks and forums, and their members have benefited from attending courses abroad. Perhaps even more important than the economic injection that these ties represent (an important contribution, as it reaches associations that have basically worked on a voluntary basis and through the contributions of private individuals) are the indirect effects on the activities of the associations: projects must meet objectives set abroad; the most-consolidated associations are bolstered to the detriment of smaller-scale initiatives, or a more 'mercantilist' mentality is fostered, associating 'resources' with 'visible results'. The bureaucratization of the movement is a reality, and so is, in a more positive vein, its professionalization.

All of these elements develop imperfectly – they start to blossom, but have yet to achieve consolidation. The blocking of liberalization processes and of the transition to democracy situates the pro-human rights movement predominantly within the phase of denunciation of authoritarian rules of play. Hence, the human rights movement cannot 'escape politics'.

A Global Civil Society in the Mediterranean?

This section briefly introduces the concept of global civil society, and then goes on to describe some general features of the pro-human rights militancy networks that span the Mediterranean, both in the form of regular (but not formalized) contacts between NGOs from the North and South, and the large transnational NGOs that include members from both sides of the sea. A third section will examine to what extent this network has an impact on the field of human rights and the issue of democratization in general.

The Global Civil Society Concept

The concept of global civil society began to be used regularly just a decade ago, from different perspectives. Mary Kaldor (2003) indicates its use, first, through the theory of new social movements, second, via international institutions and governments that use it as a 'new political agenda', and third, in post-modern theory.

Its formulation results from the application of the concept of civil society to transnational political processes, though the debate focuses on whether such organizations constitute a new realm or whether they are merely artifacts of western liberal society (Keane, 2003). As a continuation of the mother-concept, global civil society consists of a heterogeneous composition, made up of social movements, interest groups, cultural groups or global citizens, with cross-border ties. Most studies approach it more as a space than as a player, and speak of the existence of multiple global civil societies around a wide diversity of issues. These same studies question its existence (one just has to take a look at the numerous question marks in the titles) and provide different replies. Advocates of the use of the concept refer above all to its usefulness in identifying a set of phenomena, although recognizing that it is a process in progress.

Like in the case of the concept of origin (civil society), the normative weight of the concept is very high and its academic use therefore poses the same problems. Its association with the promotion of certain values, and even of democratic structures, introduces a dimension that was barely analysed in studies on the transnational phenomenon in the 1970s and 1980s. As noted by Richard Falk (2003), global civil society is the 'ensemble of transnational efforts to achieve human solidarity on behalf of a tormented and endangered planet – those movements, citizens' associations, and informal networks that are virtually oblivious to the boundaries of sovereign states'.

Another important aspect of the theory is the consideration that global civil society is capable of reshaping the political architecture of international relations. This theme is directly related to that of the 'globalization of democracy' in the debate that puts the liberal view against the rejection of certain liberal capitalist conceptions. It is also linked to the discussion on the transformation of the state (Pasha, and Blaney, 1998). The existence of a global civil society implies the rise of a 'global citizenship' and an emerging process of global governance.

According to Falk (2002: 5), in its most normative version, the concept is related to reconstructive postmodernism (as opposed to critical postmodernism), which speaks of the formation of a citizenry that places loyalty to a time (the construction of a future normative order) before loyalty to a space (a state or territory). Falk also notes that the formation of such a society implies a tension between globalization-from-above (market, state, institutions, the momentum of techno-capital) and globalization-from-below (social movements, citizens' associations, informal networks, the momentum of normative and spiritual energies). This corresponds with a normative duality (with significant exceptions), that is, players who primarily seek to expand industrial civilization vs grassroots' normative initiatives concerned with well-being and with spiritually engaged politics.

Existing Networks

For some time now, there have been regular contacts between human rights activists from the southern and eastern Mediterranean (whether organized into associations or not) and activists and associations from the northern shore in informal networks. Thus, for example, French territory has been important as an area for encounters with human rights activists from former French colonies, particularly from the Maghreb. In addition to the individual ties that were established during the colonial period, there is an important presence of political exiles who maintain their interest in the situation of their countries of origin. By way of example, in the case of Morocco, the Association of Committees in the Fight against Repression in Morocco (CLCRM) was created in the early 1970s, followed a decade later by the Association for the Defense of Human Rights in Morocco (ASDHOM), the Association of Relatives and Friends of Disappeared Persons in Morocco (APADM), and other less active groups like the Committee for Action for the Liberation of Prisoners of Opinion in Morocco (CALPOM). The presence of Moroccan political activists in associations like Amnesty International in London also doubtless contributes to focusing attention on the situation within Morocco.

French territory also hosts the main networks for contact with activists and associations from the rest of the countries of the Maghreb. In the case of Tunisia, given the grave situation with regards to personal liberties, contacts with activists inside the country are difficult and risky to establish, and there is a real problem in terms of identifying the proper representatives.

Similar networks were created during these years in other countries, as in Germany with respect to Turkey and the Kurdish issue, in Spain with respect to the Saharawi cause, or in the UK with respect to Palestine.

Although this contacts, in the decades following the respective declarations of independence one cannot speak exactly of the existence of consolidated transnational networks; rather, one can only speak of the creation of sporadic and precarious communications channels that are highly dependent on a small number of personalities.

With the passing of time, and particularly as the 1990s came to a close, these networks underwent major transformations in the context of an increased interest from different European players in consolidating civil society on the southern fringe of the Mediterranean. Pre-existing contacts would be decisive in the shaping of these new networks. Another contributing factor to the consolidation of the networks was the easing of repression in some countries, with the attending consolidation of human rights associations. Contacts are now more regular and formalized.

This consolidation of networks can be seen, both in the participation of NGOs from the South in major international human rights NGOs, and in the creation of specific networks in the Mediterranean for contact and exchanges between human rights associations.

In the first case, this participation has increased in major international NGOs such as the International Federation for Human Rights (FIDH), whose 141 members include associations from virtually all Arab countries (although some of them are organizations operating in exile), and of the 22 countries at present members of its international bureau, there are representatives from Mauritania, Tunisia, Palestine, Turkey and Morocco.

In the second case, that of specific regional networks, there are three notable initiatives. Two of them are closely linked to the reformulation of the EU's Mediterranean policy in the mid-1990s: the Euro-Mediterranean Civil Forum and the Euro-Mediterranean Human Rights Network (EMHRN). The third case is a recent one: the Mediterranean Social Forum. These three cases are very different and require a certain degree of attention. While the Network has a permanent, and independent structure, the Civil Forum is a space for encounters and exchanges, where the participants change from one encounter to the next, and the way it is run has been diverse and highly dependent on the organizing governments; and the Mediterranean Social Forum seeks the participation of all kinds of little associations without intermediaries and according to the alternative and assembly spirit of Porto Alegre.

On further analysis, the Euromed Civil Forum emerges as an important opportunity for certain players in civil society to get together, especially for those associations that address issues related to democracy, human rights, governance and development, albeit with a fairly concrete profile (in general, for instance, Islamist associations are not included). Although in theory it is the associations themselves who organize the successive Forums, there is a strong intervention from individual states and by the European Commission. The Forum takes place in parallel with the meetings of the Euro-Mediterranean foreign ministers, though it is not clear whether its activity has a major impact on the work of the Euro-Mediterranean Partnership (EMP), due, among other reasons, to the lack of an organic link.

Two models of encounter were in competition at the 1995 Barcelona Civil Forum an 'alternative' model, entirely self-run by the associations, and another model linked to (though not dependent on) official authorities. As the latter model has prevailed in subsequent encounters (Reinhardt, 2002), the Forum is not entirely independent (its main source of funding is the European Commission), nor has it been included in the structures of the Barcelona Process.

As a result of the lack of permanent structures, participating associations are not the same from one Forum to the next (although a core group of associations has remained in place throughout its first decade of existence), and the agenda is not cumulative in nature, as everything depends, to a great extent, on the national organizers of the event.[9] After the Marseilles summit in 2000, and as a result of the criticism of its current format, a period of reflection, on how to proceed with reform, was opened and the decision to launch a Euromed non-governmental platform, a common platform designed to reform the Civil Forum, was made.

The Civil Forum is doubtless an important space for encounters, exchanges and discussion, although it is far from bringing together the most representative aspects of civil society in the Mediterranean. In all its meetings thus far, the theme of respect for human rights has been very present with a large proportion of associations promoting human rights, to the extent that at the Stuttgart Forum in 1999 special attention was given to the matter.

For its part, the Euro-Mediterranean Human Rights Network was created in 1997 as a transnational umbrella organization that brings together over 60 associations, plus individual members, from more than 20 countries. The Network goes beyond an experience of exchange and encounter; it monitors the European Union's agenda and acts as a bridge between European governments and institutions and the countries where human rights violations take place (Jünemann, 2000).

Lastly, the first Mediterranean Social Forum was held in Barcelona on 16–18 June 2005. This event fits in with the proposal of the World Social Forum (WSF) of 2001 to approximate the process to local realities. Some Catalan organizations from the international council of the WSF proposed the celebration of a Social Forum linking Mediterranean groups and an initial group of 20 people started organizing the event, but the organizing committee remained relatively small only some of the militant sectors were involved in the process. Six international assemblies prepared the main axis (denunciation of the process of economic liberalization in the Mediterranean; defence of human rights and democracy; and rejection of military occupation and imperialist strategy in the region), and decided on seven thematic issues for the meeting (one of them, the most well attended, being on human rights). The objective was to look for the 'small civil society' not represented in other Mediterranean events. However, the representation was not very different from other Mediterranean transnational meetings. In spite of the alternative approach, the organization received important public financing from local and regional administrations (approximately 70 per cent of the final budget, that is, €1m).

Main Features

The following points can be gleaned from an observation of these networks:

(1) The transnational links created by human rights associations on the north and south shores of the Mediterranean are still weak if compared with those existing in

other regions like Latin America. It is symptomatic that (in 2005!) the organizers of the Social Forum still have problems to find interlocutors from the South: as a result of this, the Social Forum had to be postponed three times. This situation is understandable given the difficulties in creating independent associations within authoritarian political contexts (Jünemann, 2002: 98). But this problem also shows the lack of coordination between Mediterranean social movements, with little experience of common work. Surprisingly, after the huge effort of the Social Forum organizers to bring together associations from the southern shore, there was low attendance of Catalonian and Spanish participants (the arrival of the Spanish Socialist party to the government coincides with some demobilization); if the initial expectations were of 10–15,000 participants, the final, overall number was only 5,000! The number of seminars (200) was too ambitious, and sometimes the participants from the South did not find the right interlocutors.

(2) As a result of this weakness, there is only a small presence of Mediterranean NGOs and transnational networks within international forums, resulting in a scant contribution to broader, global networks. In comparison with Latin American or Asian NGOs and associations, those from the southern and eastern Mediterranean have taken longer to become active vis-á-vis major intergovernmental organizations, such as the United Nations, which are key in promoting the issue.

(3) The European Union's launch of the EMP in Barcelona in 1995 has significantly boosted the reinforcement and creation of new transnational human rights networks. Other dimensions have been developed around the project of creating a free-trade zone; particularly, the strengthening of respective civil societies has been fostered and the creation of networks linking them together has been promoted through the third basket of the Barcelona Process. This policy is directly linked to the promotion of democracy from a bottom-up perspective.

The EU has also launched regional and subregional cooperation programmes in addition to the bilateral aid programmes targeting civil societies of southern and eastern Mediterranean countries. The MEDA Democracy Program, created in 1996, was one of the main instruments for the funding of NGOs working on issues relating to democratization, conflict resolution, gender issues or human rights in general. The European Initiative for Democracy and the Protection of Human Rights (budget line B7-7050) is the main source of funding for programmes in this field.

(4) The most active southern associations in these networks are those located in liberalized autocracies, while there are still tremendous difficulties in finding valid interlocutors within the full autocracies. The participation of national delegations is therefore very different (at the Mediterranean Social Forum for example, the Moroccan, Palestinian and Algerian delegations were the most well attended).

Within the different countries, the associations that participate in these networks are those that have the greatest resources, which have achieved consolidation in recent years, and in general they reveal themselves, with some exceptions, to be fairly inefficient as poles of attraction for other local associations that are less consolidated but nevertheless do interesting work.

(5) Although a series of requisites must be met in order to belong to these transnational NGOs and networks, their members show signs of significant

heterogeneity given such different starting points (and this is not a negative point). In addition to this, some Arab members of these networks are associations headquartered in Europe, especially in the case of full autocracies. Thus, for instance, the EMHRN includes among its regular members the likes of the Libyan League for Human Rights, based in Germany, or Syrian associations with headquarters in France or Sweden. In the case of the Social Forum, one third of the South and East participants live in Europe.

(6) The high level of political conflict in the region is a tremendous hindrance to the creation of horizontal transnational networks, both in the Maghreb and in the Middle East, as well as in the southern and eastern Mediterranean regions as a whole. It is a fact that disturbs all networks. As evidenced at the meetings of the Euromed Civil Forum, the Israeli-Palestinian conflict constitutes a major obstacle, not only to the participation of Israeli associations in these forums, but to the normal development of these events, which are regularly blocked by demands for the application of international law by the international community as a prerequisite for other forms of collaboration (like the demands by some NGOs that the 2000 Marseilles Civil Forum be boycotted in protest against the situation in Palestine). The Western Sahara conflict is one of the political factors, among many others, that has blocked the setting-up of effective networks in the Maghreb and interferes with Mediterranean transnational meetings. In the Social Forum held in Barcelona, there were important tensions between the Moroccan and the Saharawi delegations; the Saharawi were concerned about their lack of a prominent space in the Forum when compared with Morocco's (Saharawi delegations even protested against known Moroccan human rights activists who defend the self-determination process), while Morocco sent its secret services to try and boycott seminars and the final demonstration.

In addition, one must consider the economic difficulties posed by the need to pay for travel and to set up sufficient infrastructure for these types of encounters.

In recent years there have been several attempts at coordination between generalist Arab human rights associations, which either have not had continuity (like the creation in the late-1980s of a Maghreb human rights union, which even managed to draft a charter) or else their activity takes place irregularly or is excessively constrained by official political considerations. An example of this last circumstance is the activity of the Arab Organization for Human Rights (AOHR), created in 1983 as a regional non-governmental organization to promote and protect human rights, with branches in eight Arab countries. This organization, with other partners, has promoted initiatives like the creation in 1989 of the Arab Institute for Human Rights in Tunisia, of an Arab Human Rights Information Network (AHRINET) in 1997, or the organization of the first International Conference of the Arab Human Rights Movement in Casablanca in April 1999. In the region, greater advances have been achieved in more specific areas, such as women's rights or militancy in favour of the Amazigh culture, in spite of the difficulties.

These difficulties highlight the importance of the contacts these associations establish abroad; in this regard, European territory is a major meeting ground for fostering greater mutual knowledge.

(7) The direction of transnational ties is basically vertical, between associations from the South and those from the North. It is hoped that through these ties the situation along the southern shore of the Mediterranean will be given greater coverage, placing issues that concern the region on national and international agendas.

These types of links pose important problems, including the domination of NGOs and associations from the North (where the headquarters are often located and where most meetings are held), which control the lion's share of the budget and set the agenda, in spite of the explicit objective most of them have of acting in a decentralized and balanced fashion. For example, in the case of the Social Fora, it was organized by an International Committee with representations from southern and eastern Mediterranean countries, and any organization could propose a seminar or a conference. But the structural constraints of the North–South divide are hard to overcome. Only 60 per cent of the 1,200 visas requested for the Social Forum in Barcelona were granted by the Spanish authorities.

Another question is that external support can hinder the acceptance of these associations by their own societies, and in certain cases trigger reprisals (although in the liberalized autocracies foreign ties mean greater protection for human rights advocates). In general, the challenges faced by associations in the North and South are very different, due to the diverse political situations, and personal experiences, of their respective members.

(8) Finally, there are distinctions with regards to the handling of problems in the "transnational agenda". The Palestinian question or the situation in Iraq, for instance, occupy a very important position.[10] Undoubtedly, the difficulties in obtaining information about the situation in full autocracies and in contacting other associations that can perform their work with a minimum of reliability contribute to this asymmetric geometry.

The Impact of Networks

The impact of human rights associations and their respective networks both on western democracies and autocratic regimes is achieved through a direct and independent form of non-governmental diplomacy, through channels of their own (Clark, 1995).

The Three Dimensions

The setting up of networks has served to amplify the impact of associations in their own countries. This impact has been notable, in particular, in the symbolic sphere (even in the case of the full autocracies), more subdued in the substantive sphere, and exceptional in the operational sphere.[11]

With respect to the symbolic dimension, particularly during the 1980s and 1990s, the possession of an alternative discourse that was clearly different from the official line, and with an important critical potential, contributed to the introduction of values, the transformation of the political language, and the identification and configuration of problems that, until then, had not constituted true policy targets. It therefore became a question of promotional work at the regional level carried out by the international human rights movement and through the dissemination of new human rights instruments. Yet, its success varies depending on the political circumstances of each country, but in general it can be said that a certain terminology is present in most official lines, even though only in response to criticism from abroad. The formal commitments of the different governments (e.g. the signing of international treaties) are directly related to the promotional effort of associations and their respective networks.

At present, the existing networks, which are more consolidated, continue to exert a major influence on cognitive frameworks, belief systems and values, with an ensuing homogenization of language and discourse at the transnational level. These networks contribute to the promotion of a culture of dialogue and tolerance based on recognition of cultural diversity but from a common and universal foundation. The existing networks promote the practice of close collaboration between different groups and associations, facilitate the exchange of expertise and pertinent information, and strengthen human relations across cultures. In addition, they have contributed to the creation of third-generation associations with a highly specialized jargon and work guidelines.

Nevertheless, it must be kept in mind that the netwoks link a small elite and work within difficult contexts (for the creation of regular and wide transnational networks) as analysed above.

The substantive dimension implies access to certain decision-making centres and governance networks, so they can only materialize when minimal spaces of freedom exist. In countries like Morocco or Jordan, the regime creates institutions in which the associations take part. This 'reformist' path provides the opportunity to influence, more or less directly, the formalization of legally backed decisions, including the reforms of family codes, the abolition of legislation concerning states of exception, etc. But at the same time, this option also carries the risk of being transformed into an endorsement of a change that never materializes, while the image of the regime abroad is enhanced thanks to its putative collaboration. That is why other groups reject such forms of collaboration. Certainly, inside the networks there is a debate about the extent of this collaboration along a reformist path, but in general the option is considered positive. In more repressive autocracies, this possibility is usually not on offer.

Finally, in the operational dimension (relative to the application of policies and to complement government-provided services) the issue of the relative isolation of the members of human rights movements appears once more. Only in some cases are broad national networks created which engage in drafting public policy proposals. These are networks and platforms of varying geometries, but in which the same social players usually coincide periodically. Thus, in cases like Morocco, Jordan or Lebanon, the association movement constitutes a channel of influence on public policy and of access to certain institutions. They actively cooperate with the government in specific programmes or become their privileged interlocutors. Transnational networks (together with an important collaboration of intergovernmental organizations) are usually involved in such initiatives.

The existence of networks helps to consolidate these three dimensions, contributing in an important way to the dissemination of information, and giving greater magnitude to the denunciation. It also lends greater strength and resources to campaigns and hence to the increasing demands.

From the viewpoint of the issue of 'promoting governments', and their policy-making agenda (although it is known that European governments have sacrificed the objective of promoting human rights and democracy in the Mediterranean in favour of preserving the status quo), the work of networks has been crucial in those cases where action has been taken. This is the case thanks to both the advantages resulting from the issue-specific specialization of associations as they face government bureaucracies, and their privileged access to information.

Conclusions: Global Civil Society in the Mediterranean

Are there signs of the existence of a global civil society when the transnational links relating to human rights in the Mediterranean (considered to be one of the most important fields by most studies) are analysed? Undoubtedly, communication and exchanges between very diverse human rights advocacy groups have multiplied in recent years and transnational constituencies have been forged. In addition, these transnational activities have had an impact locally, regionally and to a lesser degree, internationally.

These groups work on a common ground, based on a universal conception of human rights (one of the normative requisites of most studies), and contribute to the creation of an indispensable social capital that enables analysts to speak of a global civil society. The exchange of points of view, experiences and the organization of common events provide groups with opportunities for getting acquainted with other cultures and experiences thereby fostering closer relationships across the Mediterranean.

Another noteworthy aspect reached by the academic literature is the contribution of these groups in shaping international political organizations which in turn influence their activity, although this impact has been limited in the Mediterranean area (the EMP being a case in point).

But the existence of this 'global civil society' can hardly be identified as if it were a global player. It is necessary to recall here the low density of these networks, of communication and informational exchange, in the Mediterranean, and that effective results in this field are very far from reaching the objectives that have been set. This is particularly true when referring to even more ambitious objectives like contributing to the development of democratic institutions. Parts of the relevant academic literature establish a direct relationship between the presence of a strong civil society and democratization (Quigley, 1997; Carothers, 1997; Encarnación, 2000). Intuitively, one may think that a significant presence of socio-political players that mobilize and establish complex ties among themselves contributes to a greater plurality of the political system. But the relationship is far from being clear.

In spite of this, the presence of a vigorous civil society undoubtedly facilitates social and political interaction, making it possible for the objectives of vastly differing social players to surface and achieve more visibility, while also casting a spotlight on the contradictions. This can be extrapolated at the regional and international level as well. A strong civil society can mean a greater explicit and manifest level of conflict. Yet, at the same time, it appears as a necessary condition for the structuring of interests, enabling a greater continuity of social processes, establishing negotiations and consensus between different types of social players. Civil society adds to the identification of the collective thanks to the aggregation of individual interests. A greater density of social fabric contributes to the strengthening of social capital, and therefore facilitates the response to new problems that appear in all systems. Besides, a strong civil society contributes to the structuring of watchdog mechanisms over the public space, and helps contain the tendency to concentrate power at all levels, not only domestically.

In this context, it would be more appropriate to speak of the existence of parcels of an international (and internationalized) civil society (Peterson, 1992). There is a significant core that is transnational in nature, but it is still incipient and it is too early to say whether it will spread in the future or whether its actions will be more successful. It does not therefore seem appropriate to deal with global civil society as a phenomenon with such important implications as are attributed to it by some of the literature, with the persistence of significant factors such as national loyalties and state constraints.

The concept of a global civil society with its strong normative connotations owes itself more to will than to reality, and it distorts a situation of predominantly local ties with a partial international dimension. In any case, as Falk argues, a global political discourse has been established that has generated its own dynamic and created other realities. Thus, speaking of a global civil society is a political act, a description of what is and a desire for the arrival of something that has yet to exist.

Notes

[1] This section expands on some of the ideas set out in my book (Feliu, 2004).

[2] The Arab world is totally absent from works like those compiled by Guillermo O'Donnell, Philippe C. Schmitter and Laurence Whitehead (1988), or published by Diamond, Linz and Lipset (1988), without even an attempt to excuse such an absence.

[3] See for example the Freedom House publication *Democracy Digest*, which to a certain extent amplifies any meeting or initiative by democratic and liberal sectors in the Arab world. www.freedomhouse.org

[4] See for example Clayton, A.(Ed.) (1996). *NGOs, Civil Society: Building Democracy in Transitional Societies* (Oxford: INTRAC); Florini, A.(Ed.) *The Third Force: The Rise of Transnational Civil Society* (Washington: Carnegie Endowment) or some studies on specific fields as Howell, J. and Pearce, J. (2002) *Civil Society and Development: A Critical Exploration* (Boulder: Lynne Reinner).

[5] For a critical approach see: Scholte, J. A. (2002) Civil Society and Democracy in Global Governance, *Global Governance* (8) 3.

[6] Whitehead, L. (2001) Three International Dimensions of Democratization, in L. Whitehead (ed.) *The International Dimensions of Democratization. Europe and the Americas* (New York: Oxford University Press), p. 5.

[7] See Brynen, Korany and Noble (1995) or Norton (1995).

[8] Especially active in the Arab world are the german Friedrich Ebert Foundation or the American Ford Foundation.
[9] This became manifest for instance in the Valencia Civil Forum, where the organizers encountered difficulties in obtaining information about the previous edition.
[10] This is shared in general by the major human rights organizations. Thus, for instance, Human Rights Watch (2004) has analysed its activity in the 2002–2004 period, concluding that there was a 'highly excessive focus on Israel,' while serious cases like Syria or Libya were virtually overlooked.
[11] The following reflections were inspired by the interesting work by P. Ibarra, S. Martí and R. Gomà (eds.) (2003).

References

Al-Sayyid, M. K. (1995) The concept of civil society and the Arab world, in: R. Brynen, B. Korany & P. Noble (Eds) *Political Liberalization and Democratization in the Arab World. Vol. 1*, pp. 131–147 (Boulder: Lynne Rienner).

Brumberg, D. (2003) *Liberalization versus Democracy. Understanding Arab Political Reform* (Washington: Carnegie Endowment for International Peace).

Brynen, R., Korany, B. & Noble, P. (Eds) (1995) *Political Liberalization and Democratization in the Arab World. Vol. 1: Theoretical Perspectives* (Boulder: Lynne Rienner).

Carothers, Th. (1997) Democratic assitance: the question of strategy, *Democratization*, 4, pp. 109–132.

Clark, A. M. (1995) Non-governmental organizations and their influence on international society?, *Journal of International Affairs*, 48(2), pp. 507–525.

Collier, D. & Levitsky, S. (1997) Democracy 'with adjectives': conceptual innovation in comparative research, *World Politics*, 49(3), pp. 430–451.

Diamond, L., Linz, J. J. & Lipset, S. M. (1988) *Democracy in Developing Countries. Vol. 2: Africa* (Boulder: Lynne Rienner).

Encarnación, O. G. (2000) Tocqueville's missionaries: civil society and the promotion of democracy, *World Policy Journal*, 17, pp. 9–18.

Falk, R. (2003) Politically engaged spirituality in an emerging global civil society, *ReVision*, 25(4), pp. 2–10.

Feliu, L. (2004) *El jardín secreto: Los defensores de los derechos humanos en Marruecos* (Madrid: La Catarata, ICEI, IPADE).

Human Rights Watch (2004) *Draft Report on Human Rights Watch: A Comparative Analysis of Activities in the Middle East 2002–2004*, http://www.ngo-monitor.org.

Ibarra, P., Martí, S. & Gomà, R. (Eds) (2003) *Creadores de democracia radical* (Barcelona: Icaria).

Ibrahim, S. E. (1995) Civil society and prospects of democratization in the Arab World, in: A. Norton (Ed.) *Civil Society in the Middle East* (London: E.J.Brill).

Jünemann, A. (2000) The forum civil Euromed: critical watchdog and intercultural mediator, in: S. Panebianco (Ed.) *The Euro-Mediterranean Partnership in Social, Cultural and Human Affairs – The Human Dimension of Security as the Key to Stability and Prosperity* (Essex: Frank Cass).

Jünemann, A. (2002) From the bottom to the top: civil society and transnational non-governmental organizations in the Euro-Mediterranean Partnership, in: R. Gillespie & R. Youngs (Eds) *The European Union and Democracy Promotion: The Case of North Africa* (London: Frank Cass).

Kaldor, M. (2003) The idea of global civil society, *International Affairs*, 79(3), pp. 589–590.

Keane, J. (2003) *Global Civil Society?* (New York: Cambridge University Press).

Khader, B. (1997) *État, société civile et démocratie dans le monde arabomusulman* (Louvain: CERMAC).

Norton, A. R. (Ed.) (1995) *Civil Society in the Middle East* (London: E.J.Brill).

O'Donnell, G., Schmitter, Ph. C. & Whitehead, L. (1988) *Transiciones desde un Gobierno autoritario. 3. Perspectivas comparadas* (Buenos Aires: Paidós).

Pasha, M. K. & Blaney, D. L. (1998) Blaney Elusive paradise: the promise and peril of global civil society, *Alternatives: Social Transformation & Humane Governance*, 23(4).

Peterson, M. J. (1992) Transnational activity, international society and world politics, *Millennium*, 23(3), pp. 371–388.

Quigley, K. (1997) *For Democracy's Sake: Foundations and Democratic Assistance in Central Europe* (Baltimore: Hopkins University Press).
Reinhardt, U. J. (2002) Civil Society Co-operation in the EMP: from Declaration to Practice. Report by the Working Group on Good Governance, *Euromesco Paper*, 15.
Salamé, G. (Ed.) (1994) *Démocraties sans démocrates: Politiques d'ouverture dans le monde arabe et islamique* (Paris: Fayard).

EU Relations with Islam in the Context of the EMP's Cultural Dialogue

SARA SILVESTRI
University of Cambridge, UK

Introduction

Social scientists agree that, by the end of the twentieth century, Islam had become a permanent feature of European society and that the transnational nature of the Muslim population in Europe plays a role in the process of European integration (Allievi, 2003; Cesari, 2003; Nielsen, 1999; Roy, 2004). It has also been argued that 'much of our relationship with Islam and our capacities to understand it, both within and outside Europe, comes into play in the weave of ... two dynamics': an 'internal' or 'national' one, and an 'external' or 'international' one (Allievi, 2003: 451). Yet (and perhaps also owing to the challenges posed by this dual dimension of Islam), at the popular level, Islam and Muslims are often still perceived, both in cultural and in political terms, as a threat to European identity and cohesiveness, as well as to the integration process of the EU. The crisis of Europe and the West facing Islam became more acute in the aftermath of 9/11 (and, later, with the bombings in Madrid in 2004 and in London in 2005), when the analogy 'Muslim-terrorist' was hastily established by many. While the official US response to the terrorist attacks was primarily military and based on a Manichean discourse of absolute good versus absolute evil, the EU adopted an approach founded on the notion of dialogue between cultures and societies.

The strategy to which the EU resorted – intercultural dialogue – corresponds with the approach that is central to the third basket of the Euro-Mediterranean

Partnership (EMP), which is 'one of the main innovations within Euro-Mediterranean relations' (Pace and Schumacher, 2004: 122). The EMP is a scheme of 'multilateral relations' or a 'regional cooperation' mechanism that the EU set up, during the Spanish Presidency of 1995, with 12 southern Mediterranean 'partner' countries (originally comprising Algeria, Cyprus, Egypt, Israel, Jordan, Lebanon, Malta, Morocco, the Palestinian Authority, Syria, Tunisia, and Turkey)[1] and in which the partners commit themselves to 'conduct and to strengthen political dialogue at regular intervals' (Euro-Mediterranean Conference, 1995). The EMP, also called the Barcelona Process after the name of the Catalan city where the Euro-Mediterranean ministerial meeting took place, was the first attempt in modern history to create strong and durable bonds based on peace and political and economic stability between the two shores of the Mediterranean.[2] The statement of purpose of the EMP is spelt out in the *Barcelona Declaration*, the programmatic document that was produced at the end of the ministerial meeting and whereby the EMP was established (Euro-Mediterranean Conference, 1995). The Declaration's objectives are threefold: (1) to enhance prosperity and economic exchanges with a view to gradually establishing a free trade zone in the Mediterranean region; (2) to define a common area of peace and political stability, also through political contacts and cooperation in security matters; and (3) to encourage understanding between cultures and exchanges between civil societies (the so-called 'intercultural dialogue'), from which a more cohesive and democratic society would emerge.[3]

'Dialogue' – both in a political and a cultural sense – is a key term of the *Barcelona Declaration*.[4] In its third chapter, the Declaration provides an embryonic structure of how intercultural and interfaith dialogue should be conducted across the Mediterranean:

> Greater understanding among the major religions present in the Euro-Mediterranean region will facilitate greater mutual tolerance and cooperation. Support will be given to periodic meetings of representatives of religions and religious institutions as well as theologians, academics and others concerned, with the aim of breaking down prejudice, ignorance and fanaticism and fostering cooperation at grass-roots level (Euro-Mediterranean Conference, 1995).

The efficiency and effectiveness of this basket have often been criticized for its fuzzy terminology (Pace and Schumacher, 2004) and for the lack of a coordinated multilateral approach matching the discourse on cultural and social dialogue. However, in the face of the need to improve relations and to re-establish trust, especially after 9/11 and the 'War on Terror', between the EU and its Muslim citizens, as well as with what is more traditionally considered the Muslim world (North Africa and the Middle East), the intercultural agenda of the EMP now seems the most comprehensive answer.

Islam is intertwined in so many aspects of contemporary European life and policies (e.g. immigration from Muslim countries, integration of newcomers, employment, social cohesion, identity issues, freedom of religion, protection of minorities, diplomatic relations with Muslim countries), that European society and EU institutions need to coordinate their response to the Muslim presence within EU borders as well as to their Muslim interlocutors abroad. For a series of reasons – ranging from the heterogeneity that is inherent in Islam, to structural constraints that do not allow EU competence over religious affairs (Treaty of Amsterdam, 1997; Treaty establishing a constitution for Europe, 2004), to the fact that Islam has become socially and politically a highly sensitive issue – it is unlikely that the EU will ever develop a 'policy towards Islam and/or Muslims' (Spencer, 1997; Allievi, 2003: 469). Nonetheless, the EU has elaborated informal practices as well as policies that have an impact on Islam and Muslims living in the Euro-Mediterranean zone. There are initiatives in the sphere of immigration control, social affairs, and external relations (especially in the Mediterranean area) as well as some *ad hoc* activities (on intercultural and interfaith dialogue) sponsored by EU institutions and officials. Yet, no clear comprehensive design appears to be behind this ongoing series of separate initiatives, except for the social and cultural basket (i.e. the third one) of the EMP.

The following sections will briefly illustrate how EU initiatives relate to the theme of Islam. More specifically, I expand on the implications of those activities – such as the conferences and meetings organized by the European Commission's Forward Studies Unit/Group of Policy Advisers[5] – that are devoted to fostering dialogue with Islam within the intercultural and interfaith chapter of the EMP framework.

Undoubtedly, the treaty provisions that protect religious freedom apply to Muslims living in the EU. Declaration No.11 of the Amsterdam Treaty (1997) and Article 52 of the Constitutional Treaty of the EU,[6] although emphasizing the separation of competences between states and EU institutions over religious affairs, also suggest the formalization of EU relations with spiritual communities in the form of consultations and/or regular meetings. In addition to these general principles and mechanisms that regulate the space of religion in the EU, the EU has repeatedly dealt with Islam and with Muslim people – though indirectly and informally – by using specific approaches according to different priorities. For instance, at least three EU policy areas can be identified that are related, in various degrees and forms, to the issue of Islam. These areas are: (1) Justice and Home Affairs, (2) Social Affairs, and (3) Euro-Mediterranean relations (in particular by using the third basket of social and cultural dialogue).

Justice and Home Affairs

The area of Justice and Home Affairs – renamed at the end of 2004 as the Area of Freedom, Security and Justice (AFSJ) – includes a range of activities, from immigration and borders control to development of security and anti-terrorism measures. It is interesting to note how the new name emphasizes the link between freedom of movement and security concerns. At first glance one might think that this is the result of a securitization of EU policies and discourses in response to 9/11. In fact, the AFSJ simply implements what the Amsterdam Treaty had called for back in 1997: Article 2 of the Treaty on the European Union (as revised after Amsterdam) states that one of the 'objectives' of the Union is 'to maintain and develop the Union as an area of freedom, security and justice, in which the free movement of persons is assured in conjunction with appropriate measures with respect to internal border controls, asylum, immigration and the prevention and combating of crime'. More specifically, Articles 61 and 63 of the Treaty Establishing the European Community (Consolidated version after Amsterdam) declare that 'In order to establish progressively an area of freedom security and justice', the Union shall adopt 'measures on asylum' and 'measures on immigration policy' within five years from the entry into force of the Treaty of Amsterdam, that is by 2004.

If we divide the inhabitants of the EU into two categories – 'citizens' and 'immigrants' – we will realize that the majority of the Muslim population of the EU tends to be composed of immigrants or descendants of immigrants. Hence, controlling or restricting immigration into the EU could be seen as an attempt to create a cultural barrier between those who are seen 'European' and those perceived as the 'other', i.e. both immigrants and Muslims (cf. Zolberg and Litt Woon, 1999). Increasing immigration controls and security measures could also be interpreted as a way to check on Muslims, to identify and separate the so-called 'moderates' from the 'extremists'.[7] Especially after 9/11, the fear of violent actions by terrorist groups claiming to be inspired by Islam (Wahhabi,[8] and Salafist-inspired[9] movements such as al-Qa'ida) has led European governments to pay special attention to the typology of Islamic groups present on their territory or in neighbouring zones. They have been seeking to differentiate dangerous Islamist cells from ordinary, blameless people who are simply practising the religion of Islam. This task, however, has not been a simple one. It has met the opposition of many Muslim and citizens' associations, who have denounced the discriminatory practices and the violation of civil rights and fundamental freedoms carried out by state authorities across Europe.

Concerns with terrorism and migration have been 'at the heart of the EMP from the very start of the process' (Volpi, 2004: 156). Nonetheless, the post-9/11 emphasis on a direct link between migration and security risks has provoked a tension in EMP efforts to, on the one hand, promote democracy and liberalization in the southern shore of the Mediterranean and, on the other hand, carefully monitor potential terrorist elements or subversive political movements (Gillespie, 2003; Volpi, 2004). The consequence is that, in order to guarantee short-term security in the Euro-Mediterranean area, the EU does not engage fully in the social and political development of the Middle East and North Africa (MEDA), relying instead on the autocratic power of local regimes to keep a close eye and a firm hand on the 'Islamist' threat (Brumberg, 2000). But since in the southern Mediterranean, 'Islamic associations constitute the backbone of any non-governmental and "civil society"-type activities', any anti-Islamist measure often results in the suppression of potential sources of democratization, thus jeopardizing the purpose and the impact of the EMP (Volpi, 2004).

Social Affairs

Within the area of Social Affairs it is important to focus on the non-Discrimination principle. Although Article 13 of the Treaty establishing the European Community affirms the principle of non-discrimination ('based on sex, racial or ethnic origin, religion or belief, disability, age or sexual orientation'), it was only recently that the EU addressed the specific problem of religious discrimination by issuing, in 2000, a *Directive prohibiting discrimination in employment on grounds of religion and belief, disability, age and sexual orientation* (cf. Council of the European Union, 2000; Margiotta-Broglio, 2003). This piece of legislation is meant to protect religious minorities, including Muslims, in the EU. However, the theme of Islam emerged even more visibly in connection with discrimination and racism when, soon after 9/11, an authority of the EU – the European Monitoring Centre on Racism and Xenophobia (EUMC) – commissioned a series of country reports on *Anti-Islamic reactions in the EU after the terrorist acts against the USA* (EUMC, 2001). These were first published in 2001 and then condensed in the *Summary Report on Islamophobia in the EU* published in May 2002 (Allen & Nielsen, 2002). The following winter, European Commissioner for Employment and Social Affairs, Anna Diamantopoulou, also convened, in cooperation with the EUMC, three workshops, or 'round tables', where expert academics and policy makers discussed ethnic and religious discrimination in the EU. In particular they focused on: anti-Semitism (December 2002), Islamophobia (February 2003), and intercultural dialogue (March 2003) (see European Commission, 2002 and 2003). Nonetheless, neither these glamorous meetings, nor the European Commission-sponsored conference 'Youth and Gender, Trans-national Identities and Islamophobia' of May 2003 (European Commission, 2003c) seemed to deliver any particularly useful guideline for policy-makers on the subject of non-discrimination. What is important, though, is that through these initiatives the EU has sought to stimulate awareness about the problems and challenges that Europe is facing and also to maximize the participation of various categories of EU citizens (and inhabitants, if we include immigrants) in EU governance (cf. European Commission, 2001a). This is an example of how the EU, despite its institutional fragmentation and inefficiency, is still able to project itself, discursively, as a 'normative power' and as a 'contributor to global peace and better governance' in situations of conflict (Pace, 2006).

Islam and Euro-Mediterranean Relations

Since the Islamic tradition is a major component of the cultural expressions of the North African and Middle Eastern countries that are involved in the Barcelona Process, the 'intercultural' dialogue pillar of the EMP clearly suggests that the whole 'Euro-Med' process is about improving contacts between Europe and the Muslim context (in a broad sense: including religious aspects as well as cultural and social traditions). The incorporation of the faith dimension in the culture basket has been explicitly encouraged by the Barcelona Declaration and repeatedly reiterated by EU officials.[10] The adoption, in June 2004, of an *EU Strategic Partnership with the Mediterranean and the Middle East* (European Commission, 2004a) reinforces the idea that the Union is determined to enhance its relations with regions that are culturally and socially immersed in the tradition and history of Islam and seems to confirm that the EU is indeed determined to engage in a multi-level dialogue with the Islamic world. This indicates a particular strength of the EU, that is, its 'dialogic' attitude, its preparedness to listen and to negotiate with the 'Other' (see Pace, this collection).

However, as we have seen above in the context of JHA, the complexities of the social and political situation in the MEDA as well as the global threat of terrorism *de facto* hinder the smooth translation of the rather idealistic discourse of the EMP into coherent practices. As Ziya Önis and E. Fuat Keyman have put it, 'While the nations of Europe endorse the expansion of religious freedom, they also dislike anything that smacks of "religious fundamentalism"' and are suspicious of Islamist factions (Önis and Keyman, 2003: 106). As explained above, short-term security threats heighten this sense of suspicion and often lead EU governments to back up authoritarian regimes that can provide an immediate repression of the threat.

At the same time, the EU knows that Islamism is primarily the product of sick social, political and economic systems that need a long-term process of healing. In addition, in the southern Mediterranean region, Islamism takes up the old nationalist, Third Worldist label and plays with the North-South opposition which 'stems from an unsolved dialectic between global trends, on the one hand, and the search for identity and authenticity on the other' (Aliboni, 1996: 58). In the MENA, where government policies, social services, democratization and modernization efforts are often unsuccessful, political Islam finds a vacuum to sneak into: 'Uncontrolled population growth, large national debts, corruption and bureaucracy serve to fuel the sense of frustration felt by the inhabitants of the area and increase their vulnerability to the siren calls of Islamism' (Biad, 1996: 42).

This is why fostering democratization and civil society participation has been deemed by the Euro-Mediterranean partners to constitute the most effective way to oppose Islamism, corruption, and autocratic governments (cf. Volpi, 2004; Panebianco and Attinà, 2004). Hence, EU efforts for the democratization of the Muslim MENA region are combined with the establishment of contacts with civil society and with seeking to understand the mobilizing power of Islamic identities and traditions. This EU concern is most apparent in the fact that the EU has increasingly created opportunities for encounters between EU policy-makers and religious leaders to explore the potential of intercultural and interfaith dialogue for the formation of a peaceful, tolerant and cohesive Euro-Mediterranean society. Some of the EU initiatives with these themes – namely workshops and meetings of experts promoted by the European Commission's Forward Studies Unit/Group of Policy Advisers – are mentioned below.

Intercultural and Interfaith Dialogue, the EMP and Beyond

This final section draws attention to the growing importance of intercultural and interfaith dialogue not only within the framework of the cultural and social dialogue basket of the EMP but also in the wider international context. It also highlights EU activities that, although not explicitly defined as part of the third EMP pillar, are still closely related to it and contribute to endorse and consolidate the practice of intercultural dialogue.

A significant EU initiative aimed to support the cause of interfaith and intercultural dialogue and to broaden awareness and participation in this area was, in 2003, the official decision to set up a Euro-Mediterranean Foundation to promote dialogue between cultures and civilizations (European Commission, 2003d).[11] The original proposal for this foundation had been spelt out in February 2002, in the 'Action Plan on Dialogue between Cultures and Civilizations' of the 'Valencia Action Plan', the Commission's document prepared together with the Spanish Presidency to set the agenda for the Euro-Mediterranean Conference that was held in Valencia in April 2002 (see Commission, 2002; Gillespie, 2003). The importance of the Valencia Action Plan and of the initiatives approved by the Valencia conference relies on the reinforcement of the third basket of the EMP along two somewhat contrasting directions: the Justice and Home Affairs programme, concerned with migration and security issues, and the 'civilizational rapprochement in the cultural sphere' (Gillespie, 2003: 34–45). Further to long discussions and country-divergences over the need for, the financing and the structure of the Foundation, the establishment of the institution was formalized in May 2004 as the Anna Lindh Euro-Mediterranean Foundation for the Dialogue between Cultures. It was also specified that it should consist of a 'network of national networks' with its headquarters in Alexandria Library, Egypt, 'in tandem with the Swedish Institute in Alexandria' (Euro-Mediterranean Mid-Term Meeting, 2004: 13).

The Swedish Institute in Alexandria, opened in Egypt by the late Swedish foreign minister Anna Lindh on 3 October 2000, is itself the manifestation of the growing political support of a Nordic country, such as Sweden, for the Barcelona Process (Schumacher, 2001). Schumacher has highlighted four principal implications that are connected with the establishment of the Institute. Firstly, Sweden affirmed its interest in a region which would normally have been considered far from its 'natural' foreign policy interests in terms of vicinity. Second, the soft power of culture was acknowledged in international politics. Third, Sweden sought to give a fresh input to the third basket of the EMP by creating a forum to facilitate cultural and intellectual exchanges between the societies of both the European and the MENA region but outside the traditional top-down approach of the EU. Finally, the type of dialogue promoted by Sweden abroad – through the Institute – appears to be directly beneficial to the country's internal cohesion as well, if we consider that a large portion of the current Swedish population consists of immigrants originating from the Middle East and North Africa. The socio-cultural tensions that are normally associated with the two shores of the Mediterranean (North/EU versus South/non-EU countries) are replicated within Swedish society. This explains why, even before becoming openly committed to the cultural and social basket of the EMP, the Swedish government organized several conferences and open meetings on the impact of Islam in European society, in association with Muslim countries (Schumacher, 2001: 94) or with Muslim organizations (such as the 1996 pan-European meeting of Muslim youth organized in cooperation with WAMY, the World Association of Muslim Youth). Hence, the activities of the Swedish Institute in Alexandria can be interpreted as a continuation of this 'Euro-Islam' project (Schumacher, 2001: 95-6).

But let us go back and try to understand how the EU has gradually become involved in and supportive of intercultural and interfaith dialogue. In the mid-1990s, the Forward Studies Unit (FSU) of the European Commission promoted several conferences to study the impact of the 'religious factor' in Europe and to develop an alternative paradigm to the 'Clash of Civilizations' (Luyckx, 2000; Huntington, 1998). The first two, *The Mediterranean Society: A Challenge of Islam, Judaism and Christianity* and the *Carrefour Européen des sciences et de la culture* [*European meeting point of sciences and culture*] took place respectively in Toledo (Spain) in 1995 and in Coimbra (Portugal) in 1996 (Forward Studies Unit, 1998; Jansen, 1999). The Coimbra meeting had essentially an academic character, whereas European Christian authorities played a major role in the Toledo conference, as an 'ecumenical working group – set up by European Christian authorities with responsibility for dialogue with Islam – was entrusted with the selection of participants by the European Commission' (Forward Studies Unit, 1998: 83). Apparently, this event was integral to the social and cultural chapter of the Euro-Mediterranean Partnership, as the Work Programme of the Barcelona Declaration suggests to take this Toledo meeting as an example of the type of intercultural and interfaith dialogue to conduct across the Mediterranean (Euro-Mediterranean Conference, 1995: 14).

Social cohesion through interfaith dialogue was also the subject of a meeting of EU ministers of the interior convened in Rome by the Italian Minister of the Interior Giuseppe Pisanu, during the Italian semester of the Presidency of the EU, on 30 and 31 October 2003. It was the first time that government ministers and officials of the then 15 EU member states had met in an official way to discuss the subject of religion together with representatives of the three monotheistic religions. The conference title was 'Interfaith dialogue: Factor of social cohesion in Europe and peace instrument in the Mediterranean area'. It was also attended by three religious personalities symbolically representing the three major beliefs present in Europe: Christianity, Judaism and Islam. It is likely that on many occasions before, EU governments' representatives have discussed the issue of religious identities and religious conflicts when addressing the problems of the Middle East, for instance, or perhaps when evaluating the case for Turkey's accession to the EU, but this was the first time that interfaith dialogue was officially invoked by civil authorities as the possible instrument to overcome social and political problems across the two shores of the Mediterranean. The EU ministers in charge of Home affairs that attended that meeting in Rome even promoted a European Charter of Interfaith Dialogue, which was officially presented at a Council meeting the following December (Council, 2003).

Although the October meeting was essentially advertised as an 'interfaith' event, Islam was *de facto* the real focus of the attention; thus, the Muslim representative Mr. Dalil Boubakeur, President of the *Conseil Français du Culte Musulman* (French Council of the Muslim Religion), turned out to be the principal interlocutor, both of the ministers and of the media. The establishment of national Muslim councils across Europe, the significance of this ministerial meeting for Italian, British and European relations with Islam, and the western attempt to support the so-called 'moderate' version of Islam have been discussed elsewhere (Silvestri, 2005a; Hamzawy, 2005; Rubin, 2005). Here we will just note that the term 'moderate' Islam tends to be an artificial one; it can mean several things to several people and can be interpreted or misinterpreted accordingly. For example, certain EU governments used this ministerial conference on interfaith dialogue and social cohesion in the Mediterranean in order to bring forward their own agenda concerning Islam and to provide a model for 'suitable' religious interlocutors.

Between the end of 2002 and the beginning of 2003, President Prodi and the FSU successor, the Group of Policy Advisers (GOPA), also promoted three High Level Advisory Groups to reflect on the values and cultural and religious heritage of Europe.[12] The role of the High-Level Advisory Groups was to 'identify and rethink the fundamental principles that form a basis for societal life in a society which is shared by all the inhabitants of the EU and with due attention to our neighbours' (Prodi, 2003). The two groups that are more relevant to our analysis of the intercultural/interfaith dialogue project of the EU are: the Reflection Group on the Spiritual and Cultural Dimension of Europe, and the *dei Saggi* (wise men) Group specializing in Intercultural Dialogue in the Mediterranean Area.[13] Since the societies and cultures of the southern shore of the Mediterranean tend to be Muslim,[14] it is not surprising that the advisory group has largely focused on the future of relations between Europe and Islam. With respect to this, it is also important to remember that the whole idea of launching the UN year dedicated to the Dialogue of Civilizations (UN General Assembly, 1998) came from Mr. Khatami, the President of the *Islamic* Republic of Iran, a country often 'associated in Western minds with "terrorism" and "extremism"' (Ahmed, 2002: 21). This trend could suggest that the EMP notion of intercultural/interfaith dialogue is expanding and having an impact not only on the Mediterranean but also on its neighbouring areas. It also confirms that this dialogic framework is acquiring importance both on a practical as well as on a theoretical level, for engaging in and theorizing international relations in the twenty-first century (see Petito, forthcoming, 2005).

All these European Commission initiatives for dialogue *with* and *between* religious traditions became more and more urgent with the approaching enlargement of the EU of May 2004. EU officials, politicians and ordinary people were becoming aware that the relatively new geo-political entity of the EU would comprise a growing multiplicity of states, cultures and spiritual and intellectual traditions. These differences needed not only to be acknowledged and respected but also to be understood and placed in harmonious relationship with each other. Almost certainly, global events such as the terrorist attacks of 9/11, or the second Palestinian *Intifada* ('uprising') which began in September 2000 urged the EU to engage in dialogue with different religious groups, especially with Muslim circles. In addition, intercultural and interfaith dialogue turned out to be a political strategy of the EU to express its decision to respond to violence in a different – peaceful – way in opposition to the methods (the 'War on Terror') adopted by the US, and to establish the EU as a global actor.

In the aftermath of 9/11, many EU institutions and public figures vigorously supported mutual understanding and cultural exchanges across Europe and across the Mediterranean. Above all, European Commissioners were involved in these activities, but the conference organized by Mr Pisanu is an example of European ministers' involvement too. The relevance of the EMP in the post-9/11 international context was reaffirmed at the Euro-Mediterranean Conference of Foreign Ministers held in Brussels at the beginning of November 2001. The agenda of that meeting included the need to reinforce the Barcelona Process 'to step up the fight against terrorism and to address structural causes for extremism' and the EU's formal rejection of 'any equating of terrorism with the Arab and Muslim world' (European Commission, 2001c). It was a strident coincidence that the 9/11 tragedy had occurred in the very same year that the UN had devoted to the Dialogue of Civilizations.[15] EU leaders decided to espouse this slogan and to emphasize the need to engage in dialogue with religions, especially Islam, in order to maintain peace and stability. It seems important to remark here that, whilst strongly asserting its commitment to dialogue, the EU also slightly shifted the focus from the notion of 'civilizations' to that of 'cultures' (see also Malmvig in this volume), perhaps for fear that a 'Dialogue of Civilizations' would imply a previous 'Clash of Civilizations', an idea that the EU has always tried to dismiss.[16]

The following sections present and analyse some public EU initiatives and statements in support of this form of dialogue. Such statements and events should be understood against the background of international events and of the challenges that the EU has been facing in this turn of the century.

In the autumn of 2001, whilst the United States launched the 'War on Terror', the EU relentlessly tried to stick to a position of conciliator. Faced with the fear of falling into the announced 'clash of civilizations', the Union, and especially the European Commission, adopted a discourse focused on the notion of 'dialogue'. More and more frequently, since September 2001, European Commissioners have been adopting this terminology in their speeches. This was especially true, during their mandate, of Romano Prodi (Commission's President), Anna Diamantopolulou (responsible for Social Affairs), Viviane Reading (in charge of Culture) and Chris Patten (External Relations). 'Peace and stability are borne out of dialogue' was repeatedly stressed by EU officials (Prodi, 2002: 3). At the height of the post-9/11 anxiety, in November 2001, Commissioner Patten and President Prodi participated in important meetings, respectively at the UN and at the Euro-Parliamentary Forum, advocating the need for dialogue to promote tolerance and understanding between different cultures. In particular, Prodi emphasized the responsibility of the countries of the EMP to engage in such a dialogue (i.e. a relation of communication in which the two partner groups involved share equal rights to speak and equal responsibility to listen), with reference to the battle against terrorism and the need to establish good relations with the Muslim world:

> We must avoid at all costs the association between terrorism and the Arab and Islamic world. We are engaged in a dialogue between equals and we should promote this through cultural exchange. It is of utmost importance that we continue our dialogue. Sending a joint message of solidarity in the common

fight against terrorism is one of the best ways to demonstrate the common ground we share in our partnership (European Commission, 2001d).

In May 2004, Patten gave an all-embracing speech in Oxford on 'Islam and the West – at the Crossroads', where he used the topic of Islam to discuss a range of political issues – such as development and democracy in the Arab world – and to defuse stereotypes and fears about the future entry of an 'Islamic' country (Turkey) into the EU club (Patten, 2004). Moreover, the then German Commissioner in charge of Enlargement, Günter Verheugen, expressed his full support for Turkey's entry into the EU throughout his mandate (1999–2004) (Verheugen, 2001 and 2004). Prominent personalities within the EU who visibly broke off from this line in favour of Turkey, were: the Dutch Commissioner Frits Bolkestein, responsible for the internal market, taxation and customs-union issues; the President of the European Convention on the Future of Europe, France's former President Valéry Giscard d'Estaing; and Austrian Agriculture Commissioner Franz Fischler. Bolkestein expressed his concerns about the Islamic character of Turkey's culture, which – he argued – does not allow the country to belong to Europe (AFP, 2004; *Euractiv*, 2004a; Evans-Pritchard, 2004; Waterfield, 2004). Fischler cast doubt on Turkey's commitment to democracy and secularism, maintaining that Turkey is culturally 'oriental' and 'geographically Asian' (*Euractiv*, 2004b). Giscard d'Estaing also argued that Turkey is in Asia; moreover he attacked those institutional actors within the EU – especially the Council's ministers – who use an 'ambiguous language' about Turkey's accession, never revealing to the Turks the fact that 'the majority of the members of the European Councils are in fact against it' (*Le Monde*, 2002).

In contrast to these contestations about the accession of what is often regarded as a 'non-European' country, Prodi emphasized Europe's plural character during a discussion meeting on anti-Semitism, in February 2004, as he significantly spoke of a 'Union of Minorities' (Prodi, 2004). Although his speech was aimed at praising the capacity of the Jews of Europe to integrate in European society, it was welcomed by other religious minorities too, namely Muslims. According to Imam Dr Abduljalil Sajid (a prominent British-Pakistani Islamic preacher), for instance, the Jewish example of integration in Europe should be a spur for European Muslims to do the same (Sajid, 2005).

Transversal conferences, involving Ministers of the Interior, as well as religious leaders, intellectuals and Ministers for Social Affairs, were organized by various institutions and offices of the EU around the subject of 'intercultural and interfaith dialogue' between 2001 and 2003. As explained above, the EU had gradually developed an interest in and a specific discourse on these themes throughout the 1990s. Therefore, the EU's visible concern with intercultural dialogue in the early years of the new century cannot be regarded as a 'post-9/11 syndrome', although one cannot deny that the terrorist attacks of 2001 (and the subsequent circle of violence that spread globally, from Iraq, to Bali, to Istanbul, to Madrid, and to London) intensified the global attention to and need for cultural and social dialogue as a response to the international crisis.

In December 2001, the European Commission supported and hosted a conference, entitled 'The Peace of God in the World', which had been promoted by the Ecumenical Patriarch of Constantinople, Bartholomew. The conference was attended by EU officials and by a large number of European representatives of the world religions (though their presence did not seem to be well balanced) who then produced a declaration of mutual respect and faith in God. In March 2002, the Commission also organized a more intellectually oriented conference, where world experts and academics – including high-profile Muslim intellectuals (and modernizers) living in Europe such as Muhammad Arkoun, Tariq Ramadan and Malek Chebel – discussed the modalities of intercultural dialogue in twenty-first century Europe.

Specific initiatives to address the issue of Islam and to reach out directly to the Muslims of Europe and beyond were undertaken by the Commission, especially between 2001 and 2002, to defuse the post-9/11 hysteria. Soon after the attacks, in October 2001, then Commission President Prodi made an emblematic visit to Brussels' central mosque, to express his friendship, solidarity and respect for the Muslim communities of Europe who were facing an atmosphere of hostility as a direct consequence of the terrorist attacks that had been carried out in the US by what have since been labelled as 'Islamic fanatics' or 'Islamic extremists'.

On 29 October 2001, Commissioner Diamantopoulou had a private meeting in Brussels with the representatives of European associations of Muslim and Jewish women, whom she had invited to explore and stimulate their contribution to peace and social cohesion between religious and ethnic groups within the EU (European Commission, 2001b). A conference on 'Muslim Women in Europe: Voices to be heard in the intercultural dialogue' was also organized by then Commission Vice-President Neil Kinnock on the occasion of International Women's Day, 8 March 2002. Equal opportunities Commissioner Anna Diamantopoulou took part in this conference, urging for an end to the stereotyping and ignorance of Islam. She also stressed – by using somewhat stereotypical words – that Muslim women living in Europe should be allowed to 'exert free choice and independence in their personal and family lives' (Diamantopoulou, 2002). The European Convention's emphasis on the contribution of civil society to the debate on the future of Europe, as well as the feedback that Mrs Diamantopoulou must have received from these two events are probably the factors that pushed her to host an online interactive conference with Muslim women on 24 October 2002 (European Commission, 2002d). She had acquired visibility as a supporter of Muslim women thanks to two major events the previous year. She was invited as keynote speaker first at the conference on 'Women and the three Mediterranean Cultures: Development, Democracy and Liberty' (Seville, 23-24 November) and then at the 'Roundtable on Women's Leadership in Rebuilding Afghanistan'. This summit was organized in Brussels on 4-5 December 2001 by the European Women's Lobby, the United Nations Development Fund for Women (UNIFEM), and Afghan women themselves (cf. European Commission, 2001d and 2001e) to discuss the role of Afghan women in the reconstruction of their country after the overthrow of the Taliban regime by US-led coalition Operation Enduring Freedom. This meeting ran almost simultaneously with the UN-sponsored

Afghan peace conference – attended by Afghan men only – in Bonn (5 December 2001), which then led to the creation of the Afghan Interim Administration.

From all these initiatives devoted to 'dialogue' emerged the image of the EU extending its hands towards Muslim women and offering them support to gain confidence in themselves and thus be able to participate in public life, be it in Europe or abroad. This was neither a condemnation of the plight of women in Islam, nor an invitation to violent self-assertion breaking off with their cultural traditions. Rather, the overall impression from the type of discourse that characterized these meetings was that the EU, as a model of democracy, tolerance and equality, was smoothly proposing an important change in the lives of these women; they were shown the possibility to become engaged in the 'human' community of Europe's citizens, and to stand together – to support women's causes – irrespective of their nationality, religion and political tradition. Once again, these types of EU initiatives illustrate the normative power of the EU and the way it is projected beyond the limits of the EU.

An example of how the notion of intercultural dialogue was absorbed and re-elaborated outside the EU and then re-proposed to the EU is the Joint Forum on Civilization and Harmony (also publicized by the media as the 'EU-Islam forum'), which took place in Istanbul on 12-13 February 2002. It was organized by the Organization of the Islamic Conference (OIC)[17] and by the Turkish government with the aim of asserting their political engagement to promote harmony amongst cultures. Several EU officials and politicians participated.

The OIC is an important organization in the Muslim world. Although it is not always considered to be very successful due to a lack of coordination, the OIC has been attempting to institutionalize and represent Islam at a global level and as a major interlocutor with the EU (Haynes, 2001). However, if the EU blindly accepts the OIC as a main Muslim interlocutor – which at the moment does not seem to be the case – then the space for the articulation of identity politics of indigenous European Muslims would be jeopardized because the OIC would represent a foreign institutionalized version of 'Islam of the states' and not the Islam of the peoples.

The OIC's commitment to fostering dialogue between the West and the Muslim world started long before 9/11 and is connected with the establishment in Turkey, back in the 1980s, of the OIC Research Centre for Islamic History, Art and Culture (IRCICA). The Centre first dealt with research projects in the fields of history of Muslim nations, history of science, Islamic arts, as well as bibliographic works relating to translations of the Holy Quran and other manuscripts. Subsequently it became gradually engaged in fostering scholarly interest in the history of arts, sciences and culture in Islam worldwide and in cultivating 'both inter-Islamic dialogue and dialogue with other nations and communities'. When the OIC adopted the Tehran Declaration on the Dialogue of Civilizations, the IRCICA mandate was also reinforced. It was 'expected to play a pivotal role ... through its objective studies portraying the true image of Islamic civilisation, representing the Muslim world in multicultural scholarly forums, and helping to create awareness of Islamic culture and civilisation in world opinion'.[18] The IRCICA publication *The West and*

Islam: Towards a Dialogue (Abuhusayn and Waley, 1999), which dates back to 1999, is another tangible example of the OIC's engagement in intercultural dialogue.

Going back to the 2002 OIC conference in Turkey, one notes its political importance for Turkey if we consider the delicate position of the country at that particular point in time. As a Muslim candidate country of the EU, in the aftermath of 9/11, and in the midst of an economic crisis (*Economist*, July 2002: 20-22), Turkey probably felt under pressure to prove its distance from extreme versions of political Islam and to reaffirm its commitment to the EU and to its values of democracy, tolerance and respect of human rights.

A second meeting of the OIC-EU Foreign Ministers Joint Forum was scheduled to be held in Istanbul on 4 and 5 October 2004 but was then cancelled for political reasons that, unsurprisingly, were related to the Cyprus issue. A communiqué from the conference organizers explained that the conference had to be cancelled because the Dutch Presidency had decided not to participate – and had invited the other EU member states to do the same – 'under the pretext of the representational status of the Turkish Republic of Northern Cyprus under observer title of the "Turkish Cypriot State" at OIC' (OIC, 2004). Seeking to minimize the embarrassing situation, the same OIC source added that the Dutch Presidency's decision 'did not have a political aim but rather had the goal of providing an opportunity to discuss the political, economic and cultural dimensional mechanisms of creating a world public opinion that promotes harmony and cooperation amongst different cultures and religions' (OIC, 2004a). Whilst this diplomatic crisis prevented the OIC-EU ministerial Forum from taking place, the international symposium 'Civilization and Harmony: The Values and Mechanisms of the Global Order' that was foreseen to take place prior to the Forum, with the participation of academics, intellectuals and journalists, went on as planned. Despite the absence of the big political actors of the EU in the Forum, this conference enjoyed the contribution of the Director (Alvaro de Vasconcelos) and other members of the EU-sponsored network of experts of the Euro-Mediterranean region, EuroMeSco. EuroMeSco had hailed the previous OIC-EU meeting of 2002 as an attempt to 'create a platform of dialogue' and as 'the first high-level meeting devoted to the intensification of multicultural dialogue in the aftermath of the September 11 attacks in United States' (EuroMeSco, 2004).

In 2002, the European Commission (or, more precisely, the Presidency, together with the directorates and cabinets in charge of external relations and culture) had also become involved with the Lebanese government and with the representatives of the Arab Mediterranean countries in the organization of a conference on intercultural dialogue, to take place in Lebanon at the end of September 2002.[19] Besides the geo-political significance of hosting this event in a critical zone of the Middle East, the importance of the initiative ought to be considered perhaps more in the whole preparation process rather than in the actual outcome of the conference. The joint organization of any conference requires a great deal of exchanges, communication, capacity to interact and an agreement on the programme, on the expenditures, and so on. Perhaps this was a test, or a training process, to improve Euro-Mediterranean relations. It certainly exemplifies the meaning of the notion of partnership in the EMP and the specific dialogic attitude of the EU. Although slow and occasionally disorganized in planning and delivering tangible results in the short term, the EU possesses valuable qualities for a long-term commitment to political dialogue: flexibility and patience to listen and to negotiate.

Conclusions

This essay has sought to highlight the centrality of intercultural/interfaith dialogue practices in the context of EU relations with the Muslim world as well as with the Muslim inhabitants of the EU. Compared to various EU provisions and policies (on freedom of religion, anti-discrimination, immigration control, anti-terrorism) that affect (by protecting and indeed also controlling) the lives of many Muslims residing in Europe, the intercultural dialogue approach seems a more comprehensive and engaging method to interact, on an equal basis, not only with Muslims that live within EU borders but also with the whole Muslim world. In this study we have seen how the EU first developed its intercultural dialogue approach – with the Barcelona Declaration in 1995 – in order to establish economic and political contacts with the southern shore of the Mediterranean (which hosts a large part of the Muslim world), with the ultimate aim of creating a neighbouring area of peace and stability. Initially, EU activities in the field of intercultural dialogue tended to be a private business for the few; they consisted of meetings that took place behind closed doors or that were only accessible at the elite level (invited intellectuals and EU officials). However, with the world crisis triggered by 9/11, the EU visibly became a stronger advocate of intercultural and interfaith dialogue. This type of dialogue was considered the best way to stimulate civil society participation and social cohesion, and at the same time was seen as the recipe to fend off the violent, radical, extremists' threat. Gradually, this instrumental character was dropped and the intercultural dialogue project gained a life of its own detached from the EMP.

EU initiatives aimed at promoting civilizational, intercultural or interfaith dialogue (including the EMP) appear to have been welcome across and beyond the Euro-Mediterranean zone. Even beyond the geographical limits of the EMP, in 1998 an Islamic country (Iran) promoted the year as one of the dialogue of civilizations, to which several OIC members subscribed. After 9/11, the intercultural dialogue project gained even more importance and appeal. In a sense, one may conclude that the intercultural dialogue approach is working as a powerful statement of purpose of the EU in the face of global challenges. By successfully disseminating this new attitude centred on dialogue in order to achieve democracy and social justice, the normative power of the EU is also reinforced. As a consequence, the success of the EU's soft power (through social and cultural policies) provides added value to EU external relations and can contribute to the establishment of the EU in a symbolic new position of hegemony.

Truly believing in the dialogue of cultures, religious and civilizations means nourishing the hope that political, economic and social tensions can be resolved through a dialogic relation based on shared values, sense of responsibility and reciprocal desire to come into contact with and make space for new cultures and traditions. This is not a straightforward exercise to put into practice. Therefore, this ambitious and noble intention, centred on an honest and transparent dialogue of cultures and societies, faces two main challenges. On the one hand, it risks being hijacked by those that exploit this positive rhetoric in order to achieve visibility in the public sphere and pursue private political goals. On the other hand, none of the EU or EMP initiatives in the field of intercultural dialogue has yet produced any immediate results or clear guidelines on how to improve relations, in practical terms, with and within religious and ethnic communities in Europe and across the Mediterranean. In particular, no illuminating solution has been put forward to tackle a highly critical problem of the Euro-Mediterranean zone, the alienation of Muslim youth, who (as the July 2005 bombings in London show) can easily become prey to circles of violence. This last comment is not intended to discredit the whole intercultural dialogue project but simply to point out that this is a serious domain and it will not produce any positive outcome if exploited in a superficial way.

In general, having observed in this essay some diverse EU activities within or related to the third basket of the EMP, it may be concluded that, through the EMP, the 'soft power' of culture has been gradually acknowledged not only by the EMP partners but also in international politics and has *de facto* been elevated to a higher level. Especially when dealing with global terrorism, intercultural and interfaith dialogue seems the only effective instrument available for re-establishing trust relations and social cohesion within and between communities.

Acknowledgements

I would like to thank the editors of this volume in particular Dr Michelle Pace, for insightful comments and guidance. I am also grateful to both my mentors at the European Commission, Leonello Gabrici and Sandro Gozi, as well as Andrew Fielding, for their kind support throughout my research.

Notes

[1] With the fifth EU enlargement of 1 May 2004, the number of the partners that are not EU members has obviously decreased, since Malta and Cyprus joined the EU. Euro-Mediterranean relations clearly form a privileged area of EU External Relations and policy-making. During 2004 the Euro-Mediterranean *partenariat* became incorporated into the broader 'European Neighbourhood Policy' (ENP). As a framework designed to strengthen 'the Union's relations with those neighbouring countries that do not currently have the perspective of membership of the EU' (European Commission, 2003: 4), the ENP 'reinforces the Barcelona Process and represents an essential plank in the implementation of the EU Strategic Partnership with the Mediterranean countries' (European Commission, 2004c). It currently (2005) includes only ten southern Mediterranean states (that is, the original 12 minus those that became members of the EU in May 2004 – Cyprus and Malta – and Turkey – now a candidate country; plus Libya, which has the status of observer) as well as Armenia, Azerbajian, Belarus, Moldova, and Ukraine. For an update on the EMP and its members see the EU weblink http://www.europa.eu.int/comm/external_relations/euromed. On the ENP see Johansson-Nogués (2004) and Smith (2005).

[2] cf. European Commission (2004). As the Partnership's tenth anniversary is approaching, it is becoming evident that the Barcelona Process needs further impetus. Attention to the Mediterranean areas has thus been slightly redefined and has been included, as mentioned above, into the European Commission's vision for a Wider Europe and a Neighbourhood Policy: the *New Framework for Relations with Our Eastern and Southern Neighbours* (European Commission, 2003).

³ The third basket also includes the control of migration movements across the Mediterranean Sea.

⁴ On the meaning and importance of 'Dialogue' as 'Dialogic Understanding' in Euro-Mediterranean relations see the contribution by Michelle Pace in this volume.

⁵ The Forward Studies Unit (FSU) was re-structured and re-named Group of Policy Advisers (GOPA) with the change of College of Commissioners in 1999. In 2005, further to the installation in office of the Barroso Commission, the GOPA was in turn transformed and re-named as Board of European Political Advisers (BEPA).

⁶ The Constitutional Treaty was signed by the EU member states and candidate countries in October 2004; however, it will need to be ratified by all the 25 member states in order to be enforced.

⁷ Later on in this article I will expand on the contested notion of 'moderate' Islam/Muslims.

⁸ Wahhabism, also called *Wahhābīya*, is defined in the *Oxford Dictionary of World Religions* (Bowker [1997] 1999: 1031), as an 'ultra-conservative, puritanical Muslim movement adhering to the Hanbalite law'. Its followers regard the Qur'an and the Sunna (i.e. the tradition deriving from the Prophet's life and religious experience) as the only sources of legitimacy for Islam, thus rejecting '1400 years of development and interpretation in Islamic theology and mysticism' and forbidding 'any importation of *kāfir* (pagan) culture in their society'. Wahhabism was founded in the Arabian peninsula in the eighteenth century by Muhammad ibn 'Abd al-Wahhāb, who soon found support amongst the influential Al Sa'ūd family. The conservative kingdom of Saudi Arabia, still led by the Saudis, has since been its stronghold.

⁹ Salafism (from the arab *Salaf*, predecessors) is a sort of 'puritanical' interpretation of Islam which has been ideologically inspiring renewal of and political action in the Muslim (originally the Arab) world since the second half of the nineteenth century. It arose as a modernist response, through the re-appropriation of Islamic identity, to colonialism and the apparent European superiority; its main proponents were Jamal al-Din al-Afghani and Muhammad 'Abduh. Salafism acquired a strong political character between the 1930s and the 1960s, primarily through the Muslim Brotherhood movement of Hasan al Banna. Influential figures of the second generation of the Muslim Brotherhood such, as Ala Maududi and Sayyid Qutb, contributed to developing the activist character of the movement and reinterpreted the notion of *Jihad* (literally, the strife for spiritual purification) in violent terms. Salafist thought did not originally consider violence as an appropriate method to achieve its aim – the re-Islamisation of society. Yet, the desire to revive the authentic and true principles of Islam by renewing and purging society from injustice, corruption and infidels combined with the Jihadist ideology has produced a deadly cocktail. These ideas have provided a powerful rhetoric for terrorist groups that claim to be inspired by Islam (cf. Joffé, 2004; Kepel, 2002).

¹⁰ See for instance the contribution of Juan Prat (then acting Director of the External Relations DG of the Commission) in the 1996 conference *Islam in a Changing World – Europe and the Middle East* (Prat, 1997).

¹¹ However, the original Commission's proposal dated back to February 2002 (cf. European Commission, 2002a/b).

¹² Further information on the work done by these groups can be found in the final report. See 'Report by the High Level Advisory Group Established at the Initiative of the President of the European Commission' (European Commission, 2003e).

¹³ All the relevant information was found on the following European Commission webpages: http://www.europa.eu.int/comm/commissioners/prodi/group/michalski_en.htm (accessed 28 August 2003) and http://www.europa.eu.int/comm/dgs/policy_advisers/experts_groups/index_en.htm (accessed 30 July 2003).

¹⁴ With the expression 'Muslim countries' I do not imply any predetermined relationship between Islam and politics. It is just to define the countries where Islam is the main religion of the majority of the population and/or has strongly influenced the local culture and history.

¹⁵ See UN General Assembly 1998 and also website http://www.un.org/Dialogue (accessed 15 April 2005).

¹⁶ The most prominent proponent of the Clash of Civilizations paradigm is Samuel Huntington (1998).

¹⁷ The OIC was set up by the kings and heads of state and government of Islamic States in Rabat, Morocco, in 1969. As of May 2005, it was composed of 56 countries. Its website states that the OIC is

'the concrete expression of a great awareness, on the part of the *Ummah*, of the necessity to establish an Organization embodying its aspirations and capable of carrying out its just struggle against the various dangers which threatened it and still persist' (cf. http://www.oic-oci.org (accessed 5 May 2005)). Haynes (2001), Khan (2001) and Sheikh (2002) have studied the growing role of the OIC and its attempt to represent Islam globally and transnationally and the implications for international relations.

[18] All quotes in this paragraph from www.ircica.org, Introduction (accessed 16 May 2005).
[19] Source: privately circulated European Commission. Cf. also Prodi (2002).

References

Abuhusayn, Z. D. & Waley, M. I. (Eds) (1999) *The West and Islam: Towards a Dialogue* (Istanbul: Organisation of the Islamic Conference Research Centre for Islamic History, Art and Culture).

Agence France Press (AFP) (2004) EU Commissioner takes Ottoman swipe at Turkey's hopes, 7 September, http://www.turkishpress.com/turkishpress/news.asp?ID=26424 (13 September 2004).

Ahmed, A. (2002) Ibn Khaldun's understanding of civilizations and the dilemma of Islam and the West today, *Middle East Journal*, 56(1), pp. 20–45.

Aliboni, R. (1996) Collective political co-operation in the Mediterranean, in: R. Aliboni, G. Joffé & T. Niblock (Eds) *Security Challenges in the Mediterranean Region*, pp. 51–64 (London: Frank Cass).

Allen, C. & Nielsen, J. (2002) *Summary Report on Islamophobia in the EU after 11 September 2001* (Vienna: European Monitoring Centre on Racism and Xenophobia).

Allievi, S. (2003) The international dimension, in: B. Maréchal, S. Allievi, F. Dassetto & J. Nielsen (Eds) *Muslims in the Enlarged Europe: Religion and Society*, pp. 449–488 (Leiden/Boston: Brill).

Allievi, S. & Nielsen, J. Eds (2003) *Muslim Networks and Transnational Communities in and across Europe* (Leiden/Boston: Brill).

Biad, A. (1996) Security and co-operation in the Mediterranean: a Southern viewpoint, in: R. Aliboni, G. Joffé & T. Niblock (Eds) *Security Challenges in the Mediterranean Region*, pp. 41–49 (London: Frank Cass).

Bowker, J. (Ed.) (1999) *The Oxford Dictionary of World Religions* (Oxford: Oxford University Press).

Brumberg, D. (2000) The trap of liberalised autocracy, *Journal of Democracy*, 13(4), pp. 56–68.

Cesari, J. (2004) *When Islam and Democracy Meet: Muslims in Europe and in the United States* (New York: Palgrave).

Council of the European Union (2000) *Directive Prohibiting Discrimination in Employment on Grounds of Religion and Belief, Disability Age and Sexual Orientation* 2000/78/EC, 27 November.

Council of the European Union, Presidency (2003) Statement on Inter-faith Dialogue and Social Cohesion, 5983/03 – JAI 373, 10 December.

Diamantopoulou, A. (2002) Speech: The Voice of Muslim Women in Europe. International Women's Day event organised by the European Commission, SPEECH/02/103, Brussels, 8 March.

Euractiv (2004a) Turkish accession could make Europe 'implode', says Bolkestein, 7 September, www.euractiv.com (14 September 2004).

Euractiv (2004b) Fischler challenges EU plans for Turkey, 10 September, www.euractiv.com (14 September 2004).

Euro-Mediterranean Conference (1995) *Barcelona Declaration and Work Programme* (adopted at the Euro-Mediterranean Conference of 27 and 28 November 1995). Brussels: European Commission – External Relations Directorate General.

Euro-Mediterranean Conference of Ministers of Foreign Affairs (2003) Presidency Conclusions, Naples, 2–3 December.

Euro-Mediterranean Mid-Term Meeting of Ministers of Foreign Affairs (2004) Presidency Conclusions, Dublin, 5–6 May.

Euro-MeSco (2004) OIC-EU Joint Forum. *EuroMeSco* website, www.euromesco.net (1 February 2005).

European Commission (2001a) European Governance. A White Paper, COM (2001) 428 final, Brussels, 25 July.

European Commission (2001b) Midday Express, MEX/01/1030, 30 October.

European Commission (2001c) Press Release: Euro-Mediterranean Foreign Ministers meet to reaffirm relevance of the Barcelona Process in aftermath of 11 September, IP/01/1530, Brussels, 31 October.
European Commission (2001d) Memo, President Prodi participation in the Euro-Mediterranean Parliamentary Forum, Brussels, 8 November.
European Commission (2001e) Press Release, Anna Diamantopoulou: 'We must work for equal opportunities between men and women throughout the Mediterranean region', 21 November.
European Commission (2001f) Press Release, Afghan Women's Summit for Democracy, 4–6 December, Brussels. Fifty Afghan women leaders to attend, IP/01/1717, 3 December.
European Commission (2002a) Communication from the Commission to the Council and the European Parliament, To Prepare the Meeting of Euro-Mediterranean Foreign Ministers, Valencia, 22–23 April 2002, SEC(2002) 159 final, Brussels, 13 February.
European Commission (2002b) Press Release, Euro-Mediterranean Partnership: Commission proposes new initiatives and urges Member States and Partner Countries to reaffirm political commitment, IP/02/249, Brussels, 13 February.
European Commission (2002c) Press Release, International Women's Day: Diamantopoulou speaks out against double burden of gender and racism on Muslim women, IP/02/377, 8 March.
European Commission (2002d) Press Release, Diamantopoulou to take live Web questions on Muslim women in Europe, Brussels, IP/02/1516, 24 October.
European Commission (2002e) Press Release, First Round Table on manifestations of anti-Semitism across the EU, IP/02/1809, Brussels, 5 December.
European Commission (2003a) Press Release, Anna Diamantopoulou launches Round Table on Islamophobia, IP/03/190, Brussels, 5 February.
European Commission (2003b) Communication from the Commission to the Council and the European Parliament. Wider Europe – Neighbourhood: A New Framework for Relations with our Eastern and Southern Neighbours, COM (2003) 104 final, Brussels, 11 March.
European Commission (2003c) Press Release, Hatred of Muslims in Europe: the EU addresses Islamophobia, IP/03/735, Brussels, 22 May.
European Commission (2003d) Press Release, Sixth Euro-Med Ministerial Conference: reinforcing and bringing the Partnership forward, IP/03/1613, Brussels, 28 November.
European Commission (2003e) Report by the High-Level Advisory Group established at the Initiative of the President of the European Commission, *Euromed Report*, 68, 2 December.
European Commission (2004a) EU Strategic Partnership with The Mediterranean and the Middle East – Final Report, *Euromed Report*, 78, 23 June.
European Commission (2004b) *Enlargement Weekly*, 14 September, http://europa.eu.int/comm/enlargement/docs/newsletter/weekly_140904.htm (20 June 2005).
European Commission (2004c) Memo, The EU, the Mediterranean and the Middle East: a longstanding partnership, MEMO/04/294, Brussels, 10 December.
European Commission (2005) Press Release, José Manuel Barroso meets European religious leaders, IP/05/904, 12 July.
European Council (1999) Presidency Conclusions, Tampere European Council, SI (1999) 800, 15–16 October.
European Council (2004) Presidency Conclusions. Brussels European Council, Brussels, 16-17 December.
European Monitoring Centre on Racism and Xenophobia (EUMC) (2001) *Reports on Anti-Islamic Reactions within the European Union after the Acts of Terror against the USA* (Vienna: EUMC).
Evans-Pritchard, A. (2004) Turkey's Muslim millions threaten EU values, says commissioner, *Daily Telegraph*, 8 September.
Forward Studies Unit, European Commission (1998) *The Mediterranean Society: A Challenge for Islam, Judaism and Christianity* (Luxembourg: Office for Official Publications of the European Communities).
Fuller, G. E. (2004) *The Future of Political Islam* (New York/Basingstoke: Palgrave Macmillan).
Gillespie, R. (2003) Reshaping the agenda? The internal politics of the Barcelona Process in the aftermath of September 11, *Mediterranean Politics*, 8(2–3), pp. 21–36.

Hamzawy, A. (2005) The West and moderate Islam, *bitterlemons-international.org*, 20(3), 2 June, http://www.carnegieendowment.org/publications/index.cfm?fa=view&id=17036 (7 July 2005).
Haynes, J. (2001) Transnational religious actors and international politics, *Third World Quarterly*, 22(2), pp. 143–158.
Huntington, Samuel P. (1998) *The Clash of Civilizations and the Remaking of World Order* (New York: Touchstone Books).
Jansen, T. (Ed.) (1999) *Reflections on European Identity. Group of Policy Advisers Working Paper* (Brussels: European Commission).
Joffé, G. (Ed.) (1999) Perspectives on Development: The Euro-Mediterranean Partnership (London and Portland: Frank Cass).
Joffé, G. (2004) Global Terrorism, *EuroMeSco Papers*, 30.
Johansson-Nogués, E. (2004) A 'ring of friends'? The implications of the European neighbourhood policy for the Mediterranean, *Mediterranean Politics*, 9(2), pp. 240–247.
Jünemann, A. (2003) Repercussions of the emerging European security and defence policy on the civil character of the Euro-Mediterranean Partnership, *Mediterranean Politics*, 8(2-3), pp. 37–53.
Kepel, G. (2002) *The Trail of Political Islam* (London: I.B. Tauris).
Khan, S. S. (2001) *Reasserting International Islam: A Focus on the Organization of the Islamic Conference and Other Islamic Institutions* (Oxford: Oxford University Press).
Luyckx, M. (2000) The EU and Islam: the role of religion in the emerging European polity, *Cambridge Review of International Affairs*, 12(2), pp. 267–282.
Margiotta-Broglio, F. (2003) La Questione Religiosa nella 'Costituzione' dell'Unione Europea, *Diritti, nuove, tecnologie, trasformazioni sociali. Scritti in memoria di Paolo Barile*, pp. 493–506 (Padova: CEDAM).
Le Monde (2002) Pour ou contre l'adhésion de la Turquie à l'Union européenne, 9 November, http://www.lemonde.fr/web/article/0,1-0@2-3210,36-297386@45-100,0.html (15 June 2005).
Nielsen, J. (1999) *Towards a European Islam* (Basingstoke/New York: Palgrave).
Önis, Z. & Keyman, E. F. (2003) A new path emerges, *Journal of Democracy*, 14(2), pp. 95–107.
Organization of the Islamic Conference (OIC) (2004) Press Release, OIC-EU Ministers Joint Forum, 1 October.
Pace, M. & Schumacher, T. (2004) Report: Culture and community in the Euro-Mediterranean Partnership: a roundtable on the third basket, Alexandria 5–7 October 2003, *Mediterranean Politics*, 9(1), pp. 122–126.
Pace, M. (2006, forthcoming) EU policy-making and border conflicts: perceptions and approaches, in: T. Diez, S. Stetter & M. Albert (Eds) *The European Union and the Transformation of Border Conflicts: Theorising the Impact of Integration and Association* (Cambridge: Cambridge University Press).
Panebianco, S. & Attinà, F. (2004) Security cooperation in the Mediterranean: EMP instruments to mitigate divergent security perceptions, *Euromesco Research Papers* July.
Patten, C. (2004) Islam and the West – at the Crossroads, SPEECH/04/256, Oxford, 24 May.
Petito, F. (2005, forthcoming) Khatami's dialogue among civilisations as international political theory, *Journal of Humanities of the Islamic Republic of Iran*.
Prat, J. (1997) The Euro-Mediterranean Partnership, in: A. Jerichow & J. B. Simonsen (Eds) *Islam in a Changing World: Europe and the Middle East*, pp. 157–168 (Richmond: Curzon Press).
Prodi, R. (2002) The EU, Dialogue with Religions and Peace. Speech notes for Prof. Romano Prodi President of the European Commission. Dialogue: 'Build Europe, build peace'. Conference on Christianity and Democracy in the Future of Europe, Camaldoli (Italy), 14 July.
Prodi, R. (2003) First Meeting of the Group on the Spiritual and Cultural Dimensions of the Enlarged European Union, Speaking Notes, Brussels, 29 January.
Prodi, R. (2004) A Union of Minoritie: Seminar on Europe – Against anti-Semitism, For a Union of Diversity, SPEECH/04/85, Brussels, 19 February.
Roy, O. (2004) *Globalised Islam: The Search for a New Ummah* (London: Hurst).
Rubin, B. (2005) The myth of 'moderate' Islamists, *FrontPageMagazine.com*, 2 June http://www.isranet.org/isranetbriefings/Permanent2005/Permanent_june_2005.htm (24 June 2005).

Sajid, A. (2005) Anti-Semitism and Islamophobia: Two sides of the same coin? Paper presented at the Discussion meeting organised by the Wyndham Place Charlemagne Trust, St Ethelburga Centre for Reconciliation and Peace London: 7 April.

Schumacher, T. (2001) The Mediterranean as a new foreign policy challenge? Sweden and the Barcelona Process, *Mediterranean Politics*, 6(3), pp. 81–102.

Sheikh, N. S. (2002) *The New Politics of Islam* (London: RoutledgeCurzon).

Silvestri, S. (2005a) The situation of Muslim immigrants in Europe in the XXI century: the creation of National Muslim Councils, in: H. Henke (Ed.) *Crossing Over: Comparing Recent Migration in Europe and the United States* (Lanham, MD: Lexington).

Silvestri, S. (2005b, forthcoming) Islam in Europe and Turkey's integration into the EU, in: N. Neuwahl & H. Kabaalioglu (Eds) *Proceedings of Conference, 'Turkey's Accession Process to the European Union: Legal, Political, and Cultural Aspects of Integration'* (Istanbul: Turkish Chambers of Commerce and Industry/Turkish Association of European Studies).

Smith, K. (2005) The EU and Its Neighbourhood, paper presented at The Enlarged European Union and its Institutions: Looking Out and Looking In under the New Constitutional Framework Cambridge University, 8 July.

Spencer, C. (1997) Europe and political Islam: defining threats and evolving policies, in: M. Kramer (Ed.) *The Islamism Debate* (Tel Aviv: Moshe Dayan Center for Middle Eastern and African Studies, Tel Aviv University).

Treaty Establishing a Constitution for Europe (2004) *Official Journal of the European Union*, C310(24), 16 December.

Treaty Establishing the European Community (consolidated version) (1997) *Official Journal of the European Union*, C340, 10 November.

Treaty on European Union (consolidated version) (1997) *Official Journal of the European Union*, C340, 10 November.

Vasconcelos, Á. & Joffé, G. (Eds) (2000) *The Barcelona Process: Building a Euro-Mediterranean Regional Community* (London/Portland, OR: Frank Cass).

Verheugen, G. (2001) EP plenary debate on Turkey, SPEECH/01/487, Strasbourg, 24 October.

Verheugen, G. (2004) Turkey and the EU towards December 2004, SPEECH/04/309. Friends of Europe, Brussels, 17 June.

Volpi, F. (2004) Regional community building and the transformation of international relations: the case of the Euro-Mediterranean Partnership, *Mediterranean Politics*, 9(2), pp. 145–164.

Waterfield, B. (2004) EU's Bolkestein 'xenophobic and racist' over Turkey, *Eupolitix.com*, http://www.eupolitix.com/EN/News/200409/4676c532-a0f0-4a0d-b708-2dde1646b58d.htm (8 September).

Willis, M. (1996) The Islamist movements of North Africa, in: R. Aliboni, G. Joffé & T. Niblock (Eds) *Security Challenges in the Mediterranean Region* (London: Frank Cass), pp. 3–26.

Xenadis, D. K. & Chryssochoou, D. N. (2001) *Europe in Change: The Emerging Euro-Mediterranean System* (Manchester: Manchester University Press).

Youngs, R. (2003) European approaches to security in the Mediterranean, *Middle East Journal*, 57(3), pp. 414–431.

Zolberg, A. R. & Woon, L. L. (1999) Why Islam is like Spanish: cultural incorporation in Europe and the United States, *Politics and Society*, 27(1), pp. 5–38.

Wounded by a Divide Syndrome: The Impact of Education and Employment on Euro-Med Cohesion

JOACHIM JAMES CALLEJA
University of Malta

Introduction

The Mediterranean region is a region of contrasts. In Braudel's language it is a place where 'contradictions' converge and diverge. On the positive side, it is a region of rich cultural heritage; on the negative side, it is a region in which external and internal political forces have systematically wounded the identity of its people and their relationship with each other. From Rabat to Damascus, from Athens to Tunis, from Lisbon to Nicosia, the Mediterranean region is a cultural, economic and social area in search of a 'common language of development'. Cultures differ but yet they converge into a Mediterranean identity which scholars have defined in various academic terms but so far have failed to institutionalize into educational programmes of studies across lower and higher education institutions in the whole region. The repercussions for this failure are that investments and exchanges in the region have been sporadic and yielding insignificant economic results. Systems of communication between the Mediterranean countries are far from the standards of the 'old' continent. In fact, the Mediterranean region is a region of 'silence' broken by the horrors of civil wars and conflicts 'in the name of God'. It is a region of invisible walls that divide the northern from the southern shores; that divide religions; that divide systems of governance; that divide regional infrastructural initiatives; that divide systems of education and training; that divide ordinary men and women from achieving the same quality of life as that experienced in many parts of the Western world. It is a region which, in many parts, still looks down upon its own human resources and relies upon external influences and expertise in a mediating role among its very own forces of development.

This essay aims at bringing to the fore the need for the Euro-Mediterranean area to invest in its own capacity-building in order to move away from systems of subordination and create its own practice of economic and political growth. This does not imply reinventing the wheel, but it clearly signifies a co-ordinated response to tackle the challenges of a global economy that threatens to widen the already existing gap between rich and poor countries and exploit weak economies and labour forces. Education has always played a key role in development. In Europe, in North America, in Australia, Japan and other affluent societies, the level of education and training is synonymous with power and development. Even in developing states, the level of education of rulers and their families and friends has always been considered a tool to acquire and sustain positions of influence and decision-making. This is the challenge for the people of the region: to claim education and training as tools for development. The EU, through its Barcelona Process, the Euro-Med Partnership (EMP) and now its European Neighbourhood Policy (ENP) is offering the chance to invest in an education which addresses Euro-Mediterranean issues and problems and which, at its foundations, is marked by a deliberate and time-framed programme for capacity-building, cost-effectiveness and value for money.

The Divide Syndrome

Medically speaking, a syndrome is an aggregate of concurrent symptoms together indicating the presence of a disease. In a Euro-Mediterranean context, this syndrome is characterized by at least three concurrent symptoms: the first, the communication divide; the second, the religious divide; the third, the ethnic divide. Communication has never been rewarding in this region except for the recent developments with the start of the Barcelona Process in 1995. Regionally speaking, the area is rich in its physical and cultural heritage but often expresses itself violently in the sharing of diversity. For many centuries, religion has been the source of conflict in the region and even today the factions are still far apart from each other. Ethnicity has been the driving force for political isolation, and bridging cultures will take time and certainly involve more than one political process.

In its complexity, the geopolitical context of the Euro-Mediterranean area spells these characteristics into political, economic, cultural and social divergences. A region governed by three monotheistic religions (Judaism, Christianity and Islam), three forms of government (monarchies, presidential republics, democracies) three predominantly historical eras (the Greek/Roman legacy, Muslim expansion, and the colonial and post-colonial epoch) and three strong characters (centralists, authoritarian and conservative) have left this part of the world with a *divide* syndrome. A reflection of this *divide* can be verified in the education systems of the countries bordering the Mediterranean Sea. In their rich diversity, such systems have paradoxically, forged entire generations with a frame of mind which is exclusive and not inclusive of other cultures.[1] In fact, inclusivity has been hard to instil in the minds of young men and women who were led to believe that their own culture could be protected through an exclusion of other cultures, particularly those with fundamentally different conceptual-moral-behavioural standards that societies believe to be proper or right for themselves.

At their core, the three monotheistic religions have common roots. Yet their interconnectedness has rarely been spelt out, particularly in an educational context. As a result, entire generations have been brought up with the idea that diversity cannot be expressed in a unifying dimension or that unity can be interpreted as an expression of diversity. Luckily, in the last 20 or 30 years academics and later politicians and religious leaders have revisited this superficial yet intrinsic *divide* and sought to rectify a number of misconceptions. It is only prior to and since the Barcelona Process that decision-makers in the region have started talking about a Mediterranean ethos that is essential if this area is to find peace and development. The Barcelona Process continues to remind those capable of bringing change in this region that such change can only happen if education is geared to erase misconceptions of the past and provide the skills and the creative tools for development. From tourism to agribusiness, from sports to manufacturing industries, from ICT to gastronomy, the Euro-Mediterranean area is rich in potential and in investment. Yet the Arab, the Jewish and the Western world, although in synergy with each other on the way forward, have still to come to terms with prioritization in policy-making.

In many respects, education can and should provide the bridge to this *divide* syndrome. But unlike any other sector of development, education policies often create controversies and follow conservative approaches to the extent that generations very often miss the chance to nurture an innovative approach to culture and they still grow up with misconceptions. Notwithstanding positive notions of a Euro-Mediterranean culture, such definitions still carry the burdened weight of history and religions. As a matter of fact, history and to a large extent communication between the three cultures has shown that the great *divide* between the three religions is an institutionally-based *division*. A church, a mosque and a synagogue have architectural differences yet symbolize a spiritual reality that is common to all religions. It is based on the obedience towards the one same God. Likewise, the three forms of government yield the same result, that is, a form of organization which divides those who rule from those ruled with the exception that in practice, democracies are meant to formally express direct popular consent, while monarchies and totalitarian systems express an indirect forced and imposed consent. Without entering into the epistemological and substantive merits of such divergences, one is inclined to conclude that, in principle, the *divide* syndrome of the Euro-Mediterranean area stems from the fact that religious and political differences have been taken as insurmountable issues, and as a result the three main epochs quoted earlier on have brought a system of schisms rather than partnerships which still exist and which have only lately been addressed at the regional level through the EU.

In her comments on 12 April 2005,[2] Commissioner Benita Ferrero-Waldner said that the European Commission is proposing a 50 per cent increase of EU funding for education as from 2007 if the EU's Mediterranean partners commit themselves to a programme of measures, such as to increase reading standards and eliminate gender discrimination. With one third of the population of the Mediterranean partners under 15 years of age, education, for Commissioner Ferrero-Waldner, is top priority. In real terms, although this is a programme for promoting literacy and equality, it is also an indication that the Euro-Mediterranean area lacks the basic tools of development that have forged the quality of life of affluent societies. Eradicating illiteracy, ensuring primary education for all and rooting out gender discrimination throughout the education systems is no mean feat. On the contrary, it means that the Euro-Mediterranean *divide* syndrome is based primarily on the fact that inequalities cannot guarantee communication, cooperation and confidence-building between partners. The establishment of partnerships could also be jeopardized by such a *divide,* as the term 'partnership' implies 'common ground' upon which to invest cooperation. Having one partner in a more hegemonic position than the other (the northern affluence as contrasted to southern development) may threaten to break such a partnership as it expresses inequality.

It is therefore interesting to note that Ferrero-Waldner's priorities for the period 2007–13 are those related to education and training. If the Lisbon goals are centred around the need to create a 'competitive knowledge society', then it is of paramount importance that the Euro-Mediterranean area also participates in a policy of education and training aimed at preparing a workforce with knowledge, skills, competences and attitudes conducive to growth and synergy between the various sectors of development. This is indeed a huge challenge for education as well as an opportunity for governments to invest in an educational dialogue which bridges the cultural and social divides that history and religion have artificially constructed for political purposes. The people of the Euro-Mediterranean area are the descendents of hegemonic empires and cultures that gave birth to the western world and to Arab and Jewish traditions. In many respects, these traditions have forged the cultures not only within the Euro-Mediterranean area but also beyond, including North and South America (Christianity) and the Near and Far East (Islam). While religions and cultures have clearly segregated and organized people by territory and region, education has reinforced this tendency and unfortunately manipulated the way people feel, think, act and react to development.

The divide syndrome was therefore seen as a means to protect conceptual, moral and behavioural patterns of the nation-state which either incarnated the principles of religion and made them its own or coexisted with such principles in order to secure its own existence. The crusades and the wars in the name of God are an example of how religion managed to manipulate and brainwash the minds of millions of men, women and children who believed that the elimination of the so-called 'enemy' would guarantee peace and security. Historical facts proved this position wrong. Wars have provoked further wars and genocides and widened the divide between cultures and ethnic groups. The legacy of such praxis is reflected today in the hard-fought divide between Islam and Christianity, between Christianity and Judaism and between Islam and Judaism. The three religions have lived separately on separate territories with random tolerant instances in southern Europe and in some parts of Northern Africa.

But the educational challenge must start as part of a community of communication of the Euro-Mediterranean area that regards human beings as equals irrespective of ethnicity or creed. Unless this is addressed in an institutional manner and reaches the grassroots of Euro-Mediterranean societies, a regional educational process will be difficult to launch, let alone accomplish. The coexistence of conceptual-moral and behavioural patterns or standards of behaviour is the first step towards the dismantling of this *divide* syndrome. More specifically, education must make way for inter-faith education so that young people from different religious backgrounds can be educated in a manner which facilitates co-operation and confidence-building.

It is this perspective that, in the long run, will eradicate the *divide* syndrome in the Euro-Mediterranean area. Alternatively, people will remain entrenched in their cultural position, and this will inevitably hinder their need to open up politically and economically. In other parts of the world, such as Europe, Australia and America the religious dilemma has been superseded by the need for concerted growth beyond the blinkers of religion in its institutional expression. Efforts are already evident in the three monotheistic religions of a *rapprochement* which will hopefully eliminate prejudice and insecurity. The passing away of the Head of the Roman Catholic Church in April 2005 was the first global mourning of a religious leader who sought to unify people through religion but not through religious doctrine in its fundamental and divisive elements. This event marked, for the first time in modern history, a concrete example of unity in diversity which augurs well for future relations, particularly among religions within and beyond the Mediterranean region.

A Unifying Vision

Is there a unifying vision for the Euro-Mediterranean region? Is this vision endogenous in nature? To what extent is this vision participatory? The Euro-Mediterranean area in the terminology used by Braudel is 'a thousand things at once' (Braudel, 1972: 4) where 'everything has converged' into what Churchill Semple terms as 'a melting pot for the peoples and civilizations which have seeped into it from its continental hinterlands' (Churchill Semple, 1931: 235). On the other hand Amin believes that 'the Mediterranean area, by virtue of its past and many of its present characteristics, is evidently a region where diversity does not preclude unity and both are products of geography and history' (Amin, 1989: 16). Clearly, such historical reflections challenge the idea of a unifying vision for the Euro-Mediterranean area. On the one hand, the region must be recognized as 'many things at once' – social, cultural and political systems superimposed on each other and therefore a homogeneous position is practically impossible. Yet, such diversity has been melting through many centuries into what peoples of the area represent today. A Tunisian, a Cypriot, a Spaniard, a French, an Italian and a Lebanese citizen have 'things' in common (such as landscapes, temperament, physical features, related languages) but have other 'things' which are not at all common (such as frames of mind, political priorities, gender relations, religious influence, legal characteristics), yet they have to search for mechanisms that can help them coexist into a system of cooperation that could lead to confidence building. In a more academic fashion, one could term this as the mission statement of Euro-Mediterranean relations for the next decade: to identify specific political and economic mechanisms that could lead to endogenous developments through systems of education that promote knowledge, skills, competences and positive attitudes for a Euro-Mediterranean union.

A unifying vision for the Euro-Mediterranean area can only be built through an educational programme which looks into endogenous developments as its driving political forces. This must be based on two important premises:

1. The actual circumstances of societies and the needs and aspirations of their populations, and
2. The existing potential resources, whether human, material, technical, or financial, which any such societies may possess (Cao Tri, 1986: 5).

The goals of such a vision are (1) to revive values, spur on creativity and mobilize the energy of the peoples, (2) to invest heavily in capacity-building at all levels of development and, (3) to make the Euro-Mediterranean zone a union of human resources that within two decades can have the capacity to implement a programme of development which can transform this part of the world into a sustainable economy. Furthermore, such strategy could be transferred into the poor states of Central Africa and create equally viable economies. Linking education to economic development is the backbone of a 'knowledge society' that considers lifelong learning as the tool to sustain quality of life. This must be a vision based on endogenous development. It must be meaningful to the Portuguese as well as to Palestinians, Moroccans and Greek and Maltese citizens – it must be inclusive of all human capacities and exclusive of long-term dependency. It is a fact that most countries in the Euro-Mediterranean area have not yet recovered from long periods of colonization or domination or the repercussions of the process of decolonization. The trauma suffered by populations in the region continues to persist beyond their gaining of political independence. A look at their education systems clearly indicates this reality. British, French, German and Spanish (and to a lesser extent American influences) are still evident in many education systems in the region. As a result of this process, the Euro-Mediterranean area is a zone in which the erosion of cultural identity has led to a high level of dependency upon former colonial countries; it has led to the de-personalization of the individual to the extent that 'foreign' expertise is highly valued even if in substance it may have, in the long run, no added value and drains budgetary resources.

It is therefore not surprising at all to observe phenomena of introversion, as well as of dependence and the 'divide and rule syndrome' in former colonized societies.

Such introversion may manifest itself as either a rejection of the dominant system by a return to traditional values or institutions or as an escape from realities (Rocher, 1968: 236). A unifying endogenous vision for the Euro-Mediterranean area would be a step towards reducing these tendencies particularly in avoiding the possibilities that societies take refuge in their past, their history, their former structures, their manners, their customs, their myths and their folklore to which they attach disproportional weight. The recent rejection by the French and the Dutch of the EU constitution may also be interpreted as a sign of refusal by people to be governed by structures that do not reflect the actual circumstances of their societies and that do not address directly the needs and aspirations of societies. A Euro-Mediterranean area governed by external forces, that is the EMP and the ENP, may yield results which in the long run will not change the economic and social fabric of the same societies that may have participated with a short-sighted attitude. This is one of the major challenges of the EU and of the Euro-Mediterranean partners in particular for the forthcoming period of 2007–13.

Looking back there is no doubt that the MEDA programme, for instance, had a clear vision for the Euro-Mediterranean area. Five priority areas which were selected for their regional added-value had an initial positive impact on:

- Initiating the process towards a Euro-Med free trade zone;
- Promoting regional infrastructural initiatives;
- Advancing the sustainability of Euro-Mediterranean integration;
- Enhancing the rule of law and good governance;
- Bringing the partnership closer to the people.

The EU's objective is to support the implementation of the Barcelona Process, a multilateral framework of relations establishing a comprehensive partnership which has become the centrepiece of the EU's policy towards the area. In its objectives, the EMP is a means through which the EU supports Mediterranean partners in their political, economic and social reforms while at the same time building closer EU-Mediterranean partnerships. The Euro-Mediterranean Association Agreements (EMAA) and the MEDA programmes assist each country on the way towards the declared Barcelona objectives. In this context it is important to note the three main goals of the EU's Med policy as set out in the Barcelona Declaration in the Common Strategy that was adopted by the European Council in Feira in June 2000:

- the creation of an area of peace and stability based on the fundamental principles including the respect for human rights and democracy;
- the creation of an area of shared prosperity through sustainable and balanced economic and social development, and especially the gradual establishment of free trade between the EU and its partners and among the partners themselves. This process should be accompanied by substantial EU financial support to help partners deal with their economic transition and the resulting social, economic and environmental challenges;

- the improvement of mutual understanding among the peoples of the region and the development of an active civil society (Barcelona Declaration, 1995).

In a nutshell, these goals imply structural reforms, economic and political stability, the strengthening of democracy, the rule of law, respect for human rights and fundamental freedoms and the promotion of good neighbourly relations as well as the respect of obligations under international law, intensified regional cooperation and integration, furthering of sustainable market economies and promotion of greater understanding between cultures. Such an agenda requires a regional approach, intensification of South–South cooperation and a trans-national dimension in tackling issues. Furthermore, it requires European and southern Mediterranean countries to work with each other, to use every possibility for regional and sub-regional cooperation and to build multilateral networks of close contractual relationships on all development sectors particularly those that favour mobility, exchange of personnel from one place work to another and cultural interaction especially between higher education institutions and colleges in the Euro-Mediterranean zone.

A unifying vision built on this foundation also requires support at the grassroots of society. But the only effective way of reaching this level of society is through an educational and training programme which should start as early as possible and include a lifelong educational component. Having been the birthplace of various civilizations, this is a region with a very rich cultural heritage. At the same time, it is a region characterized by two conflicting strands, namely the co-existence of a great diversity of cultures and the risk of undermining such co-existence by the persistence of negative perceptions between civilizations, stereotypes and xenophobia. Therefore one of the main challenges of education is to eradicate racism and xenophobia and to foster greater mutual knowledge and understanding between cultures which are rich in their diversity. Such tasks require a clear understanding of the role that education and training could play. So far, universities and higher education institutions have played a leading role in forging moral, conceptual and behavioural standards and patterns of living which may not have resulted in the kind of communication and cooperation that promotes confidence building between the peoples of the region. On the contrary, higher education has been elitist in its structures and in its programmes of studies as well as in its attraction. It has managed, as in other prosperous countries, to reiterate the already existing divide between professional and vocational education and provided societies with a workforce that is not flexible enough to meet the challenges of economies in transition and of work ethics which require major changes in mentalities. In addition, a number of higher educational institutions, particularly those with a religious vocation, were set up to consolidate an orthodox approach to co-existence.

In the future, Euro-Mediterranean co-operation must be guided by EU processes which lay the ground for co-operation at an institutional level and which encompass a wide range of structures that would indeed improve the quality of life of entire populations and bring prosperity, peace and security. At the core of such processes, and building on European experiences, is the principle of unity in diversity, as well as the need to eliminate the possibilities of conflicts within the region. The Barcelona Process, MEDA and the ENP are initiatives which, coupled with other initiatives, networks and joint ventures, should provide a unifying vision for a region in search of endogenous development.

If development is a cultural project, then it cannot be disconnected from what Pierre Pascallon calls 'the sum total of a people's creative activities, its method of production and of appropriation of material assets, its form of organization, its beliefs and sufferings, its work and its leisure, its dreams and its successes' (Pascallon, 1982: 25). It implies that development is culture and culture is development. Such a relational approach to development in the Euro-Mediterranean area signifies that processes in the region must be governed by a unifying vision built upon a sustained democratization process of culture, so that change and integration will come through conviction and not imposition.

The participation of populations in an alternative form of regional development can be seen on two levels: production and direction of economic processes. On the first level, a productive organization must be elaborated. This will absorb manual and non-manual labour and displace inadequate technology or methods of production through high degrees of productivity. Consumer habits and work practices will also be transformed so as to end ostentatious and unnecessary products, replacing them with services and goods capable of providing marginal groups with well-being in a development model they can fully internalize. With regards to the second level, what is expected is the increasingly extensive and active participation of the present and future workforce within the economy's orientation so that they can themselves make decisions concerning the productive processes to be followed. This would be a controlled, constant and decisive production from which every individual will acquire a feeling of fulfilment and dignity. Certainly, the education sector has a pivotal role to play in this unifying vision. Building on existing unifying structures provided by the EU, education should seek to list the priorities in line with the Lisbon goals and promote in vocational and higher education training programmes and research, values, which would increase the possibilities of cooperation and confidence-building in the region.

Euro-Mediterranean Priorities

In a region charged with negative emotional feelings resulting from historical and religious fanaticisms, a list of education priorities should be based on a rational model of development. In a way, 'rationality' is the means to prioritize sensitive areas of development so that goals are achieved according to set deadlines in a cost-effective manner. In political science, sociology and economics, a decision or situation is often called rational if it is in some sense the most advantageous, and individuals or organizations are often called rational if they tend to act somehow optimally in pursuit of their objectives. Thus, one speaks, for example, of the rational allocation of resources (in which fairness and prioritization control behaviour) or of a rational corporate strategy (in which 'macro' objectives are subservient to 'micro' ones). In this concept of rationality, the individual's goals or motives are taken for granted and not made subject or conditioned to pre-conceived ideas based on traditional behavioural or ethical implications. In a sense, rationality implies the success of goal attainment, whatever the goals may be. Sometimes, in this context, rationality is equated with behaviour that is self-interested, reaching the negative aspects of egoism.

Over the years and in particular after independence, governments in the Euro-Mediterranean area have not always been rational in their political and economic objectives but rather have been submissive to outside influences. Consequently, conflicts in the region have always been triggered by forces external to national or regional interests. Unfortunately, communication and education systems have not been given enough attention. What is required is policies that promote effective communication and education which ensure that populations interact and build among themselves levels of trust that permit development in trade, commerce and exchange of ideas, capital and know-how. It is through education at all levels that such development can take place. However, systems of education are so diverse and lack so much synergy that the region remains alien to itself, whereas similar situations in North America, Western Europe and Australia were resolved through political cooperation. In fact, organizations such as the Council of Europe and the Organization for Security and Cooperation in Europe had as their main objective the goal of keeping in constant communication, even if only at the political and bureaucratic levels.

In many respects, the Barcelona Process is a process of communication in a region which lacks the structures of dialogue on a cultural level. The idea of a Council for the Mediterranean never really took off, and similar initiatives taken during the early and late 1990s never brought any significant paradigm shifts. To its credit, the Barcelona Process has been a breakthrough in communication among its members. It has sought to integrate development on a multilateral basis and has kept conflict and inter-religious controversies under control. It is therefore natural to make a further step in this development by focusing on the processes that will ultimately influence the widest possible spectrum of societies so that any political manoeuvres will be welcomed without scepticism and hopefully with a resolved energy for change. It is perhaps in this spirit of renewed commitment toward a more tangible and sustained dialogue that on 12 April 2005, the European Commission unveiled a wide-ranging work programme to reinforce the EMP over the next five years. In its communication to the Council and Parliament, the Commission outlined three major priorities, namely: education, sustainable economic growth, and human rights and democracy. In the words of Ferrero-Waldner, the work programme has all the ingredients to 'reinvigorate the EMP as it enters its second decade'.[3]

On education, the Commissioner took a holistic approach which ties the third to the second and first baskets of the EMP. There can be no 'security and stability' as well as 'shared prosperity and economic growth' in the region if populations lack the education and the skills necessary to accomplish what other populations in affluent societies have done over the last 60 or 70 years. The message is clear in the Commissioners' outline of the main objective: increasing the quality of education for all and ensuring a more equitable access are the focal points of the EMP for the next five years. In particular the Commissioner proposed the following goals:

- to promote a substantial increase in EU and member states' support for education and vocational training with the objective of increasing by at least 50 per cent the proportion of financial assistance devoted to education;
- to seek a commitment from partners to a new target of 2015 for the eradication of illiteracy in the region, full enrolment of girls and boys at primary school and elimination of gender disparity at all levels of education;
- to launch a scheme offering scholarships for university studies in Europe, with a percentage of places reserved for women.[4]

Of significance is the emphasis on vocational education and training, the eradication of illiteracy and gender discrimination, access to primary education for all, and studying in European universities. Will this strategy in education help to create by 2010 a Free Trade Area, the liberalization of services including agricultural liberalization and political reform to achieve security and stability? Will the new focus on issues such as the protection of human rights, the empowerment of women, the strengthening of democracy, pluralism and independent judiciary be accomplished through education and training? The answer to this set of questions is that the area needs a system of education which is able to trigger, establish and sustain the political reform necessary to connect a region disconnected by non-regional priorities. If the EU convinces its southern Mediterranean partners to achieve this objective, then a rational approach to such processes will be to coordinate efforts to sustain such process. The societies on the southern shores of the Mediterranean can only benefit from this development tool to eradicate centuries of slow or irrelevant development, poverty, submission and prejudices that have inflicted entire generations with a lethargic expression of their own belief in themselves, their identity as well as their form of well-being.

Clearly, Euro-Mediterranean priorities are education and training. Most partners in the Barcelona Process have launched reviews of education, labour and training policies as well as fundamental reform programmes to make these policies responsive to the new economic and social realities of a region in constant growth and flux. An example of this is the MEDA-ETE regional project launched in November 2004 with a budget of €5m. The project objective is to support Mediterranean partners in the design of relevant technical and vocational education and training policies that can contribute to promoting employment through a regional approach. Through the European Training Foundation (ETF) this project is a prototype of the projects that the area requires in the field of education. It is an initiative at the regional level which has at its core education, training and employment. This is one of a number of features upon which the region can build a prosperous future. Despite the heterogeneity of partners in terms of population, size, culture, religion, systems of education and training, economic and social development, the common features identified in the EMP for the period 2002–2006 remain as relevant today as they were before: the analysis and monitoring of the quality and relevance of education, training and labour market systems; access to finance; occupational certification and training standards; analysis and role of education and training institutions and definition of relation between employment and labour market measures.

To a large extent, the EU is also in a phase of revisiting such *common features* in the education and training of its own member states. In fact the Bologna and the Copenhagen processes launched a series of initiatives for higher and vocational education which should lead to a number of goals applicable also to the Euro-Mediterranean area. Both the Bologna and the Copenhagen declarations, and particularly the Maastricht and Bergen communications of 2004 and 2005 respectively, gave priority to transparency, comparability, transferability and recognition of competences and/or qualifications, so that the principles of unity and mobility are strengthened among and between all member states. Linked to these initiatives, taken by European Universities and Colleges, the Commission also launched in 1997 the European Employment Strategy as part of the Lisbon Goals in order to improve the capability, efficiency and competitiveness of the European labour market and employment.

In many ways, the EMP and the education, employment and training sectors of southern Mediterranean partners are in their initial stages of development. The latter are obliged to accomplish the Lisbon goals within a framework which would overlap with their direct involvement in the EMP for the period 2005–10. It is therefore interesting to note that such processes have reached a stage in which symbiosis and cross-fertilization of ideas and programmes could provide platforms of cooperation across the whole region. It is in the interest of EU member states to ensure that systems of education, training and employment are systematically addressed not only to achieve the results set by the EU for individual member states but also to involve in legislative and economic contexts the non-European countries of the Barcelona Process. The Commission's open method of co-ordination may also apply to the EMP, so that the best practices in these interconnected areas of concern run across all participating countries. If much more needs to be done to increase labour participation, especially for women and older people and to improve productivity and flexibility in EU member states, the same holds true for the southern Mediterranean partners.

The commonality of issues and problems merits concerted action between and among EU and non-EU member states within one process of development. Comprehensive reforms and action plans should be drawn up so that financial and human resources are used efficiently in cost-effective ways. Education, employment and training in the EU and in the Euro-Mediterranean area have two fundamental goals: the first, to provide relevant skills and competences to young and adult job-seekers, for rapid occupational integration and to promote equal access of special groups exposed to social exclusion, and the second, more effective measures for employment, particularly in the transition from school/college/university to work, strongly integrated into the overall strategies for social and economic development and based on the partnership model.

This rational approach to Euro-Mediterranean development requires that the Bologna and Copenhagen processes, as well as the Lisbon Strategy are somehow connected to the next phase of the EMP so as to waste no time and resources in accomplishing common goals and objectives and in bringing about political reforms concurrently and within attainable time-frames.

The *Neighbourhood* Process

The implementation of EU policies across member states and non-EU Mediterranean partners concerning education, employment and training is the key indicator of a successful Barcelona Process designed to bring political reform, peace and stability, as well as shared prosperity to economies in transition. The target is to address the Social, Cultural and Human Chapter of the EMP through employment strategies aimed at strengthening the first and the second Chapters of the Process. Hence, it is a holistic approach to education and training that the EMP requires, in order to transform policies into concrete action by all stakeholders. A process which has limited ownership is a process doomed to formalize inertia. Now that the Commission has declared that it wants to boost education in the framework of the EMP, no efforts should be spared to implant into the educational process three conceptual dimensions namely:

- the need to think of education and training as a *meta-framework* which will add value to the existing national systems but which would at the same time strengthen transparency, supporting transfer and facilitating recognition of programmes of studies and qualifications at all levels of education;
- the development of educational policies consistent with employment strategies with an accent on vocational education and training;
- the provision of institutional infrastructures which allow cultural synergies between the various cultural systems of the Euro-Med region with the aim of promoting peace and stability, financial partnerships and the gradual establishment of free movement of goods, services and people across the region.

The process of the development of a meta-framework for education and training in EU member states is still in the making. Following the Bologna, Copenhagen, Maastricht and Bergen conferences,[5] there is a general consensus that education and training on the mainland should follow a structure which would make it easier for employees and employers to engage in employment possibilities and development. The proposed European Qualifications Framework (EQF)[6] aims at providing read-across systems of education which would not hinder transnational cooperation and development and subsequently labour mobility. Such an EQF will facilitate communication and recognition of training between EU member states.

The same should apply in a Euro-Mediterranean context, particularly if countries such as Portugal, Spain, France, Italy, Greece, Cyprus and Malta have already endorsed this initiative taken by the Commission. A Mediterranean Qualification Framework in line with EQF will enable:

- citizens to move within complex systems of education in the region and therefore support employability;
- educational experts and decision-makers to compare systems of education and thus strengthen transparency and confidence building measures between different models of education and training in particular at vocational and higher education institutions;
- an authentic Euro-Med labour market to emerge particularly in view of Commissioner Ferrero-Waldner's objective 'to launch a scheme offering scholarships for university study in Europe with a percentage of places reserved for women';[7]
- the idea of a globalized system of education by making it easier for students in developing countries to obtain recognized qualifications.

The Euro-Mediterranean area also requires systems of education that channel their energies and resources into providing skills that are needed in employment within and beyond the region itself. This has been largely the position taken by the United Kingdom vis-à-vis the future of the Barcelona Process.[8] According to the UK, an 'outcome-focused rather than a process-driven' approach should be adopted in 'establishing education systems that fully support open, knowledge-based and empowered societies across the Euro-Med region'. In concrete terms, the British government is suggesting a number of measures such as the opening of ERASMUS (and other EU programmes) to Mediterranean partners; the development over the next ten-year period of partnerships in education; the enhancement of the education of girls; the alignment of knowledge and skills to investment and employability; the introduction of 'standard' university qualifications that achieve both EU and international recognition, and sector skills development through work schemes which allow skilled youth to build and gain experience for a number of years before returning back to their country.

If the EMP aims at constructing a zone of shared prosperity, the sharing of knowledge is the first step towards this goal. As a matter of fact, the Lisbon Strategies define such goals in a way which is significantly relevant to the Euro-Mediterranean area in particular: better regulation, investment in research and development, innovation and change, more and better jobs, an adaptable workforce and better education and skills. The accent on the relationship between education, training and employment is one of the key factors which would integrate the three main objectives of the EMP for the next decade or so. A region-wide consultation which involves all Euro-Mediterranean countries, social partners, employers and non-governmental organizations is the first step in a process which would ultimately create a programme for concrete action among Euro-Mediterranean partners. Certainly, an educational process-in-the-making among EU member states that excludes non-European partners could be counterproductive to the EU's objective to

> share the benefits of the EU's 2004 enlargement with neighbouring countries in strengthening stability, security and well-being for all concerned...designed to prevent the emergence of new dividing lines between the enlarged EU and its

neighbours and to offer them the chance to participate in various EU activities, through greater political, security and cultural co-operation.[9]

As a number of southern Mediterranean countries are developing countries, the need to invest in infrastructure should be seen as a priority if the Commission's objective for the EMP for the next five years, especially the eradication of illiteracy, access to education for all and support for vocational education and training, is to be achieved. Functional buildings, advanced information and communication technology, equipment, teaching aids, *in-situ* expertise, effective communication systems, road networks, trained personnel and adequate legislation are among the first priorities that the EMP should encourage if region-building and identity-building processes are truly the objectives. Adequate infrastructures play a pivotal role in creating a feasible pathway to learning, to dialogue and to an active participation by all citizens. Defining Mediterranean education in terms of quality, access and employability would be giving the Euro-Mediterranean area the right to join the development bandwagon that most EU countries enjoy in this field of concern.

While it is understandable that a Euro-Mediterranean identity, in its classical form, can be expressed through religions, cultures, languages, landscapes, folklore, traditions, physical features and civil societies, a Euro-Mediterranean identity of the twenty-first century may have to be further articulated to include the context of communication, cooperation and confidence-building. In this vein, the EMP is indeed a unique and ambitious project. However, further investment in young generations particularly through information and communication technologies may bring about the much-needed leap in quality in the region (that such processes have been targeting since 1995 but with results that are still negligible)

Towards 'an unlimited Community of Communication'

In the wake of new initiatives by the EU, particularly the ENP, Libya's openness to the West, the developments within the Palestinian Authority, Turkey's position in the EU, Syria's withdrawal from Lebanon and the continued cooperative relations between partner countries of the EMP, the time is ripe to discuss and agree on a *renewed political and economic identity* for the Euro-Mediterranean region. Such a new context must overcome the chains of prejudice and mistrust and seek to achieve common ground on which to build development through education, training and employment. Karl Otto Apel offers an interesting conceptual framework based on the realization of an *ideal* community of communication from a *real* community of communication (Apel, 1977: 258–68). In his celebrated book *Transformation der Philosophie* he proposes the foundation of ethics on the 'unlimited community of communication' which stimulates political, economic and cultural expediency. Using a Kantian approach to philosophy, Apel believes that the rational use of an unlimited applicability of communication (in the widest sense possible) is the prerequisite for coexistence at the political and cultural levels of development. There are two regulatory principles that govern such a philosophy: the first is survival of humanity and therefore the survival of a real community of communication at all costs, and the second is the realization of an *ideal* community of communication within the real community of communication. The survival of societies as a system of auto affirmation is the means to achieve unrestrained autonomy. Such liberation, or unrestrained autonomy, channelled through an unlimited community of communication results into a new form of inclusive identity, in which every individual plays a functional role in their attainment of a moral collectivity. While the socialization process, particularly in the early years of life, determines a person's *real* community of communication, the sense of judgement of arguments that led to a relative truth resolves the ideal and 'unlimited' community of communication. It is through the inter/intra-cultural communication of subjects who are morally and legally entitled to judgement, thus ethically responsible for any form of social, political, economic and cultural action, that ultimately determines the validity of the political and cultural action needed to ensure justice and prosperity. Democracy therefore plays an important role in such a process of communication which determines the form that civilization takes in the history of humanity.

Like Kant, Apel's complex political philosophy is governed by his strong belief in a rational process of democratization and political governance as the determining factor in human endeavour. What is interesting from a Euro-Mediterranean perspective, although his philosophy has universal appeal, is that the means to overcome the divide in this region is to apply communication, that is an unlimited and unobstructed response to dialogue, to a Euro-Mediterranean identity which is totally inclusive of an endogenous point of view and exclusive of exogenous influences that do not respect the authenticity of the cultural framework of the region. Such an approach does not exclude intercultural and international relations. On the contrary, it uses such interaction to serve the purposes of people who have no such access but who may ultimately be the victims of so-called processes of globalization. Apel's philosophy focuses on the need of every individual with dialogical capacities to act as the 'subject' of their own destiny in order to avoid marginalization and exclusion.

In this scenario, education and training can serve as the means to help individuals achieve three main goals: the first, a level of communication which allows them to interact on a local level – literacy and education for all; the second, a level of communication which allows them to move in a regional context – societies built on partnerships; and the third, a level of communication which spells out competences, skills and an ethical formation – vocational and higher education and training. In such an educational context, all three levels should run parallel with the first level, thereby providing the point of departure of survival and socialization: the second level represents the point of departure of freedom and identity in a regional context, and the third a point of departure is related to one's own personal preparation for the world of work and leisure well-being. Run concurrently, these three levels of education and training prepare individuals, as citizens of a given territory in a meta-territorial context understood and owned as part of their immediate geopolitical environment. The third level of training relates to every person's role in the world of productivity. A Euro-Med process which manages to design educational programmes targeted towards regional objectives within an employment perspective, is a meaningful political commitment which will mobilize individuals for a personal and collective purpose.

So far, the Euro-Med process has adapted a pragmatic approach to the three main chapters of the Barcelona Declaration. The implications of this have been that, while at the political elite level, significant progress has been registered across the board, at the grassroots, the feeling is still that of a divided region in which North and South have been conditioned to grow apart. Applying Apel's philosophy to a Euro-Mediterranean context also implies that a new form of identity for the region is gradually inculcated into young generations; a culture of communication, of openness, of inclusively, of mutual respect and of the management of enriching diversities. A regional identity which is poised to promote developmental factors can minimize the traditional and emotional contexts of meta-cultures and increase the value of wealth and security.[10] Rather than blocking differences, such a culture of communication for the Euro-Mediterranean area will enable people to build confidence in the institutions that represent them and have a direct bearing on their lives and in the policies that aim at establishing a new form of cooperation through communication. In this respect, media and information and communication technologies play an important role. Similarly, cultural tourism, investments in industries that generate productivity and the provision of services in areas such as building and construction, pharmaceutical products, automotive technology, transport, entertainment (including the film industry), marine technology, communication services, sports and food production are sectors that will effectively enhance identity and the quality of life of the region's populations.

Transforming identity into a *working* hypothesis for Euro-Mediterranean development is the next step in a process of change that will give to the region a new form of ownership not only at the highest levels of decision and policy making, but at all levels of societies and through an established plan of action. Tied to this goal is the need to apply European guidelines of the qualifications framework to the whole region in the context of the ENP programme. Achieving such an objective will be an enormous step towards invigorating growth and employability in the region.

Conclusions

The European Neighbourhood and Partnership Instrument, which for the Euro-Mediterranean area will be reflected through the Barcelona Process, has 25 key areas of development among which is political dialogue and reform, the promotion of legislative and regulatory approximation, the strengthening of national institutions, support for employment policies and higher education and research, and the promotion of understanding between cultures, people-to-people contacts, cooperation between civil societies and exchanges of young people.[11]

From a conceptual point of view, this ties with Apel's idea of an 'unlimited' community of communication which, in the long run will guarantee openness, transparency and confidence-building among partners who adhere to the principles of communication as the vehicle of development. Moving away from Kant's 'categorical imperative', Apel advocates for dialogue as a form of communication based on fairness and mutual respect. Communication inevitably leads to complementarity, partnerships, co-financing, compatibility, coordination and coherence in defining and implementing projects and programmes among partner countries. In the spirit of the Barcelona Process, the ENP should consolidate, in agreed sectors of development, a harmonization of policies and procedures and a regular exchange of relevant information in particular at field level in a regional context. As stated in the ENP Strategy paper, the ENP will reinforce existing forms of regional and sub-regional cooperation and provide a framework for their further development with the next step being that of negotiating European Neighbourhood Agreements (ENA).[12]

However, the strategy for the Euro-Mediterranean area concerning education and training needs further elaboration. The vision is clear but the roadmap is blurred. While it defines action on issues such as infrastructure/interconnection projects, the environment, justice and home affairs, trade, regulatory convergence and socio-economic development, the paragraph on people-to-people projects is too vague although there is specific mention of 'intercultural dialogue through educational and youth exchanges, as well as human resource mobility and transparency of qualifications'.[13] The issue of qualifications is supreme in achieving a truly 'unlimited' intercultural dialogue. Vocational and higher education institutions must act fast and provide an education, which features the Euro-Mediterranean area as a hub for cooperation in research and development. Whether it is information and communication technologies or agribusiness or mechanical engineering or maritime studies or building and construction or law or commerce, an effort should be undertaken to promote a people-to-people research project on how such areas of development can be learnt within a Euro-Mediterranean context. Such a project will include common programmes of study for vocational and higher educational institutions, a common qualifications framework based on the European Qualifications Framework and competency and occupational standards which would make it easier for both the emerging workforce and employers to apply skills and competences to industry and service provision.

Thus an 'unlimited' community of communication is the answer to eradicate a *divide* syndrome and the perception of a region of manifest diverging rather than (hidden) converging contrasts. Education, training and employment can serve as political platforms to achieve a neighbourhood which makes use of partnerships to commit people in understanding and sharing values through close and cooperative relations.

Notes

[1] In response to the implementation of the 2004 OSCE Ministerial Council Decision Number 12/04 on Tolerance and Non-Discrimination, the OSCE *Conference on Anti-Semitism and on Other Forms of*

Intolerance which was held in Cordoba on 8 and 9 June 2005, addressed this *divide* and in particular how the media can avoid anti-semitic messages in systems of mass communication and the internet.

[2] Commission Launches 5-year work programme to reinforce Euro-Mediterranean Partnership – Press Release downloaded from http://europa.eu.int/rapid/pressReleasesAction.do.

[3] Press Release, 12.04.05 IP/05/419 downloaded from http://europa.eu.int/rapid/pressReleases Action.do.

[4] See, Commission Launches 5-year work programme to reinforce Euro-Mediterranean Partnership – Press Release downloaded from http://europa.eu.int/rapid/pressReleasesAction.do.

[5] Since 2000, member states of the EU committed themselves to a transformation of the systems of higher education into a framework for qualifications of the European Higher Education Area. This process, known as the Bologna Process, led to the creation of the European Credit Transfer System and the framework for qualifications of the European Higher Education Area. In 2002, a new Copenhagen Process was initiated to achieve a Vocational Education and Training Qualifications Framework. The two processes are now converging into a European Qualifications Framework which will be operated through an EU Integrated Programmes Initiative. Member states of the EU are currently undertaking reforms in education and training with a view to achieving the goals set in the Lisbon Strategy. Such a strategy has the key objective to make the Union the 'most competitive and dynamic knowledge-based economy in the world capable of sustainable economic growth with more and better jobs and greater social cohesion', http://europa.eu.int/growthandjobs/index_en.htm. Knowledge and employment are the key factors which will determine the success or failure of such a strategy.

[6] The European Qualifications Framework was presented during the Maastricht Ministerial meeting, held in December 2004, and re-elaborated during the Bergen meeting of May 2005 to include a Framework for Qualifications of the European Higher Education Area. The Framework is based on eight levels in response to three main elements: a set of common reference levels to formal qualifications and to competences acquired through combinations of formal, non-formal and informal learning; a range of common references and principles agreed at the EU level on quality in vocational education and training, guidance and the validation of non-formal learning which aim to achieve mutual trust, and finally the European Qualifications Framework, which will provide citizens with a series of instruments such as the EUROPASS, European Credit Transfer System and EU Vocational Education and Training. Such instruments will support job mobility across EU member states, improve matching of labour needs through the modernization and strengthening of labour market institutions notably employment services, greater transparency of employment and training opportunities at national and European levels, and better anticipation of skill needs. See Education Committee doc DS 193/05. See also Minutes of Directors General of Vocational Education and Training [DGVT] meeting held in Luxembourg 18–19 April 2005. For further information including EU reports and papers see www.cedefop.eu.int, and http://europa.eu.int/comm/education/policies/2010/doc/jir_council_final.pdf.

[7] Commission launches 5-year work programme to reinforce EMP, http://europa.eu.int/rapid/pressReleasesAction.do.

[8] See *Achieving a Common Vision: A UK contribution to the future of the Barcelona Process*. See also EUROMED Report 90, 1 June 2005, and Conclusions from the VII. EUROMED Conference of Ministers of Foreign Affairs in Luxembourg, 30–31 May 2005.

[9] http://europe.eu.int/comm/world/enp/policy_en.htm.

[10] The emphasis of this paragraph is on shifting the current focus of identity, exclusively based on religious and cultural identities, to one based on development, prosperity and security. The terms 'development' and 'prosperity' are being used to express the notion in the widest possible sense excluding notions of 'territorial and religious' hegemony. The term 'security' encompasses the physical territory, as well as the individual's health, well-being, safety and the satisfaction of basic needs.

[11] See COM (2004) 101 and COM (2004) 487. The reasons leading to this proposal were explained by the Commission to the Council and Parliament in her communications on the financial perspectives. See also COM(2004) 628 final and 2004/0219 (COD).

[12] See COM (2004) 373.

[13] Ibid.

References

Apel, K.-O. (1977) *Comunita' e comunicazione, 'Transformation der Philosophie'* (Torino: Rosenberg & Sellier).

Amin, S. (1989) Conditions for autonomy in the Mediterranean, in: E. Yachir (Ed.) *The Mediterranean* (London: Zed Books).

Braudel, F. (1972) *The Mediterranean and the Mediterranean World in the Age of Philip II Vol. I & Vol. II* (Glasgow: William Collins Sons).

Cao Tri, H. (1986) *Strategies for Endogenous Development* (Oxford: UNESCO).

Churchill Semple, E. (1931) *The Geography of the Mediterranean Region* (New York: Henry Holt & Co.).

Pascallon, P. (1982) *The Cultural Dimension of Development* (Paris: UNESCO).

Rocher, G. (1968) Introduction a' la sociologie generale, in: G. Rocher (Ed.) *Tome 3. Le Changement Social*, 3 (Paris: Editions HMH).

Conclusion: Cultural Democracy in Euro-Mediterranean Relations?

MICHELLE PACE
University of Birmingham, UK

Challenging Times, Challenging Concepts

Post-9/11, the wars in Afghanistan and Iraq, the Madrid bombings of March 11, 2004, the London bombings of 7/7 (2005), threats from the 'South', the rise of radical fundamentalism in the Middle East and other securitization discourses about the southern Mediterranean (Malmvig, this volume) have drawn the attention of academics, policy-makers, civil society actors and wider societal communities.[1] As the contributors of this volume have highlighted, the Huntingtonian discourse of the 'clash of civilizations' is being debated more than ever before. Historically, *Islam* has nearly always been the principal Other in the Western dialectic of imagination, fear and domination.[2] At a time when the perception of the irreconcilable nature of cultures is growing, it is important to take these concepts and discourses seriously, in particular the concepts of culture and democracy (Del Sarto, this volume). The progressive adaptation of Euro-Mediterranean cultural co-operation under the third basket of the EMP needs urgent examination: what is the *raison d'être* behind this policy? what drives the EU to act in the southern Mediterranean in the social, cultural and human field? is there a presumed link between third basket efforts and economic, political and social development in the Mediterranean? What is the role of permanent education in all this? Is efficient cultural provision possible? What are the limitations to democratization in the southern Mediterranean? This concluding section of the volume attempts to address some of these questions although it does not endeavour any definitive answers.

Democratization of Culture and Cultural Democracy

The EU's Civilizing Mission

Intrinsic in colonialism was the idea of self-legitimation, the most powerful tool of which was the colonizers' claim to bring the fruits of progress and modernity to the subject peoples. According to colonial logic, people who were different because they were inferior had to be made similar – and hence equal – by 'civilizing' them.[3] When European powers took over territories in the southern Mediterranean, they argued that they brought civilization to the barbarian peoples of the region, enlightenment to the heathen, prosperity to the impoverished, law and social order to the brutish primitive. Most of the European powers saw no reason to apologize for forwarding European economic interests in the colonies, and their imperialist expansion and adventures found further justification in their self-declared missions of spreading 'civilization, commerce and Christianity' across the globe.[4]

This 'civilizing mission' philosophy still seems to be ingrained in the minds of European Union policy makers today. In the context of the theme of this volume, the EU has, thus far, represented its EMP third basket policy aims to its members and its Mediterranean partners in a highly idealized fashion (as Tobias Schumacher puts forward in the introduction): the three main objectives of the Partnership, which are clearly interrelated, are declared as follows:

1. The definition of a *common* area of peace and stability through the reinforcement of political and security dialogue (Political and Security Chapter).
2. The construction of a zone of *shared* prosperity through an economic and financial partnership and the gradual establishment of a free-trade area (Economic and Financial Chapter).
3. The *rapprochement* between peoples through a social, cultural and human *partnership* aimed at encouraging understanding between cultures and exchanges between civil societies (Social, Cultural and Human Chapter).[5]

But, if we analyse this policy deeper, as the contributors of this volume have attempted to do, the EMP as a whole and as it still emerges today, in effect is a compromise between different conceptions of the EU's own identity that structure different approaches to the Mediterranean area and the ways in which this area is securitized. The discursive merging of a continuum of threats ranging from terrorism to illegal migration are the primary objectives of the Barcelona Process. Where does this leave us in terms of EU efforts aimed at the democratization of Mediterranean Non-Member countries (MNC) through the third basket of the EMP?

Democratization of Culture

First, it is important to query what the EU actually means by democracy in the southern Mediterranean area? What does the process of democratization in the southern Mediterranean actually entail? Or, can we put the question differently and ask whether the third basket is in fact an aspect of the EU's experimentation in the southern Mediterranean – a form of imperial hegemony? What does the third basket tell us in terms of the societal and political role of Islam, the functioning of modern states in the southern Mediterranean, cultural and individual rights of every citizen in the region, the monopoly of corrupt leaders versus a transparent and equitable system of shared resources?

The idea that culture is a natural good, first articulated in the Renaissance, was extended during the Enlightenment and the emergence of industrial society. It was renewed in the post-war period with the democratization of culture promoted as a mechanism for the re-civilization of a European society that had demonstrated how close to the surface lay barbarism.[6] The philosophy behind the idea of the democratization of culture asserted that it is a missionary obligation of the state to make culture (in a narrow sense) accessible and attractive to the masses.[7] Early cultural co-operation was largely confined to issues concerning the interchange of information and facilities for the arts (with arrangements between politicians and administrators responsible for the arts and artists) and to educational systems. Eventually, governments started to rethink outside the boundaries of these traditions: they began to look into the cultural needs of their societies against the changing backgrounds and emerging life-styles and to lay stress upon the quality of life. Matthew Arnold and Raymond Williams (with notable interventions from distinguished social scientists) initiated a long – albeit inconclusive – debate on the concept of 'culture'.[8] However, while administrators and 'experts' moved on to a new understanding of culture, the public at large continues to equate culture with the arts (in particular with the productions and performances of professional artists). Underlying this view is a related assumption that there is a superior minority in society who act as guardians of all that is 'culture'. It is therefore crucial to question the relevance of culture to people at large and to their daily life. This brings us to a new rationale where the health, wealth and happiness of people are accepted as governments' obligations. This broad understanding of culture requires those in power to ensure that democracy becomes increasingly 'real' for people, so that their wishes and concerns are voiced and sought and responded to by their governments. The concept of cultural democracy which seems to lie behind the *raison d'être* of the third basket of the EMP is aimed at developing human resources, promoting understanding between cultures and exchanges between civil societies in the Euro-Mediterranean area.[9] Efforts under this basket are aimed at enhancing educational levels throughout the region (with special emphasis on the MNC). Moreover, municipalities and regional authorities are to be closely involved in the operation of the EMP. In the promotion of mutual understanding, the third basket encourages cultural exchanges and knowledge of languages. Certain fields are highlighted as being of primary importance, including: cultural and creative heritage, cultural and artistic events, co-productions (theatre and cinema), translations and other means of cultural dissemination, as well as training. Support is also given to representatives of religions and religious institutions with the aim of breaking down prejudice, ignorance and fanaticism and fostering cooperation at grassroots level. The media is also supported, with the objective of enhancing cultural understanding. Youth and civil society organizations are the key target groups of the EMP's third basket.

The EMP also aims to contribute to improving the living and working conditions (including the development of public health services) and increasing the employment level of the population in the MNC, in particular of women. But the third basket is also overshadowed by discursive practices relating to terrorism, drug trafficking and organized crime and illegal immigration. What do these discourses tell us about the state of cultural democracy in the Euro-Mediterranean area today?

Cultural Democracy

The idea of cultural democracy encompasses several inter-related concepts. If we apply this notion to the third basket of the EMP, it envisions that:

- Euro-Mediterranean cultural traditions can co-exist and none of these should be allowed to dominate and become an 'authoritative culture' (Pace, this volume). Thus, European culture is not superior and cannot be enforced on southern Mediterranean peoples 'for their own good' (Stetter, this volume). Diversity in cultural life is not a problem; it is not something to be eliminated but actually something to be celebrated. Cultural democracy thus places great value upon cultural diversity. In this vein, the objectives of the third basket of the EMP are based on appropriate measures that seek to preserve and promote cultural activities from the full array of traditions present in Euro-Mediterranean communities (not just from European traditions). This approach is based on a belief that mutual respect is a prerequisite to survival in a multicultural Euro-Mediterranean society.
- A second element of the idea of cultural democracy is participation. If the third basket is to be comprehensive, any programmes or efforts must be related to the socio-economic life patterns and to educational systems in the southern Mediterranean (Calleja, this volume). Doctrines of cultural pluralism and cultural democracy must be enacted through the active participation, creativity and activity of the people of the southern Mediterranean themselves. These activities in turn will highlight the role of southern Mediterranean partner governments as well as that of the EU. The administration of cultural programmes under the third basket requires a decentralization approach wherein partners from different municipalities in the southern Mediterranean are given the opportunity to 'own' their own efforts in forging closer human and social as well as cultural relations between the peoples of both sides of the Mediterranean. Cultural democracy thus proposes a cultural life in which everyone is free to participate. At the practical level, this means the right to free expression that must be protected. A dynamic cultural life is not compatible with censorship and restriction of freedom, as Laura Feliu clearly argues in her contribution to this volume people must have access to the means of expression, including help in learning to use them. Access to the powerful mass media which so profoundly affect our view of the world is important in this regard, but participation should not stop there (there is a danger that

television, for example, discourages people from participating in community cultural life, undercutting their opportunities for active participation). The task of building a community of active, democratic participation requires people to leave their homes to enjoy conversation, music, film or theatre – to express themselves in a variety of ways.
- A third aspect of cultural democracy is that cultural life itself should be subject to democratic control. Peoples in the Euro-Mediterranean space need to participate in determining the directions that cultural development takes. They should all be able to have a say in public cultural issues that concern them – for example, how they are educated, what they are taught, what facilities are made available, what types of cultural institutions and art works are supported, how they are housed and transported, how their political system operates. Thus, the motor of cultural democracy is human agency – people in the Euro-Mediterranean area *can* affect EU-Mediterranean third basket policy and they *must* somehow be engaged in affecting and sustaining all aspects of cultural life if culture is to be a vital drive and a 'live' concept.

Towards a Wider Definition of Culture

In light of the discussion above it is pertinent to ask what exactly is Mediterranean culture and democracy enshrined in? The contributors to this volume have highlighted the conceptual limitations that have so far been generally accepted as orthodox. The type of policy that the EU and its Mediterranean partners have adopted has thus far been framed to promote causes that, albeit idealistic and generous, do not necessarily address the concerns and needs of the people of the Mediterranean. The achievements thus far are by no means negligible or useless. But a clearer definition of culture is called for.

Culture as we understand this concept here is an all-encompassing idea: it includes the arts, politics, the built environment, the entire array of voluntary activities that are part of human life, people's way of life. We identify culture not as some marginal embellishment of daily life but as a determinant of it, a reflection of people's social conditions including those which press heavy upon them every day – over-population, poverty, illiteracy, prejudices, deterioration of the environment, to name but a few. A broad understanding of culture means that problems like the latter are only susceptible of solutions through widespread changes in attitudes, patterns of thinking and ways of life. If the EU and the southern Mediterranean partners of the EMP are to act effectively in the region, then an understanding of the inter-relatedness of all aspects of culture is called for. Rather than subscribing to the view that each aspect of culture is a specialized enclave, best left to experts, culture must be seen as a public interest. In this respect, we urge the need to go beyond the artificial divisions within the third basket as well as the division between the three baskets of the EMP, to encourage the involvement of societal actors in the Euro-Mediterranean area. Social consultations should be the basis of a truly dialogic Euro-Mediterranean community. Establishing the procedures to make such consultations viable should be the main agenda for the coming months in rethinking Barcelona on its tenth year anniversary.[10]

Towards a Desirable Euro-Mediterranean Society: Some Policy Recommendations

How can the EU square its commitment to promoting democracy in the Mediterranean with longstanding EU economic and security interests in the region?

Human Rights and Civil Society Organizations

The human rights situation in some southern Mediterranean partner countries is still very difficult. For example, drawing upon two MNC cases, the authorities in Syria refuse to grant human rights organizations a license to work legally with the effect that such organizations work without being registered. For NGOs to gain licenses and work freely from government interference and harassment, Syria's association laws need to be modernized. Because they work in such harsh contexts, civil society organizations inside Syria find it particularly difficult to secure funding. The authorities maintain laws as tools for threatening human rights organizations in particular – exceptional law number 6 of 1965(!) penalizes with capital punishment any person who receives any kind of support from 'outside' for any reason.[11] In light of the initiation at the end of 2004 of the Association Agreement between the EU and Syria, in which article 2 it is clearly stated that the Parties commit themselves to respect for human rights, the continual harassment of Syrian human rights defenders is indeed of concern. The EU is empowered to insist that the Syrian authorities translate their rhetoric into action when it comes to reform before signing the EMAA. The European Parliament should also act along these lines before giving consent to this agreement. The Syrian authorities on their part must recognize the rights of human rights NGOs by granting these organizations legal registration and allowing them to work freely. In a similar vein, the EU needs to adopt a stick approach and exert firm pressure on the Tunisian authorities with respect to the prevention of human rights NGOs from freely undertaking their activities. To mention one example, the Tunisian authorities recently froze the funds of the Arab Institute for Human Rights (a member of the Euro-Mediterranean Human Rights Network). The Tunisian authorities should abide by article 2 of the EU-Tunisia EMAA and respect its human rights commitments in accordance with international standards.

Building in part on the EMP, the ENP is aimed at offering a privileged relationship with neighbours and relating this to mutual commitment to common values including the respect for human rights. The Action Plans cover a timeframe from three to five years and contain a set of priorities and actions including human rights. They build on differentiated approaches where each Plan is designed in collaboration with each neighbour and according to a degree of commitment to 'common' values and the capacity to implement jointly agreed priorities (Commission of the European Communities, 2003a). Thus, for example, in light of the recent conclusion of an action plan for Tunisia (within the framework of the ENP), the EU is in a strong position to reiterate Tunisia's responsibilities with respect to international human rights law. However, although the ENP opens new opportunities for the promotion of human rights in the southern Mediterranean area, Action Plans have thus far been negotiated with neighbouring governments without any consultation with civil society. The result is that some Plans are well developed on human rights, others less so. It is crucial that human rights local NGOs are involved in the elaboration of their country's Action Plan and in the follow-up processes on implementation. These local actors can, in turn, assist in making the ENP more easily accessible to ordinary citizens in southern Mediterranean neighbouring countries. Moreover, the ENP should be linked more unequivocally to the implementation of the recommendations in the May 2003 Commission Communication *Reinvigorating EU Actions on Human Rights and Democratisation with Mediterranean Partners* (Commission of the European Communities, 2003b) which explicitly suggests the setting of benchmarks for the implementation of human rights activities.

Media, Youth

As already mentioned above, a running theme throughout this volume relates to the urgent need for Euro-Mediterranean issues to be brought closer to the people of this regional space. For this purpose, initiatives like TV broadcasts addressing such matters have a wide audience reach and are welcome. The MEDA funded Information and Communication Regional Programme, managed by the European Commission Delegations in the southern Mediterranean and steered by the Commission's EuropeAid Co-operation office is a very useful instrument in this regard. One such TV programme entitled 'Across the Mediterranean' series was broadcast on 27 June 2005 by the Pan-Arab channel Al-Arabiya, with young people from seven countries discussing 'Europe: From Colonialism to Partnership'. The co-ordination of this broadcast was entrusted to the Commission Delegation in Beirut and is a clear example of a Euro-Mediterranean partnership in action.[12] On 28 June 2005, TV5 transmitted features on three central Maghreb countries as well as a debate on 'Europe-Maghreb: Partners on both Shores' as one of the *Rideau Rouge* (Red Curtain) programmes as part of a co-operative effort between the French-language channel and the Commission Delegation in Tunis.[13] Exchanges between young people across the Euro-Mediterranean area should continue and should be further encouraged. A recent example of cultural activities comprises a programme designed to facilitate such exchanges including social educators across the Mediterranean which ran in parallel with the 15th Mediterranean Games opened on 24 June 2005 in Almeria, Spain.[14]

Towards Cultural Democracy in the Euro-Mediterranean Area?

In light of cultural democracy efforts, an increase in the quality of EU financial support for third basket activities can be achieved by better targeting resources on the key policy priorities of the people of the Mediterranean, for example, the rights of women and children, strengthening the capacities of civil society organizations and professionals concerned with human rights and citizenship issues, which will, in turn, impact upon their government's reform agendas. Through the Euro-Mediterranean Parliamentary Assembly, parliamentarians from both sides of the Mediterranean have an opportunity to stand united to promote freedom of speech and democratic values across the region. In encouraging tolerance, compassion and participation, third basket programmes have been crucial in allowing the space for dialogue to ensue, but more needs to be done in terms of engaging the people of the Mediterranean and giving them the lead to seeking strategies for cultural development which takes account of the facts of everyday life and which is, at the same time, consistent with the values and aspirations that these people hold and that constitute 'the Euro-Mediterranean conscience'.

The events of 9/11 and thereafter have severely challenged the social values and patterns which have governed Euro-Mediterranean life since Barcelona. These changes have recently accelerated and proliferated to the point of causing critical dissension among those who are charged with policies and their administration and the people of the Euro-Mediterranean area. The third basket of the EMP has been the main instrument through which the EU has attempted to respond to this 'cultural crisis'. To enhance these efforts, the contributors of this volume call for a Euro-Mediterranean drive towards participatory development in this region. One of the main underlying assumptions about the lack of social and economic development in southern Mediterranean societies is that members of the latter are oppressed by the power-holders of their own societies, who control the relevant economic resources including capital, services, wealth, agriculture, land and industry. Hence, as Calleja argues, the main remedy for overcoming this oppression lies in an 'unlimited' community of communication. Through education and critical learning, this process will enable the oppressed to become aware of their condition and position as well as empower them (the people of the southern Mediterranean) to take pragmatic actions.
[15] What is missing in the third basket of the EMP is a Mediterranean political equation. The missing link in the southern Mediterranean's political development lies in the modification of southern Mediterranean cultural values to suit contemporary situations, and in a reconstruction of the southern Mediterranean nation-state. The need for cultural democracy in the southern Mediterranean comes from a type of democracy which is compatible with its culture: the need for continuous consultations with the people of the southern Mediterranean is more urgent than ever. To see the Mediterranean exclusively in a European way has never worked and does not work; prescribed European solutions to problems and arrested development of the southern Mediterranean do not serve southern Mediterranean aspirations. Therefore, what we call for here is to see the Mediterranean's heritage of thousands of years and of its cultural values applied to the issues of politics and reconstruction of southern Mediterranean nation-states, economics, the environment, family structures, conflicts and wars. Democracy in the southern Mediterranean area has long been enshrined in kinship, and we now need to extract from these social systems, with their consensual culture intact, a mould of

representation connected to the national level. We need a modernization process in the area by forgoing certain traditional practices which are no longer necessary. Southern Mediterranean political structures need to fit with their environments: Elites in the region can modify the incompatible political systems to suit the specific challenges today by re-education, and this re-education requires an ideology. And the ideology we envisage is Pan-Mediterraneanism to emancipate peoples from mental blockages and to enable them to value their own culture. The danger thus far with programmes within the third basket of the EMP is that southern Mediterranean peoples are encouraged to emulate European values – with the danger of forgetting that they are Mediterranean peoples and can solve problems only in their own ways. What the EU should therefore encourage is initiatives which come from the people of the southern Mediterranean and which are then supported by Europeans. As Silvestri points out in this volume, the third basket of the EMP offers a comprehensive context through which EU member countries can communicate with Mediterranean partner countries (in the context of the latter's main religion, Islam, which influences local Mediterranean cultures). EU discourses have recently indicated an appreciation of the deep cultures of southern Mediterranean countries: in fact these discursive practices have highlighted the importance of reaching out to non-violent Islamist political movements in the Arab world and integrating them in the EU's democracy promotion efforts – although clear policy guidelines that structure such a dialogic EU encounter with Islamist movements has yet to be enunciated.[16] Current developments in some Mediterranean partner countries offer windows of opportunity for the EU and its Mediterranean partners to engage in a true dialogic encounter: for example, the EU can support efforts of the Egyptian movement for change, *Kifaya*, which are aimed at a free, democratic Egypt that respects the rights of its citizens.[17] Change in Arab-Mediterranean countries has to come about from the people and their awareness of their full economic and social possibilities.

Social commitment and creativity, the voices of youth and women, and the role of educational systems are thus the three main pillars for the evolution of cultural democracy in the Euro-Mediterranean space. A Euro-Mediterranean cultural charter could be developed to highlight the foundations for such developments in Euro-Mediterranean relations. A Council of the Mediterranean could also be created as an operational structure to constitute a moral force striving to express the quintessence of Mediterranean ideals, aspirations, knowledge and expertise and thereby give a lead in these matters to central and local governments as well as NGOs in member countries of the region to secure the sound development of their peoples. Cultural affairs in the broadest sense should be the driving force behind the Council's philosophy.

Invitation for Arab Colleagues: The Dialogue Continues ...

This volume brings together contributions by a group of European scholars who have been working for some years on the way that EU policy on the southern Mediterranean is forged. It suggests some theoretical reflections on the concepts used in this policy-making process and the impacts on southern Mediterranean societies. Our contributions represent an attempt at presenting critical reflections on the policy-making process not as personal insights or expressions, although these are difficult to exclude from any writing. The contributors however share the desirability and feasibility of a liberal and egalitarian Euro-Mediterranean society and we see this possible through a new type of human relationship and social behaviour. The society towards which we are trying to work is one in which there is a multiplicity of free dialogue on the basis of a genuine equality of the social partners involved in Euro-Mediterranean relations, transcending differences and celebrating commonalities; where the opinions and convictions of European and southern Mediterranean peoples are all given the same courteous and serious consideration in the making of EU policy towards the southern Mediterranean. This Euro-Mediterranean society that we envision is one where the 'ordinary wo/man in the street' has a fully accepted right to question authoritative decisions and propositions, whether made by politicians, or social scientists or 'experts' (including cultural experts), and where these authoritative decision and proposition makers feel compelled to give due attention to this questioning. A Euro-Mediterranean social system of this nature is one where the least noticeable member of the 'masses' can feel assured that they have a voice they can raise in the decisions which affect their life. Such a voice is too often only given to the selected and privileged few – the influential, elitist groups in the Euro-Mediterranean community who have established themselves in their profession, be this politics or the arts/entertainment industry: put differently, people who know the rules of the 'game'. This privilege should be extended to everyone. The Euro-Mediterranean road towards a more just community is a long and demanding one and will involve everyone compromising. The path that is suggested in this direction is one of a true cultural dialogic relationship between European and Mediterranean partners alike (see Pace in this volume). For this purpose, we invite our Arab colleagues to continue the dialogue we have initiated here and to advance their ideas on cultural dialogue in the Euro-Mediterranean area in a future collaborative effort. We invite them to bring with them the distinct national preoccupations, routines and challenges that reflect those of the people of the southern Mediterranean to produce ideas and proposals of greater scope and more far-reaching vision, an ensemble of concepts which constitutes a moral force, a Mediterranean conscience. We hope that this dialogue will continue to develop. Economic indicators give us a very bleak picture of the development of southern Mediterranean societies. For this reason, it is all the more important to promote efforts for effective policies of social, human and cultural development – for the cultivation and nourishment of human resources.

Notes

[1] The terms civilizing mission, democratization of culture and cultural democracy used here are not new to readers working in the field of cultural policy and other related disciplines. However, these concepts can be effectively applied and adapted to the EU's Mediterranean policy, and in particular to the third basket of the EMP.

[2] Alam Shahid (2005).
[3] Fischer-Tiné & Mann (Eds) (2004).
[4] Livingstone (1992).
[5] Barcelona Declaration (1995).
[6] Matarasso (2000).
[7] Simpson (1976).
[8] Arnold [1869] (1981); Williams [1958] (1979); and Williams (1981) Culture.
[9] Barcelona Declaration (1995).
[10] Pace (2005).
[11] Euro-Mediterranean Human Rights Network (EMHRN), http://www.euromedrights.net.
[12] http://www.dellbn.cec.eu.int.
[13] http://www.tv5.org.
[14] EuroMed Synopsis, 30 June 2005, http://europa.eu.int/comm/external_relations/euromed/publication.htm.
[15] See also Khan (2005).
[16] Hamzawy (2005).
[17] Carnegie Endowment for International Peace (2005). Interview with George Ishak.

References

Arnold, M. [1869] (1981) *Culture and Anarchy* (Cambridge: Cambridge University Press).
Carnegie Endowment for International Peace (2005) Interview with George Ishak, founding member of the Egyptian Movement for Change (Kifaya), *Arab Reform Bulletin*, July. Available at: http://www.carnegieendowment.org/publications/index.cfm?fa=view&id=17183&prog=zgp&proj=zdrl#Interview.
Commission of the European Communities (2003a) Wider Europe-Neighbourhood: A New Framework for Relations with our Eastern and Southern Neighbours, COM(2003) 104 final, Brussels.
Commission of the European Communities (2003b) Reinvigorating EU Actions on Human Rights and Democratisation with Mediterranean Partner, COM (2003 294 final, Brussels, May.
European Commission (1995) Barcelona Declaration. Adopted at the Euro-Mediterranean Conference, 27–28 November 1995, Barcelona
Fischer-Tiné, H. & Mann, M. (Eds) (2004) *Colonialism as Civilising Mission. Cultural Ideology in British India* (London: Anthem Press).
Hamzawy, A. (2005) The West and moderate Islam, *bitterlemons-international.org*, 20(3), 2 June, http://www.carnegieendowment.org/publications/index.cfm?fa=view&id=17036.
Khan, S. (2005) The legend of participatory development (Mukto-mona organization), Available at: http://www.mukto-mona.com/Articles/shazzad/Freire.htm (accessed on 11 July 2005).
Livingstone, D. N. (1992) *The Geographical Tradition: Episodes in the History of a Contested Enterprise* (Oxford: Blackwell).
Matarasso, F. (2000) To save the city: the function of art in contemporary Europe society (3rd Delphi Encounters), Available at: http://www.comedia.org.uk/downloads/TOSAVE-1.DOC Accessed on 11 July 2005.
Pace, M. (2005) The impact of European Union involvement in civil society structures in the southern Mediterranean, *Mediterranean Politics*, 10(2), pp. 239–244.
Shahid, Alam M. (2005) America's new civilizing mission, *CounterPunch*, Available at: http://www.counterpunch.org/shahid01152005.html (accessed 11 July 2005).
Simpson, J. A. (1976) *Towards Cultural Democracy* (Strasbourg: Council of Europe).
Williams, R. [1958] (1979) *Culture and Society 1780–1950* (Harmondsworth: Penguin Books).
Williams, R. (1981) *Culture* (Glasgow: Fontana).

Author Query

Q1   Please check the shortened book title throughout the book.